Humors of Blood & Skin

ALSO BY JOHN HAWKES

The Beetle Leg

The Blood Oranges

The Cannibal

Death, Sleep & The Traveler

The Innocent Party

The Lime Twig

Lunar Landscapes

The Owl

*The Passion Artist** *

Second Skin

Travesty

*Virginie: Her Two Lives** *

*Published by Harper & Row. Limited Edition, New Directions

Humors of Blood & Skin

A JOHN HAWKES READER

AUTOBIOGRAPHICAL NOTES BY THE AUTHOR

Introduction by William H. Gass

A New Directions Book

First published clothbound and as New Directions Paperbook 577 in 1984
Manufactured in the United States of America
Published simultaneously in Canada by George J. McLeod, Ltd., Toronto

Library of Congress Cataloging in Publication Data
Hawkes, John, 1925-
    Humors of blood & skin.
    (A New Directions Book)
    I. Title.
PS3558.A82A6   1984   813'.54   84-4890
ISBN 0-8112-0906-7
ISBN 0-8112-0907-5 (pbk.)

New Directions Books are published for James Laughlin
by New Directions Publishing Corporation
80 Eighth Avenue, New York 10011

Table of Contents

Introduction

We feel, first of all, that we—you and I—that we can't miss it: fineness, excellence, quality; it is there like an address at the end of some elaborate directions we've been given: larger, more bovine, than life; and we believe that although, conceivably, others may be obtuse or spiritually absent on occasion, certainly we (it is ourselves, after all, of whom we speak) won't overlook Eden, Etna, or their Equivalences; yet—alas!—at one time or other we surely shall: we shall fall asleep in the train window while, beneath the trestle, a painted canyon opens like a lily; we shall blink in the middle of a beautiful pirouette; blunder into the wrong street and never find the Duomo; pick the squid out and shove it to the side of our plate; yawn in the face of the vast Pacific; sneeze on the President's hand as he fastens the medal to our chest; quarrel about love in Syracuse and thereby lose Sicily, a land our embittered memory can't return to; yes, similar incidents will happen often: ancient, medieval, modern history, as well as present life, continually repeats and records such oversights, such nodding, such detumescence; there is a coolness which clings to us sometimes even when we are wrapped in flames and pretending to be a phoenix.

I record with shame the several times I failed to complete the first chapter of *Under the Volcano*, my tardy appreciation of Turner's burning boats and smoggy sunsets, the jokes I made about a Gertrude Stein I hadn't read, the deaf ear I turned to *Eugene Onegin* just because it had been composed by Tchaikovsky; the foolish idea I had that Ford

Madox Ford had hung around Conrad's neck like a ten cent St. Christopher's medal. My grudging regard for Walt Whitman is still a blot upon my scutcheon. And in 1959, while reading manuscripts for a little magazine named *Accent*, I nearly fell asleep over my first pages of John Hawkes. In the tall sloppy stack of stories which were victimizing me, I had turned up a piece called "The Horse in a London Flat," by an author whose name was unfamiliar. It was a title not strange enough, by itself, to make me sit up, though it should have. Afterward I made excuses for myself: it was winter in Urbana; an infant had mewled its alarming way throughout my night; the stories in the slush pile I'd been assigned were artless and awful. So my eyes had run over perhaps five pages like rain down a window when somehow my consciousness was penetrated by his prose. There was fog on a river, I remember. What else was going on? They—dim figures, men—were lifting a horse by means of a sling from the bottom of a barge to a place on the quay . . .

> The whistles died one by one on the river and it was not Wednesday at all, only a time slipped off its cycle with hours and darkness never to be accounted for. There was water viscous and warm that lapped the sides of the barge; a faint up and down motion of the barge which he could gauge against the purple rings of a piling; and below him the still crouched figures of the men and, in its moist alien pit, the silver horse with its ancient head round which there buzzed a single fly as large as his own thumb and molded of shining blue wax.

. . . and I woke as if something scalding had fallen in my eyes. I did not complete the paragraph which followed. My cheeks were burning with embarrassment. The pride I took in my taste, as well as the protective arrogance of an unbudded artist, were, in that moment, removed. I found myself in dirty underdrawers.

> He stared down at the lantern-lit blue fly and
> the animal whose ears were delicate and unfeeling,
> as unlikely to twitch as two pointed fern leaves
> etched on glass . . .

I don't know why it was this particular passage which woke me rather than another; it should have been the brilliant opening paragraph that did it, the paragraph to which I now returned in order to enter a beautiful and dangerous new world. From the first, John Hawkes' prose had sounded what Henry James would have said was "the right note," and I had not heard it. As I read the pages I had previously dozed through, those two leaflike ears were etched on my imagination, and image after image went to join them. I hope that the book which you are holding now will provide a similar exhilaration, for these lines are alive as few in our literature are; it is a prose of great poetry; it is language linked like things in nature are—by life and by desire; it is exploratory without being in the least haphazard or confused; and, for me, at least, it is fundamentally, and in the best sense, exemplary: it shows me how writing should be written, and also how living should be lived. *It is a prose that breathes what it sees.*

So I shortly went next door with the shock of my recognition, its author's pages beating in my hand like a fresh heart, only to have a choral scatter of voices say,

"O, yes, John Hawkes. Of course. Haven't you read *The Cannibal*?"

"Or *The Goose on the Grave*, for god's sake."

"What about the beginning of *The Beetle's Leg*?"

"That's *The Beetle Leg*."

"He's like no one else. I'd recognize his work in a minute."

"Hawkes was still practically a baby, you know, when he wrote *The Cannibal*; right after—like the infant Hercules—he strangled a snake in his bed."

So I suffered, in a matter of moments, my second humiliation. I didn't know; hadn't read; wasn't up. Yet it is true, as I told myself, that in our society a major writer can work for years, and have a hardy and devoted following, even achieve an international reputation, without interrupting the insipid flow of the culture by scarcely so much as a comma. Hadn't Faulkner been safely sealed in indifference for three-quarters of his writing life? There comes a time, for most of us, when, with respect to some fine film-maker, novelist, poet, or painter, the seal gets broken. Originality escapes like a genie from a jar.

The secret is in the sentences. Of course, the sentences must add up; they must amount to something more than themselves; they must create that larger sentence which every fine fiction passes upon us in the course of its composition; but if those phrases which form a face, for instance, have not themselves some features; if there's no "look" to them, no character; then the unremarkable will remain as unremarked as it deserves to be; just consider when you last regarded with love some inclining head, and ask yourself if it was ever true that the eyes were without allure, the nose without distinction, the mouth not worth a mention, its smile without consequence, while the whole, on the other hand, was wonderful: attractive, generous, appealing?

In a sense, the pieces which make up this *Reader*, then, are fragments, and can only beg us to restore them to the complete text they somewhere else are; to return us, as my eye was returned, to the beginnings of all these endings; but the fragments we have here, like the even smaller shards that are the sentences themselves, are not useless nothings like bits of broken bottle, but rather they are "details" as details are depicted in the careful study of a painting: magnifications, points of focus, centers of concentration. They invite the closer look, the savor of the silent reader's speaking tongue; they invoke that special state, the literary reverie, which, unlike the day dream, as Gaston Bachelard has argued, circles its subject and returns us repeatedly to places of thoughtfulness and appreciation. I draw out a few sentences from here and there in this book or that:

> The damp smell of the river rolled over soldiers' leggings and trousers that had been left in doorways, and a cow lying dead in a field looked like marble.

> Even the dialogue of the frogs is rapturous.

> Precious brass safety pins holding up their panties, and then I saw the pins, all at once saw the panties, the square gray-white faded undergarments of poor island girls washed in well water morning and night and, indistinguishable from kitchen washrag or scrap of kitchen towel, hung on a string between two young poplars and flapping, blowing in the hard island wind until once more dry enough and clean enough to return to the plain tender skin, and of course the elastics had been worn out or busted long ago and now there were only the little bent safety pins for holding up their panties and a few hairpins for the hair and a single lipstick which they passed from girl to girl at country crossroads or in the high school lavatory on the day of the dance.

> For a moment she stood there waiting, allowing
> him to see through his tears and his swollen lids
> her chest, her knees, the little belly that was the
> same shape as her face.

Though taken almost at random from several novels, don't they call for fresh intensities of inspection, these extraordinary combinations? and the nature and effect of each is quite different, for our author knows many modes and can be breathless and romantic or harsh and succinct, as seems best— formal or colloquial, circumspect or blunt. The 'ands' of my first example, we might settle on them, our eye like a fly made of blue wax; or we might consider the character of those trousers that have been left in doorways, repeating the expression until its oddness is engraved upon us; or we might simply listen to the dialogue of the frogs; or match, as we move our minds from word to word, the pace of the beautiful sentence about the panties, with its characteristic Hawkesean slide, in this case, from pins to hairpins, hairpins to lipstick, lipstick to lavatory, and lavatory to dance; or we might appreciate the sight Hawkes has permitted us of a belly the same shape as a face.

Each such sentence, and there are thousands of them— thousands—creates not a new world so much as a special and very alert awareness of one; and that awareness is so controlled, so precise, so intense, so angular while remaining uncomfortably direct, so comic, too, as if a smile has been sliced by a knife, that many readers have recoiled as though from reality itself, and pretended to be running from a nightmare, from something sur- or un- real, restoring the disguise which Hawkes' prose has torn away. In Rilke's great novel, *The Notebooks of Malte Laurids Brigge*, there is a passage in which Malte perceives an old woman with her face implanted in her hands, as if put there by Rodin, so that when—startled by a sudden sound in the street—she pulls her hands away, her face must adhere to her hands, and she (and Malte, too) must then look down at the inside of herself as one might at the inside of a mask or the inner peeling of a fruit. Above the compote of the palm, the peeled face Malte cannot confront is presumably moist. This is the effect of Hawkes' fiction: it sees the world from just inside its surface, a surface at which it looks back the way Orpheus so dangerously did, thereby returning an unlamenting Eurydice to Hades. It is as if a wall were examining, from its steadfastly upright side, the slow peel of its paint. The position is unprecedented. And the final result is the merging of two surfaces as if the print of this page were bleeding through the paper to shadow the obverse side; or, again, we might imagine a stained-glass window made of what could be simultaneously seen from both sides. We cannot pretend, then, that the world has only one side. There is a second skin. So those panties we encountered a moment ago are observed not only from the point of view of a voyeur who might enjoy their innocent flaglike alignment, but from the vantage of the flesh which will wear them—the two contemplations pressed together then as though by thighs.

Rilke wrote that beauty was the start of a terror we could only just barely endure, and I think the reader will feel that tension, that doubleness, here; but I want to rejoin those thighs for a moment, pay heed to the warmth they generate, for among the more prominent qualities of John Hawkes' prose is its glorious sensuality:

> So while the spring kept Oscar cool, the five
> of us sprawled close together and held out our
> hands to the fat black arm that disappeared inside
> the pot and came up dripping. Calypso herself
> couldn't have done better. Sweet guavas and fat
> meat that slid into the fingers, made the fingers

breathe, and crushed leaves of cinnamon on the
tongue and sweet shreds of coconut. We ate together under the dark speckled covering of the
tree, sprawled together, composed, with no need
for wine, and the cows stood about and nosed us
and a blackbird flew down and sat on Sonny's cap.
We ate together among the smooth green oval calabashes that were as large as footballs, and lay among
the calabashes and licked our fingers.

Such language nourishes more certainly than lunch, and within
its context the song it sings contains a smile, for Oscar is a vial
of sperm, and this is artificial insemination day.

The world is not simply good and bad on different week-
ends like an inconsistent pitcher; we devour what we savor
and what sustains us; out of ruins more ruins will later, in
their polished towers, rise; lust is the muscle of love: its
strength, its coarseness, its brutality; the heart beats and is
beaten by its beating; not a shadow falls without the sun's
shine and the sun sears what it saves. These are not the
simplicities my saying has suggested. In our civilization, the
center has not held for a long time; neither the center nor
the place where the center was, can now be found. We are dis-
ordered, arthritic fingers without palms. Inside the silence of
unmoving things, there are the sounds of repeated explosions.
Perhaps it is catastrophe breathing. Who has rendered this
condition more ruthlessly than Hawkes has, or furnished our
barren countrysides with their hanging trees and human
sluices more honestly, yet with wealth? with the attention
one lover has for another? for his work has always refused
ruin in the act which has depicted it, and this collection is the
joyful showing forth and celebration of such a healing art.

William H. Gass, Washington University, St. Louis

Humors of Blood & Skin

Short Fiction

In most of my novels I have written with nearly obsessive intensity about the comedy and violence of sex and about the family—from the sexually dead families of *The Cannibal* and *The Beetle Leg* to the incestuous, broken families of *Second Skin* and *Virginie*. And I have written increasingly about the imagination itself, especially in *The Blood Oranges*, *Travesty*, *The Passion Artist* and *Virginie*.

From my asthmatic childhood and from my late adolescent experiences as an ambulance driver in Italy and Germany in the last months of the Second World War, have come the main materials of my fiction as well as my working beliefs as a writer: that design always emerges from debris (the theme of *Travesty*) and that the beauty of the nightmare is that it inevitably shows forth some unattainable ideal. When *The Cannibal* (my first novel) was published in January of 1950, a fellow undergraduate conducted an interview for *The Harvard Advocate* and in the course of it asked me how it felt to be a writer. I answered that it had never occurred to me to want to "be" a writer and that I was only interested in language and the work itself, and this has been my attitude from then to the present. The following short selections have in common that they were culled and shaped from longer narratives and have the same concerns as the novels excerpted in this collection.

In the early 1960s, I tried to write a short novel about two brothers, one a weak and loving man, the other a wealthy patriarch. I wanted to endow a German family with aspects of my father's Irish background, and though that narrative finally proved intractable, still two remnants yielded "The Traveler," based on one of my father's favorite anecdotes about a blistering sunburn he once suffered, and "The Grandmother," which in part travesties my father's love of food as well as his condescending attitude toward one of his brothers.

"A Little Bit of the Old Slap and Tickle" (an English expression referring to sex) is an episode that so strained the form of *The Lime Twig* that I was forced to leave it out of that novel. But I am still partial to this eroticizing of ordinary family life and so include it here.

"The Universal Fears" owes its existence to a former student of mine who, for a brief period, took the place of a teacher ruinously beaten by a class of violent girls in a London reformatory. My former student, a highly inventive person, won over his pupils, thought to be unteachable, by tape recording and playing back in class their street stories and dirty jokes, thereby engaging their interest in language but finally earning for himself the loss of his job. I was unable to transform this material into a short novel as I had hoped but at least gleaned a story from the effort and had the satisfaction of trying to create sympathy not only for the so-called delinquent girls but for the teacher who had probably deserved their nearly fatal assault.

The Traveler

Early one morning in a town famous for the growing of some grape, I arose from my bed in the inn and stepped outside alone to the automobile. I smelled the odor of flowers thirsting early for the sun; deep green fields stretched to either side of the road, wet and silent; it was the cold dawn of the traveler and I wished suddenly for a platter of home-cooked sausage. The car was covered with the same white dew as the grass, and when I opened the door I smelled the damp leather, the still cold oil and the gasoline that had been standing the night long. Soon the hot day would be upon us; the dust of driving would whirl us into villages, every hour or two whirl chickens and small children across the roads like weeds.

Down the road came a young bent-backed girl. On her shoulders she carried a yoke from either end of which hung a milk can, and over her shoulders she wore a shawl. Her legs were bare and scratched by the thistle. Slowly she came into the inn yard and approached me, each step loudly sloshing the milk.

"Your name, Fräulein?"

"Just Milkmaid," she said.

"Well, Milkmaid, how many cows have you milked this morning?"

"Five, Mein Herr," she said. Her arms were pimpled with a curious raw color as if they had been sunburned the day before but now were cold. The girl tugged at her shawl, trying to hide the hump of her spine below the yoke. She seemed to know that I, Justus Kümmerlich, would miss nothing. She took the lid from one of her buckets—a steam rose from the white milk lying flat now inside—and offered me a ladleful small and thick.

"But it is still warm," I exclaimed.

"Yes," she laughed, "I have only now stripped it from them." And she made a milking motion with her hands and peered up at me.

I put the wood to my lips and quickly drank down the milk still raw with the warmth of the cows that gave suck to this community. I paid her and she walked again to the road, herself sloshing like a cow. Long and carefully I wiped my mouth.

Then, having drunk of the rich countryside, I climbed behind the wheel of my car and started the engine. I leaned from the door: "Auf Wiedersehen, Milkmaid!" I put my foot on the accelerator, once, twice, and the engine rocked full throttle in several explosions of cylinders and exhaust. Smoke filled the yard. I raced the engine again and took hold of the hand brake; the pressure of the automobile filled the dashboard; vibrations possessed the automobile in all its libertine mechanization, noise, and saliency.

"Wait!" At first I hardly heard the cry, "Wait, wait!" But from the inn ran my wife, calling loudly the word shaped in vapor, twisting her ankles with every step, and one could see she felt the possibility of being left behind, left all alone, so driven was she to run like a wasp across this strange and empty yard. I imagined how she must have been wakened from her country sleep and how she must have started, frightened at the roar of the racing engine.

"What, Sesemi," allowing the engine to cool down and idle, "no hat?" But she did not smile and did not stop her trembling until I had silenced the machine.

So we journeyed, bearing always south, bearing down upon the spike-helmeted policemen of small villages, coming abreast of flocks of geese by the road, driving toward some church spire in the distance, racing down our rich continent all that summer and settling ourselves to sleep each night in the spring-weakened hollows of familiar beds which, no matter how old we grow, tell us always of mother and father and sick child as we roll from side to side through the years.

"Justus, do you know what day this is?"

"No," I replied and kept my eyes to the road so flat now against the contour of the sea.

"They sent little Mauschel out of the house. . . ."

"No riddles, Sesemi. No riddles."

The sun was hot on the roof of the automobile and I sat with my chin lifted. Always I drove with my head raised slightly and looked clearly and relentlessly at the space ahead and now and then swabbed my neck, leaving the handkerchief to soak, so to speak, around my collar. That day the country-side was sunswept and a pale blue as if at any moment the earth itself might turn to water.

"Don't you recall it, Justus? Don't you recall the wreath?" Sesemi peered out of the window into the blue stratum of air spread over the sand. She was remembering, of course, and seemed to be washing her little eyes in that blue air, cleansing her sight if only to enjoy the scratching progress of the impurity across the conjunctiva. What memories she retained: only the unpleasant ones, the specks of gloom, the grains in the eye which, months later, she would tell me about. But the eyes of certain people are never without a redness inside the lids.

"I do not remember. Perhaps this is not a special day after all, Sesemi."

"It was evening, Justus."

"Then perhaps it was not a special evening, Sesemi."

"Oh, yes. How lonely your brother would be now, except for Metze and Mauschel. And you and me, Justus."

"Don't taunt me, Sesemi. Please."

Late that afternoon we approached a small city and I steered the automobile quickly as I could through the outskirts to the center of this traveler's resting place until I found the bank and parked in front of it. A group of children collected immediately around my automobile and began to touch the hood, the fenders, the spokes in the wheels.

There are banks all over the world and I am always at home in a bank. Nothing else is needed when one brushes off his coat and makes his appearance before the faceless tellers of these institutions. The clerk did not ask to see my credentials, sensing at once that his bank with its gold clock was my hostel, that some of my assets, a stranger's assets, were vaulted there waiting only upon my demand and my signature—Justus Kümmerlich. I noted that the pen trembled when he thrust it, his fingers pinching the wet point, through the grille.

"Thank you," I said shortly and raised my eyes.

There was a hair on the pen point. I handed it back to the clerk, indicating the dirt, and lit a cigar. I could not hurry bank business. I looked around the room—the same, all the same, this very bastion in Zurich, Parish, Milan, even small Tiergarten, retaining faithfully all one's fortunes, the scruples of one's piety and reserve.

"A traveler must be cautious, I imagine," came the sudden whisper.

"I beg pardon?"

"Cautious with money, Mein Herr. I imagine one does well to carry little." He dropped the pen, then reappeared, attempting to wipe dry that face and quiet those round eyes. "Traveling, sir, I should think one would take only the barest amount . . . thieves, chambermaids, accidents. Nicht wahr?"

I began to write. The round worried face hovered there behind the mesh.

"If one is ordained to have it, one's money is not stolen, my friend. If there is money in your pocket, it will stay. If money is your domesticity, you will have only to be a good housekeeper. When traveling, my friend, it is simple: one has merely to know how to pin one's pocketbook inside the pillow." I laughed and pushed the pen and the check into those reaching fingers.

He murmured something and then, smiling, sucking his breath, began to count with a terrible aimless dexterity, an inhuman possessiveness, confident but suffering while my money passed through his hands.

"Mein Herr," he whispered, "don't leave these bills in your hotel room."

I took the packet and counted it quickly myself. The grillwork closed without a sound.

I reached the automobile and wrenched open the door. "Mein Herr, Mein Herr," begged the children, "take us with you!" Against the hot leather seat I lay back my head and smiled though the eyes were shut. "Well, Sesemi. The Riviera?"

I paid the hotel manager in advance. I stared into his small French eyes carefully and signed my name on his register. I guessed immediately that there was no sand in his shoes and that he drank a good deal of wine.

"But the linen," staring at him again, "what of the linen?"

"Herr Kümmerlich, smooth and white, of course! Perfectly white!"

The room was small. It contained a white bed and a few white mats placed on the empty table and on the arms of the chair, a room facing the ocean and filled with that tomb odor of habitations built by the sea. Each time I entered there was the sensation of a mild loneliness, a realization that it was not one's own.

In the beginning I thought that if we tired of going to the beach, we might sun ourselves on the porch completely encircling our floor of the hotel. But those who walked the porch at night spoiled it for the day. It was not long before I moved my chair so that it blocked our own screened doors, which opened upon the rotting and down-sloping porch. The first night the sea was loud; we could hear it green and barbarous, having emptied itself of humans there below. The sun sank like a woman into a hot bath; it became dark and the night was suddenly singing with mosquitoes and violins.

Sesemi was at last done with her kneeling at the bedside and climbed in beside me. We lay in the dark. Someone, perhaps a child, had fastened two large starfish to the screens of our porch door and now I saw them, silhouetted in dead sea fashion, between the blue night outside and the blackness within, all around us. From the next room came a little voice:

"Mamma, a drink of water, bitte."

We lay still. The starfish rustled against the screen in a slight wind. The sea was beginning now to turn to foam, the hopeless separation of day and night, against all shores.

"Mamma. A drink of water, bitte."

"Sesemi," I said in the dark, "if the child will not be quiet and go to sleep, you must fetch some water."

"Ja, Justus."

My eyes would not close. Even an older man—I was pleased to count myself among them—watches the stars when he lies down in a strange place, watches them in their cold heaven as he wonders what he may find on the beach when next the sun rises and the sea grows calm. I reached out and reassured myself of the light switch, relaxed my arms straight by my sides, thought of the meal I should order at dawn, and subsided into that state of alertness which for those who have found the middle of life is called sleep.

But I woke and the violins, not the insects, were still. Some equatorial disturbance was reflected now in the sea, which mounted steadily upon the scales of the shore, that sea which drowned the midnight suicides. I lifted my head quickly. There were two in embrace. Together they leaned heedlessly into our screened doors as if they thought the room empty, the two become a single creature that rolled its back and haunches into the mesh, scraped its four feet now and then on the porch wood. Their single body moved, scratched the wire, intent upon the revealing introspection of the embrace, immobile, swept by the black sea breezes.

"Pfui! Pfui!" I cried, clutching at the top of my pajamas. And they were gone, drifting down the porch.

I got out of bed and trembled in the cold. Deftly, overcome with conscience, I pulled the billfold from my linen coat and opened my valise.

"Justus. What are you doing?"

"The pins," I hissed over my shoulder, "the pins!"

I did not eat heavily the next morning. But with the ringing of the gong and the screeching of a pack of gulls that early took flight from the roof of the hotel, Sesemi and I appeared among the first breakfasters and met, as we met morning and morning again, those old ladies who sat one to a table drinking their black coffee. It was said in the hotel that we Germans would not miss a meal, and that we even sat in the midst of the deaf ladies that we might eat the sooner. The old ladies were all grandmothers who had survived their young. All of them wore violet shawls over the quick irregular protrusions that were their backs and shoulder blades. They stayed in the dining room a precise time, each of them; and then, before the sun was fully risen, they retreated up to their drawn rooms to wait through the long day for sundown. They preferred the cool, they sought the shade like snails, and feared what they called the stroke.

Whenever we entered the dining room Sesemi helped one of them to sit; whenever we left the dining room Sesemi helped one of them to exit. Every morning the hotel manager came among the tables and spoke to each old woman and finally to myself, urging his guests to enjoy some special luxury, but knowing all too well the fruitlessness of his invitation. The dining room was a quiet place; the old women hardly tinkled spoon to cup until, in French, one of them would say, "Ladies, ladies, here comes the sun!" And, putting down their napkins they would faintly stir, then flee.

And a moment later the beach would be turned to fire, scattered over with the burning bathers and their umbrellas, bathers who were as eager to lie in the violet rays as the ladies were to escape them. The young ate no breakfast but went directly from their beds to the beach as if their youthful bodies and anonymous lively figures needed no food, except the particles of sunshine, to exist upon. The Germans were good at volley ball. The others, the French, rarely played the game, but paired off, man and woman, woman and man, to lie on their bright blankets and hold hands, inert about the beach like couples of black and slender seals.

The sun was always upon its dial, sending down to the beach intangible rays of heat and fomenting over this area its dangerous diffusion of light. The world came to us behind shut eyes. A silent bombardment descended upon the women with dark glasses while old gentlemen stuck out their legs as for treatment, expecting the sun to excite those shrunken tendons. Feet ran close to our heads on the sand. The catchers of starfish came dangerously near and a small boy stepped on my arm at midmorning. The immensity of the sun was challenging, all the biology of myself, Justus, my lungs and liver, my blood-pumping system, cried out to meet the sun, to withstand the rising temperature, to survive the effects, the dehydration, of such a sun. We saw the child who had called for water in the darkness; well might it thirst.

When I went down to the water, Sesemi, sitting upon a towel, waved good-by and admonished me to return if the seas were too cold or if I felt cramps. Women have no place in the water. What is the sea if not for the washing of dead relatives and for the swimming of fish and men? On this trip, only a few steps, I left behind my wife, my housecoat, the muffler, the partially smoked cigar that marked me for this world, and then, feeling the sands go wet, braced myself for that plunge into the anonymous black.

When I began walking upon that nearer undersurface which can never breathe the air upon which the less heroic sea creatures move, I saw the thirsty child standing knee-deep and not far off, watching me. The child did not wave or smile but merely watched as if its parents had perhaps told it something about Herr Kümmerlich. But no, as I splashed forward, I realized that the child was speculating, trying to calculate the moment when I should leave my feet and trust myself to ride upon the waves. I shut my eyes and heard it calling suddenly for its papa to come and see.

I was an excellent floater. I could drift farther from shore than anyone, buoyed and perfectly calm, flat on my back, so unsinkable was my body, classic and yet round with age as my father's. Floating is a better test of character than swimming—creatures that float are indestructible and children beware of them. Their parents have only admiration for him who moves effortlessly, purposefully, out to sea.

"That is Herr Kümmerlich out there."

"What? That far?"

"Ja. Herr Kümmerlich. And, see, not a splash."

Now I was floating, perfectly proportioned, helmeted in my old bathing cap and rocking steadily. What a swim it was, what sport! The water carried me fathoms high and I lay on the surface, the plane, from which the winds started and across which grew the salt in its nautical gardens. I was the master and the ship. Now and then my breast went under, I rolled for a long while in the hollow of a swell. My feet cut the water like a killer shark's fins, I breathed deep—Justus

Kümmerlich—in the world of less-than-blood temperature. The knees float, the head floats, the scrotum is awash; here is a man upon the sea, a rationalist thriving upon the great green spermary of the earth!

I might never have returned. The sea is made of male elements and I was vigorously contented there on the crest of it all. But at that instant there came suddenly the cutting of two sharp arms and the beating of a swimmer's legs. He made straight for me and at the last moment lifted his mouth to exclaim: "Mein Herr, Frau Kümmerlich is worried. She would be pleased if you returned to shore," and he shot by, racing, his head buried again in the foam of his blind channel. He was carrying on his back his little thin thirsty son, the boy sitting upright as on a dolphin and unconcerned with the violence of his father's strokes.

Sesemi was waiting on the dry sand with the towel. It was a noon sun, straight above us and near to the earth. I exposed myself to it and the thousand molecules of salt crystallized on my freshened skin. My hair was suddenly dry as straw. I heard her saying, "Justus, Justus," but I never moved and heard nothing but the swishing of the sun's tails. After all the peace of the ocean, now there was none; there was only the immoderate heat and a sudden blackness that fell upon me in the form of a great dead gull filled with fish. And so I stayed in the sun too long, and so I burned.

For three days I lay in our room occupying the bed alone, and blistered. A thick warm water swelled under the skin of my red body, my temperature would drop suddenly, chilled, and nausea would come in a storm. I knew the twilight of the sunburn, the sheet stuck to me like a crab. In the dead of night I would hear the speechless methodical striking of my compatriots' fists into the gasping sides of the volley ball. All memory, the entire line of my family, was destroyed in the roaring of the sea and the roaring of the sun. What horror when the bed turned and rocked gently out on the thick swells.

At last I woke. Like a gangrenous general waking from a stupor in his hot, fly-filled field tent, I peered through the sticky substance of eyeball and eyelid and saw the gray of the late afternoon, the gray of the dying window blinds tightly drawn. The room was disheveled and torn as if their attendance upon me had been a violent thing. But now they too were serene.

Sesemi and the child were huddled together in the corner in the half-turned chair. They were watching me and smiling. Wearily and happily they were hugging each other—little Frau Kümmerlich, her hair undone, was hugging the child about the waist. They came to the bed together; Sesemi held his hand.

"Justus," she said, and looked into the diffused parts of my eyes. "Justus," she whispered, "it has been a long while."

Then I was able to think of them and my lips slid open long enough for me to say, "Yes, Sesemi. Yes, it has."

"O die Fröhlichkeit!" she whispered, dropping her head to the tepid, sun-smelling sheet. The boy picked up the pan and went out the door, as habit had taught him, to empty it.

When I was able to travel, when I was able once more to hum the *Lorelei*, and we quit the town, I stopped the automobile before a butcher's shop and ordered the throat cut and the lamb packed whole with ice and rock salt in a wooden box.

"The whole lamb," I explained to Sesemi, "is for my brother. For Lebrecht! You see, Sesemi, I am the father after all."

We started home.

The Grandmother

"Lebrecht! I'm here, I'm here, Lebrecht!"

It was with all the old impatience that I cried to them, with all the old affection that I announced myself, and my hands were outstretched. A window slammed in the back of the house. How little it had changed; yet I seemed to bring with me the dust and aching of long travel and separation. At that moment, looking up the path, beating my jacket, waiting, I felt the wanderer come home.

"Why, look, Mauschel, it is your Uncle Justus!"

The door opened a crack, then it was wide, and suddenly the four of us intermingled in our confused and unexpected embrace. I shook my brother Lebrecht by the arm, bumped against Metze, his wife, and felt them gather around me.

"And do I smell the stove, Metze?" I threw my chin high, laughing.

"No," she replied in a low flat voice, "you do not. The stove is cold."

With clouds above us and a slight wind ballooning our trousers and sweeping away the summer, I caught hold of Lebrecht Kümmerlich. He was not so much younger than his brother Justus now.

"Lebrecht, Lebrecht, it is so, nicht wahr?"

"Ja, ja, ja, Justus."

Our hands were on each other's shoulders, we faced each other and I cared nothing for the rest.

"Well, then," I whispered, "laugh, Lebrecht, laugh . . ."

And he did so.

The grass was long, the wind blew coldly among us. We all

shook hands again, and I noticed that Metze had many wrinkles on her throat. Suddenly I pushed between them and ran back to the car. I pried loose the wooden box I had brought with me, and though I was hardly able, carried it to them before the house.

"Lebrecht—for you, Lebrecht!"

Metze insisted that we put the box down immediately, there on the path, and open it. She scraped away the ice until they could see the white of fat and the redness of cold meat. Lebrecht began to thank me, he was serious and turned his face from side to side, but he was whispering so softly that I could not hear.

"Mauschel," said Metze, holding tightly to the edge of the box, "bring some coal, bitte."

"Metze," I smiled quickly, sure she would understand, "the lamb is for tomorrow's Mittagessen . . ."

"We will eat it tonight. And tomorrow also."

The three of them hurried inside with the box. I followed.

"Metze," I called, "the meat must season, it must hang in the open air!"

But she disappeared into the kitchen and began washing the pots.

We were silent a moment. Mauschel had climbed down into the darkened cellar, we heard him through the thin floor, moving slowly beneath us; suddenly there came from below, amid barrels and coal dust, a distinct and vituperative profanity as from the other side of Berlin. We sat still. What sort of boy was Mauschel now, shaking the coal scuttle by the throat? He grunted and drove the shovel deep again into the bin. Lebrecht walked softly to the door.

"Mauschel. Will Papa help you with the coal?"

The boy, man-sized, immeasurable, suddenly big in his shadow, emerged from the little stairwell and swung the sack of coal into view. Lebrecht stepped away quickly as Mauschel crashed his burden against the walls and to the kitchen. We could hear the two of them, mother and son, whispering.

"He is so big."

"Bigger than I," said Lebrecht softly.

"That is the way with you family men," I laughed, feeling my forehead, "you have your taxes, your dedication, the satisfaction of your big sons to wrestle with."

"Only one son, Justus."

"Ja. Remember how he needed a beating once, Lebrecht? He was always my favorite. Ah, he knows the character of his Uncle Justus." I smiled in the dark.

We began to smell the smoke of the roasting meat. And Mauschel was sharpening the knives. I noticed Lebrecht's slippers under the window, I was light-headed and content, sitting there, waiting for the meal to be served.

"And Metze, Lebrecht, has she overcome her grief for der Blumenstrauss?"

He lifted his eyes slowly. "Ja," he said.

I nodded.

"She talks to her mother some nights, Justus, but without grief, I assure you."

"So?"

"Ja. She talks. But there is Herr Popanz and the lady from Augenstrasse, neighbors in grief. And God forgives such things, Justus."

I did not answer. I was hungry and would eat a good meal.

"I have been ill, Lebrecht."

"Ill?"

"Ja, Lebrecht, seriously. Perhaps as sick as Papa when he died . . ."

But as soon as our father's name was mentioned, Metze called out that the lamb was done.

"Give the knives to your Uncle Justus, Liebling," said Metze as we entered the dining room, and Mauschel thrust the blades at me.

"In my brother's house . . ." I murmured and extended the knives to Lebrecht, and he was quick enough to take them. Pushing his arms out of his coat sleeves, he worked to free his shoulders.

There was a heavy, gasping, uncontainable sigh at the head of the table as Lebrecht raised his two hands—in one was the great carving fork, in the other a knife—and held them above the smoking lamb as in some kind of feverish dying benediction. His eyes looked straight down at the crackling skin, peering, taking aim at the roast which had been rushed to the table. Lebrecht's head became wet, and still the fork and still the knife hovered powerfully as if he could not bring himself to begin. But his nose was over the meat and he was sniffing it. And with the very smell of the fat and the meat, the juices were already filling his mouth and the acids seeping into his stomach's pit. He seemed so to be smelling that he could not bring his knife down, could not drive the point into the leg of the lamb. Then suddenly he sank back and half turned away, lowering his arms until the steel rested helplessly against the wood. He licked his lips and smiled.

"Ach, Metze, I've forgotten how . . ."

For answer, unable to wait longer, she reached out piercingly through the tumblers and from the platter snatched up a small potato which she immediately began to smash in the bottom of her plate.

"Pardon," he said softly and once more took up knife and fork.

"I'm not hungry," I said cheerfully, smoothing the napkin, "I'll take just a little of the skin, if you please, Lebrecht."

"Not hungry!" Mauschel pushed back his chair and rose

menacingly on his big haunches. "Not hungry, Uncle!" He looked as if a fish had been smacked against his eyes. His hands clutched the empty plate. "Ah," he began to sit down again, "you are fooling me, Uncle Justus." Then, he put a large dirty finger into each corner of his mouth and pulled wide. After which he said, "Empty, you see, Uncle, hungry as all that!"

I smoothed my napkin. A shrill tinkle rang from one of the crystal glasses; at last it had been barely touched, nicked by Lebrecht's knife large as a scimitar. Lebrecht pushed his chair to one side of the table.

"Potato. Plenty of potato for me," said Mauschel loudly, peering at the carver. With a black finger he rubbed the bottom of the plate.

Lebrecht nodded, he had heard his son. Then, whispering, holding the knife up to the aging chandelier, "Mauschel. Give me a hair, Knabe."

"I'll give you my whole scalp if you'll cut us some meat . . ."

"Only a hair, Mauschel."

The coal carrier, the only child, pulled a hair from his head and Lebrecht, taking it, began testing the edge of the blade against it, cutting and swinging emptily in the air.

We watched. He leaned down and immersed himself in the delicate clutter of the table, and faced the lamb; obviously he wanted nothing more than to carve and eat.

"If you cannot do it," came the woman's hissing, "then give the knife to Justus."

So he began, as his wife coaxed him and his son leaned toward him salivating like a street dog. Lebrecht carved. But in the last pitiful instant he was unable to wield the fork—the knife alone was quite enough for him—and now one hand was clasped upon the lamb. That hand lay embedded in the fat, the fingers curled down the sides of the meat, squeezing their prints into the golden skin. He perspired, bit his lip, and with the very palm of his hand, and with the fingers—on one was a gold ring—pushed the roast firmly into its platter, despite the hot juice that trickled across the knuckles, the grease that splattered his white cuff. He began triumphantly to smile.

"Metze, you'll forgive me if I serve my brother Justus first . . ." And the plate was passed to me, heaped high.

Then Lebrecht sat and looked at the last filled dish, his own. But as he swung the knife down from its striking position, giving hardly a thought to the blood-covered blade, he brought another tinkling from a goblet, and now, after all his care and watchfulness, it fell over and emptied into his lap.

"Mauschel," said the boy's mother, "bring a cloth."

"Later. After we eat," came Mauschel's voice out of the deep and rattling plate.

"It's all right, Metze," whispered my brother, "eat your food, meine Herzliebste."

"Well," I said when the meal was half-done, at last spreading a piece of bread with preserves from a little pot, "well, I was sick."

"Ah," Lebrecht roused himself, "you were sick, Justus!"

"I was."

"Mama has been sick too, haven't you?" said Mauschel. He grinned at his mother, but Metze's eyes were toward me. Arching her brows and without thinking, she sat holding herself, the ache, under one breast. Her jaws chewed irrevocably and silently behind those pale lips.

"I have been nearly dead. Sick, yes, but worse, Mauschel, your Uncle Justus, mein Neffe, nearly died."

"Ah, Justus," Lebrecht apologized, pushing back his chair, "you had not made it clear. Ah, ah, was it bad as that?" He walked around the table, behind his wife, still carrying the full fork in one hand, and then returned quickly to the head of the table, smiling for their luck in having me that night, then frowning and shaking his shoulders.

"Yes, it was that bad," I said and tasted the jam which was quite sweet. "Yes. I did not think I would come out of it. But other than that I had my holiday . . ."

"Holiday?" Metze stopped chewing.

I nodded. "I stayed at the Gasthof. There was the beach, real sea water. All that."

"How then," her hard yet almost tearful eyes turned sharp like the sights on the end of a gun, and from the twisting of her hand beneath the heart, the pain must have been growing. "How, then, did you nearly die?"

"Sunstroke," I said calmly. "Lebrecht," raising my voice, "I was nearly burned to death by the sun down there."

"Were you, Justus!" he exclaimed, plunging the fork into his mouth and looking from his wife to his son and back again to his plate. "Scheusslich, scheusslich!" he faltered and banged his knife handle on the table.

I took a mouthful of potato. Then I pushed the dinner away.

"There is nothing worse than sunstroke!" exclaimed Lebrecht, wiping his mouth thoroughly.

"Ja. Nothing so bad, Lebrecht, I could actually hear the hoarse cries of the angels, my brother."

"Is that true?" he asked.

"True, Lebrecht. True indeed. And the blisters were big as pullet eggs. It is true: near death, near death."

I glanced at Metze. She was lifting the breast now to probe at her pain. All of a woman's hurt collects there, all of the nerves seem to end there under the breast.

"Did you," turning the wrinkles of her forehead into a cold smile, "did you enjoy swimming in the ocean, Justus?"

"It was perfect," I said briefly.

"Poor Justus, poor Justus," sighed my brother, clacking again at his food, pausing to stare at me as at a man in his coffin. "How many days did you lie there, Justus?"

"Well taken, Lebrecht. I don't know. It was long enough for that burned body of mine to cool off, long enough for it to cool down like a comet that plunges into the shore and steams in agony for weeks, until the night air and sea breezes cool it a little, and the fires die out. Then, my skin turned to water. And, of course, there was the odor, Lebrecht."

"But you should have called me, Justus. You should have communicated. Metze," turning suddenly upon his wife, "didn't you dream, didn't you get a message? Didn't you know that Justus was slipping from us? Metze never fails, Justus, she is a receiver of the sparks from beyond. We rely on her, Mauschel and I, to interpret for us, to tell us . . . Didn't you know, Metze?"

"I did not," she said.

"You must not have been listening for me, Metze!" I laughed. "Yes," I went on, leaning back to pluck off the end of my cigar as they poked in the debris of gristle and cutlery, "I was red as the lamb's tongue. Red and rather yellow too, I believe. Metze," I held out my glass, "may I have some more water? Sunstroke leaves a man dehydrated, leaves him with a thirst in every cell of the flesh. May I have some water, bitte?"

Mauschel watched his mother. She said nothing and did not move. She simply remained white and perhaps trembling, as if that mechanism inside her bosom had missed a revolution or two.

"How restful it must have been for your Uncle Justus on the beach, Mauschel," she murmured at last.

Mauschel looked at her a moment more, then drew back his elbows, relinquished his massive guard over his plate, got to his feet and fetched the water pitcher from the kitchen.

"Ja, Justus," his mother began, without looking at me, "I have been ill."

"What, Metze! You, too?"

"Ja, Justus. We shall accompany each other," and she touched my hand with one of her frozen fingers.

"Ah, too bad," I answered. "But then, Lebrecht," I looked down the table, "Metze had no blisters after all!" We laughed. "Here, Mauschel," I said, holding out a cigar, "give this to your father."

"Thank you, Justus," my brother said softly and felt in his pockets for a match. I thought that he was going to eat more, but no, he could not and began instead to smoke.

Metze suddenly pulled her fingers away from the breast—gone the pain!—and laughed like a charming mother.

"Mauschel," leaning forward, "Mauschel, my son, go put on your swimming suit. Let us see you in it, Mauschel."

"What? Has Mauschel a swimming suit also?"

"Ja," said Metze proudly. "Hurry, Mauschel!"

It was as if she had asked him to play a piece on the flute or to recite Goethe. His head hung like a sheep dog. He kicked the legs of the table a moment, then left us.

We remained waiting around the drafty and ruined table. Metze smiled. But her eyes were blank and white as the knucklebones of an old woman. Lebrecht Kümmerlich was no longer hungry, he held the burning cigar in his teeth and sent the smoke up into the blue of the ceiling.

"Tell me, Lebrecht," I said out of the silence, pushing back from the table and crossing my knees, "how is the old wireless?"

He did not answer. His mouth made only a small, violent puffing gesture, like a noiseless engine. I watched my cigar ash grow, and sat with them in this room suddenly cold for summer, filled with shadow and plaster, this world full of family dinners and Mauschel's growing pains, far from the sea.

"Come in, Liebling," said Metze toward the dark door, "don't be shy." Then I saw one of Mauschel's bare feet dangling, showing itself just over the edge of the jamb, feeling its way timidly as if into a pool of cold water.

"Gut, gut," exclaimed his mother and smiled upon him.

Mauschel was naked except for a pair of bright black trunks which fit his loins tight as the skin of a melon. They were cut high on the buttocks. He was white, grinning, and came around the table to stand beside Metze. He had large legs and enormous arms; and every section of arm, of leg, was nipped tightly at the joint where it ended, but was otherwise fat. I noticed a few babyish freckles on the white slopes of his shoulders.

"Is he quite fully grown yet, Lebrecht?" I asked.

"Oh, indeed yes. We can get no more out of him. You're not going to grow any bigger, are you, Mauschel."

The boy shook his head. He grinned and slapped his arms loudly.

"Next year," Metze pronounced, trying to twist about to see him, "we're going to take Mauschel to the beach."

"Fine, fine," I answered.

"And you won't get sunstroke, will you, Mauschel?"

"No," he said, "not me." Then, taking courage from the laughter: "This is the way I shall dive!" he exclaimed and suddenly thrust his arms above his head and shook his very gelatinous soul into the swimmer's fishlike form.

"Ah," Metze reached and touched his flesh.

"Mauschel," I spoke softly and drew out my purse. "Come here, Mauschel." Feeling him close by, suddenly obedient, I gave him the bank note. "Don't spend it, Mauschel. It is to bring you good luck."

I heard the earliest sounds of birds outside and, louder than the birds, a woman's sharp voice. I pulled on my trousers, went into the bathroom, carefully raised the green glass window, thrust my head through the opening and looked down. Metze was standing below on the stoop talking loudly. A market boy, leaning on an iron cart filled with food, watched her, grinned, but made no move to unload his packages.

Against the fence that bordered the yard stood Lebrecht's row of birdhouses, and the sun lighted the houses while the birds hopped in and out, quickly, noisily, fluttering and ill-prepared for the morning.

"Put the food in the kitchen," Metze commanded. The boy laughed and scraped one of his muddy boots on the iron spokes. He had only one eye and wore no patch to hide the withered empty bed of the other. His fingers were red from handling wet carrots and sides of beef, his leather apron was splashed from the road; he pulled a green stalk from a bundle in the cart and began to eat, scratched his blood-stained cheek, under the skin his jaws moved sideways back and forth. He looked at Metze. The birds sang loudly.

"No, Frau Kümmerlich. I might leave you this little bag, but no more."

"The kitchen!" Her voice rose to my window. "The whole wagon load goes into my kitchen!"

"No, Frau Kümmerlich," eating more of the green, "why only yesterday the butcher said, 'The Kümmerlichs have stopped eating meat. And they eat no garden produce either. When Herr Kümmerlich's wife grows thin,' he told me, 'leave them a box of meal.' You don't look thin to me, Frau Kümmerlich."

Still leaning on the cart, he began slowly to push his weight on it, swinging and moving it in Metze's direction, and the iron wheels ground slowly with a muddy, metallic noise, slipping, clanging, the cart turning as if to run her down. The boy's bent uncombed shape—I could see that he had brushed against dead fowl and smoked half-cigarettes in the butcher's meat locker—sidled close to Metze. He lifted up a package, shook loose the paper exposing a large beef heart and dropped it again into the wagon.

"Have you a good fire, Frau Kümmerlich?" he whispered and, reaching out stubby fingers, tweaked her arm.

"I want the food," she said, "all of it!"

He stood straight up and with both hands took hold of the cart's pushbar, wheeled the iron-walled vehicle around and ran off, laughing and bouncing the wagon so that a few soft oranges flew from it and fell to the roadside. I shut the window and washed myself.

Downstairs Metze was trying to build a fire in the kitchen stove. The shades were pulled tight in the living room. During the day we ate in the kitchen and there was a plate—a sausage, a piece of bread—for each of us. Metze kept Mauschel's meal on the stove in a large double pot with a black lid.

"Where is the boy?" asked Lebrecht after a long silence.

"He is not late," said Metze. "Mauschel is never late."

Then I saw my nephew's face at the kitchen window: only the head, the face, staring at me over his father's shoulder. He had taken a bit of yellow leaf and wadded it into one eye socket. He winked his visible eye and raised one hand. Satisfied that we were already at the table, he must have walked around the house, for we heard him tramping near the front entrance and the door banged. Lebrecht nodded and smiled. We waited. The forks lingered in the broken skin of our sausages.

"Come in, Mauschel," his mother called, "we've only been eating a moment!" Lebrecht stood up and took the pot off the flame, filled the dish at Mauschel's place and blew lightly on it. Lebrecht sat down. Our heads—Lebrecht's contented, Metze's starched, mine massive—turned toward the door.

Mauschel was leaning there. His belly swayed sleepily, his shoulders massed themselves against the wood, a jacket hung over one arm, the seeds of his eyes were black.

"Welcome, Mauschel," murmured Lebrecht. "Monday's greeting, Mauschel." Lebrecht lowered his eyes and began spreading a piece of bread for his son. The boy said nothing. At the top of his shirt I could see the broad expanse of thick flesh white and damp as a drake's breast.

"Wouldn't you like to eat just a spoonful or two?" his mother asked him.

"You had better join us," I agreed quickly, laughing, "or I will eat your portion, Mauschel!"

Mauschel then started forward. He was fat, he seemed more ready to burst a clod of earth than to rest at the table. His hair was wild and his shirt wet, his bulk cut off the sunlight from the window.

Mauschel walked around the table and stood for a moment beside Metze, letting the jacket slide off his arm. He put his arm like a dead reptile across her shoulders and pushed his face into her hair; his free hand crept to a pocket in the tight trousers and, while Lebrecht and I watched, the fat fingers produced a single bank note and stealthily placed it in the middle of his mother's plate, draped it over the two split sausages.

When he moved, the sun danced thoughtlessly across the kitchen tiles and poured itself into the empty potato bin, swam in the empty sink, cast our four shadows on the white wall. The morning seemed to flow forward and backward, flooding the day with its light and the smell of hungry children, as if all our lives had come here to rest, to stop, and our fortunes were to be found in Mauschel's untouched plate. I heard the sound of a far-off dog, heard the bark that bites into life itself. We sat still and straight.

Then Metze saw the bank note, there on her plate and already soaking up the sausage fat. How she looked! How wide the eyes! To be kissed, yes, but then to find this tender money on the tip of her fork! Metze at that very moment must have felt this bit of paper safe in her bosom, finding a meager breakfast flowered to a fortune. A strand of hair came loose and scraped at her neck, the blue veins sang on the backs of her hands and she reached out, trying to pick up the bill with calm, trying to take it at last between icy fingers.

But Mauschel was quicker than Metze. He snatched the bank note from under her eyes, caught it, leaned and turned in front of her. And then, clicking his teeth in a moment of joy, he stretched the bank note wide, pulled it suddenly until it measured a good foot, elongating the rubber bill wide as his smile, and let one end go, snapped it in Metze's face.

"What shall we buy, Mamma?" he cried. "Look, it is bigger than that even!" And he stretched the hundred marks again. "What do you want, Mamma? A leg of lamb?" He laughed and stuffed the piece of rubber counterfeit into his hip pocket. "It is a good joke," he said flatly as if to himself and walked from the room, leaving his coat on the floor.

"Ach, Mauschel," whispered Lebrecht, hanging his head, "ach, my dangerous son," and slowly emptied the plate into the waiting pot.

With a cold gliding motion Metze went straight to the livingroom couch, still tumbled and stale as it was when Mauschel roused himself at dawn. She lay down but did not close her eyes. I saw her ear, a kind of muscular shell, quite separate from the head; I saw the mole on her throat; I saw the line where the hair grew upon the scalp. I watched her, making no sound, and waited to see what she would do. Her wedding hand hung down forgotten. Then, like die Leichenfrau who cares for the dead, her lips moved, her eyelids narrowed, and she began to talk to her dead mother.

"Mamma?"

"Metze?"

"Shall we speak to him, Mamma?"

"Natürlich, Metze!"

"Mamma, we must be firm with him."

"Bring him to me, Metze. Bring him to his Grossmutter . . ."

"Oh, he loves you, Mamma!"

"He is a good boy baby, Metze. Bring him to me . . ."

"Mamma?"

"Ja, Metze?"

"Talk to him, Mamma, talk to him . . ."

When Mauschel stood in the doorway, his mother groaned from the couch. I pushed past him and up the stairs.

A Little Bit of the Old Slap and Tickle

Sparrow the Lance Corporal knew he would find his family by the sea.

Now through the underground and in a public bus with wooden seats and on foot he traveled until under the dusty tree tops he smelled the surf and brine and stood at last atop the great cliff's chalky edge. On the upward footpath the trees had fallen away and at the head of the ascent he was alone, windswept, with the sun in his eyes and a view of the whole stretch of coast before him. It was a peaceful sea, worn down by flotillas of landing boats forever beached. And away to either side of him the cliffs were crumbling, these desolate black promontories into which gun batteries had once been built. Now it was all won, all lost, all over, and he himself—a tiny figure—stood on the crest with the seawrack and the breeze of an ocean around him. He was wearing his old battledress and a red beret.

The war-worn flotillas lay a hundred feet below. Down there, spread at the cliff's bottom, was the mud, that softly heaved between the line of water and the first uprisings of dry stone: and down there lay the iron fleet half-sunk in the mud. For ten miles in either direction from the stump on the cliff's high windy lip—a flat tin helmet was nailed to the stump and it was Sparrow's sign, marking the steep descent he had found for himself—he could see once more the wreckage and this low mud of the coast, washed with foam, slick, cleaving to the sky. Terns sat with ruffled, white, still faces on the spars; the ends of cables sucked up rust from the low pools; the stripped hull of a destroyer rose bow first from the muck.

Here was Sparrow, come back unannounced. Leaning forward, resting his kit, grass tangling up about his boots and the wind blowing tight wads of cloud in his direction, he gazed down upon the scene and knew it was home after all. His own spot was there, the sweeper lying straight and true in the mud up to her water-line, his salt and iron house with chicken wire round one portion of the deck where the children played, the tin pipe at the stern with a breath of smoke coming up, the plank run out from her bow to a sandy place ashore. It was like living in a war memorial, and letting his eyes swing back from his own ten windy miles of devastation, fixing upon the tiny figure of a scrubby black dog that was barking at the abandoned shape of a carrier listing not fifty yards to the lea; seeing the dog at her game, and seeing a handful of slops come suddenly from one porthole, now he knew that his sweeper was inhabited and that, once aboard, he was father of this household respectable as a lighthouse keeper's station.

The terns set up a terrible cry that afternoon as he made his way down the cliff, and the dog—Sparrow loved her bent tail, the sea lice about her eyes, loved the mangy scruff of her neck—the dog leaped, then floundered out of the mud to meet him. So with kit and cane, red beret hanging off the tip of his skull and dripping dog in arm, he climbed the plank and shouted the names of his kiddies, limped round the capstan to see that the rain-water pan was full.

"You back?" The woman stepped out of the companionway and stopped, her eyes already simmering down on Sparrow, sharp fingers unfastening the first three buttons of her khaki shirt. "Well, it *is* a good day." And then, coming no closer, speaking in the hard voice wreathed with little trails of smoke, standing with the dirty ocean and derelicts behind her: "The boys have been wanting to search the *Coventry* again. We'll let them go. And we'll put the other buggers in the brig for an hour. Funny . . . I've had it on my mind all day."

"Good girl," said Sparrow. "Good old girl."

It was the home air that he breathed, smells of mid-ocean, a steady and familiar breeze pungent on the deck with the woman, a sweeter fragrance of grass and white bones on the cliff top, an air in which he sometimes caught the burnt vapors of a far-off freighter or, closer at hand, the smells of his own small dog. Scraping paint or splicing rope, or sitting and holding a half cup of rum in the sun on the bow, or following the boys down the idleness of the beach, he smelled what the woman washed or what a hundred-foot wave discharged into that whole long coastal atmosphere. In the dawn the red sun stretched thin across the line of the eye; throughout the day there was some davit swinging and creaking; and at supper they all ate black beans together and drank their ale.

There were old ammunition boxes for Sparrow and the woman to sit on at dusk when at last the terns grew quiet. Man and wife smoked together while the night blew in across the cold slickness of the sea. A bucket of old rags at her side, her legs no more than two white streaks, the starlight making the sock or shirt turn silver, she hunched forward then and sewed, and he liked her best in the beginning of the blue night when she was thin and preoccupied and without children, digesting her meal and letting him sit with his arm across the shoulder hard as a rocker-arm. No park benches, no dancing or walking out for the woman and Sparrow. They turned to a great pile of anchor chain or to the deck when the sewing was done. In union their scars, their pieces of flat and no longer youthful flesh touched and merged. He liked her to leave the impression of damp potatoes on his belly, he liked to feel the clasp-knife in the pocket of her skirt. And love was even better when they were sick, the heart of it more true with aching arms and legs. It was a good red nose that pleased him, or the chance to kiss the water from her eyes. Love, not beauty, was what he wanted.

In the beginning of night—the time when at last the woman leaned far forward so that the shoulders disappeared from under his arm and his hand traveled down until the four glossy tips of his fingers were thrust into the crevice between her flesh and the lid of the ammunition box, feeling her more desirable than the girls he had seen in Chisling or Squadron Up—in this beginning of the night, Sparrow knew the privacy of marriage and the comfort to be taken with a woman worn to thinness, wiry and tough as the titlings on the cliff.

And the second night, after the moon had gone into the sea and after the woman had returned from helping Arthur out of a bad dream: "You're a proper fire-stick, little cock," she said. "You could spend more time at home, I should think. It's been on my mind."

He nodded, taking the offered cup of rum and the cigarette. "I could do that." He put the cup to his mouth as if the burn of the rum and the fire of his own lip and loin could bring to life the great amphibious shadow around them. In the dark he looked at the bridge wings and dipping masts. "I could stay home rightly enough. No doubt of that."

The woman took the cigarette from between his lips, put it to hers and spoke while exhaling: "Why not set up for yourself?"

He shook his head. "I'm not big enough for that."

"I've thought you were. Like the old girl with the glass ball said."

He nodded. "It's the risks, that's all. You take them alone if you try it alone." And after a moment, shifting, wetting his lips for the cigarette: "Shall I send down a packet of skivvies for Arthur?"

"Oh, give us a kiss," she answered, and she was not laughing.

For the two days and nights that was all they said. Sparrow watched the woman throwing out her slops, putting the youngest to play under the cover of chicken wire, or smoking at the rail with broom in hand and eyes coming down to him. In a few old jars she put up wild berries picked from the cliff.

Once, wearing a short mended garment styled before the war, she stepped slowly into the deeper brown water off the stern, pushed her chest down into the warmth of the water while the boys clapped and Arthur, the oldest, cried: "Coo, Sparrow, why don't you teach her to swim?" Until he saw the look on his father's face and his mother's own humorless eyes and soaking wet hair turned up to him. The dog, that often lay panting in a little black hole in the mud against the carrier's enormous side, danced in after the woman and pulled abreast of her with spongy paws. While Sparrow, toes dangling in the silt and the faded old red beret tilted sharply forward on his brow, found everything in the woman that the boys were unable to see. The awkward movement of her hands and legs, the faded blue of the suit tied carefully across the narrow back but wrinkling over the stomach and stretching loose from the legs, the clot of seaweed stuck to her shoulder, the warnings she gave the dog, all this made Sparrow pause and lift himself slightly for a better view.

"Arthur," he called. "Show more respect for your mother."

At that moment he took in the swimming woman and paddling dog and sighed. For beyond those two, beyond the sweeper with its number still faintly stenciled on the bow, there lay in muddy suspension the entire field of ships, encrusted guns and vehicles. And he thought of the work it would take to set the whole thing afloat again—seeing the splash, the snort of the dog—and knew it could not be done, and smiled, clasping his knees, sucking the sun. All won, all lost, all over. But he had his.

So the leave passed. He shook Arthur's hands and the

woman went with him to the end of the plank. "Send the skivvies along," she said.

Then Sparrow stood on the cliff with home flashing through his head. Then he was gone, leaving small footprints below in the mud. He chucked his cigarette as he limped back into the world from which he had come.

The Universal Fears

Monday morning, bright as the birds, and there he stood for the first time among the twenty-seven girls who, if he had only known, were already playing the silence game. He looked at them, they looked at him, he never thought of getting a good grip on the pointer laid out lengthwise on that bare desk. Twenty-seven teen-age girls—homeless, bad-off, unloved, semi-literate, and each one of their poor unattractive faces was a condemnation of him, of all such schools for delinquent girls, of the dockyards lying round them like a seacoast of iron cranes, of the sunlight knifing through the grilles on the windows. They weren't faces to make you smile. Their sexual definition was vague and bleak. Hostile. But even then, in their first institutional moment together, he knew he didn't offer them any better from their point of view—only another fat man in the mid-fifties whose maleness meant nothing more than pants and jacket and belted belly and thin hair blacked with a cheap dye and brushed flat to the skull. Nothing in the new teacher to sigh about. So it was tit for tat, for them the desolation of more of the same, for him the deflation of the first glance that destroyed the possibility of finding just one keen lovely face to make the whole dreary thing worthwhile. Or a body promising a good shape to come. Or one set of sensual lips. Or one sign of adult responsiveness in any of those small eyes. But there was nothing, except the thought that perhaps their very sullenness might actually provide the most provocative landscape for the discovery of the special chemistry of pain that belongs to girls. Still he was already sweating in the armpits and going dry in the mouth.

"Right, girls," he said, "let's come to order."

In a shabby display of friendliness, accessibility, confidence, he slid from behind the desk and stood leaning the backs of his upper thighs against the front edge of it. Through the south window came the sounds of whistles and windlasses, from closer came the sounds of unloading coal. It made him think of a prison within a prison. No doubt the docks were considered the most suitable context for a school, so-called, for girls like these. Yes, the smells of brine and tar and buckets of oil that rode faintly in on the knifing light were only complementary to the stench of the room, to the soap, the thick shellac, the breath of the girls, the smell of their hair. It was a man's world for an apparently sexless lot of girls, and there was only one exotic aroma to be caught on that tide: the flowery wash of the sweet bay rum that clung to the thick embarrassed person of their old teacher new on the job.

"Right, girls," he said, returning warm glance for hostile stare, tic-like winks for the smoky and steady appraisal of small eyes, "right now, let's start with a few names. . . ."

And there they sat, unmoving, silent, ranked at three wooden benches of nine girls each, and all of their faces, whether large or small, thin or broad, dark or light, were blank as paper. Apparently they had made a pact before he entered the room to breathe in unison, so that now wherever he looked—first row on the left, first on the right—he was only too aware of the deliberate and ugly harmony of flat chests or full that were rising and falling slowly, casually, but always together.

Challenging the prof? Had they really agreed among themselves to be uncooperative? To give him a few bad minutes on the first day? Poor things, he thought, and crossed his fatty ankles, rested one flat hand on the uphill side of the belly, and then once more he looked them over at random, bearing down on a pair of shoulders like broken sticks, two thin lips bruised from chewing, a head of loose brown hair and another with a thin mane snarled in elastic bands, and some eyes without lashes, the closed books, claw marks evident on a sallow cheek.

"Girl on the end, there," he said all at once, stopping and swinging his attention back to the long black hair, the boy's shirt buttoned to the throat, the slanted eyes that never moved, "what's your name? Or you," he said, nodding at one of the younger ones, "what's yours?" He smiled, he waited, he shifted his glance from girl to girl, he began to make small but comforting gestures with the hand already resting on what he called his middle mound.

And then they attacked. The nearest bench was going over and coming his way like the side of a house undergoing demolition, and then the entire room was erupting not in noise but in the massed and silent motion of girls determined to drive their teacher out of the door, out of the school, and away, away, if they did not destroy him first right there on the floor. They leaped, they swung round the ends, tight-lipped they toppled against each other and rushed at him. He managed to raise his two hands to the defensive position, fingers fanned out in sheer disbelief and terror, but the cry with which he had thought to stop them merely stuck in his throat, while for an instant longer he stood there pushing air with his trembling outthrust hands. The girls tripped, charged from both sides of the room, swarmed over the fallen benches in the middle, dove with undeniable intent to seize and incapacitate his person.

The pointer, yes, the pointer, it flashed to his mind, invisibly it hovered within his reach, burned like a long thin weapon with which he might have struck them, stabbed them, beaten them, fended them off. But of course the pointer was behind him and he dared not turn, dared not drop the guard of his now frenzied hands. In an instant he saw it all— the moving girls between himself and the door, the impenetrable web of iron battened to each one of the dusty windows, and he knew there was no way out, no help. A shoe flew past his ear, a full-fifty tin of cigarettes hit the high ceiling above his head and exploded, rained down on him in his paralysis and the girls in their charge. No pointer, no handy instrument for self-defense, no assistance coming from anywhere.

And then the sound came on, adding to that turbulent pantomime the shrieks of their anger, so that what until this instant had been impending violence brimming in a bowl of unnatural silence, now became imminent brutality in a conventional context of the audionics of wrath. His own cry was stifled, his head was filled with the fury of that small mob.

"Annette . . . !"

"Deborah . . . !"

"Fuck off . . ."

"Now . . . now . . ."

"Kill him . . . !"

Despite their superior numbers they were not able to smother him in the first rush, and despite his own disbelief and fear he did not go down beneath them without a fight. Quite the contrary, because the first to reach him was of medium height, about fourteen, with her ribs showing through her jersey and a cheap bracelet twirling on her ankle. And before she could strike a blow he caught her in the crook of his left arm and locked her against his trembling belly and squeezed the life from her eyes, the breath from her lungs, the hate from her undersized constricted heart. He felt her warmth, her limpness, her terror. Then he relaxed the pressure of his arm and as the slight girl sank to his feet, he drove a doubled fist into the pimpled face of a young thick-lipped assailant whose auburn hair had been milked of its fire in long days and nights of dockyard rain. The nose broke, the mouth dissolved, his fist was ringed with blood and faded hair.

"You fucking old bastard," said a voice off his left shoulder, and then down he went with a knee in his ribs, arms around his neck and belly, a shod foot in the small of his back. For one more moment, while black seas washed over the deck and the clouds burst, the pit yawned, the molten light of the sun drained down as from a pink collapsing sack in the sky, he managed to keep to his all-fours. And it was exactly in this position that he opened his eyes, looked up, but only in time to receive full in the mouth the mighty downward blow of the small sharp fist of the slant-eyed girl whose name he had first requested. The black hair, the boy's gray workshirt buttoned tight around the neck, a look of steady intensity in the brown eyes, and the legs apart, the body bent slightly down, the elbow cocked, and then the aim, the frown, the little fist landing with unexpected force on the loose torn vulnerable mouth—yes, it was the same girl, no doubt of it.

Blood on the floor. Mouth full of broken china. A loud kick driven squarely between the buttocks. And still through the forests of pain he noted the little brassy zipper of someone's fly, a sock like striped candy, a flat bare stomach gouged by an old scar, bright red droplets making a random pattern on the open pages of an outmoded Form One Math. He tried to shake a straddling bony tormentor off his bruised back, bore another shock to the head, another punch in the side, and then he went soft, dropped, rolled over, tried to shield his face with his shoulder, cupped both hurt hands over the last of the male features hiding down there between his legs.

They piled on. He saw the sudden blade of a knife. They dragged each other off, they screamed. He groaned. He tried to worm his heavy beaten way toward the door. He tried to defend himself with hip, with elbow. And beneath that struggling mass of girls he began to feel his fat and wounded body slowing down, stopping, becoming only a still wet shadow on the rough and splintered wood of the classroom floor. And now and then through the shrieking he heard the distant voices.

"Cathy . . ."

"Eleanora . . ."

"Get his fucking globes . . ."

"Get the globes . . ."

They pushed, they pulled, they tugged, and then with his eyes squeezed shut he knew suddenly that they were beginning to work together in some terrible accord that depended on childish unspoken intelligence, cruel cooperation. He heard the hissing of the birds, he felt their hands. They turned him over—face up, belly up—and sat on his still-breathing carcass. One of them tore loose his necktie of cream-colored and magenta silk while simultaneously his only white shirt, fabric bleached and weakened by the innumerable Sunday washings he had given it in his small lavatory sink, split in a long clean easy tear from his neck to navel. They flung his already mangled spectacles against the blackboard. They removed one shoe, one sock, and yanked the shabby jacket off his right shoulder and bounced up and down on his sagging knees, dug fingernails into the exposed white bareness of his right breast. Momentarily his left eye came unstuck and through the film of his tears he noted that the ringleader was the girl with the auburn hair and broken nose. She was riding his thighs, her sleeves were rolled, her thick lower lip was caught between her teeth in a parody of schoolgirl concentration, despite her injury and the blood on her face. It occurred to him that her pale hair deserved the sun. But then he felt a jolt in the middle, a jolt at the hips, and of course he had known all along that it was his pants they were after, pants and underpants. Then she had them halfway down, and he smelled her cheap scent, heard their gasping laughter, and felt the point of the clasp knife pierce his groin.

"He's fucking fat, he is . . ."

"The old suck . . ."

In his welter of pain and humiliation he writhed but did not cry out, writhed but made no final effort to heave them off, to stop the knife. What was the use? And wasn't he aware at last that all his poor street girls were actually bent to an operation of love not murder? Mutilated, demeaned, room a shambles and teacher overcome, still he knew in his fluid and sinking consciousness that all his young maenads were trying only to feast on love.

"Off him! Off him!" came the loud and menacing voice from the doorway while he, who no longer wanted saving, commenced a long low moan.

"Get away from him at once, you little bitches . . . !"

There he was, lying precisely as the victim lies, helplessly inseparable from the sprawled and bloodied shape the victim makes in the middle of the avenue at the foot of the trembling omnibus. He was blind. He could not move, could not speak. But in customary fashion he had the distinct impression of his mangled self as noted, say, from the doorway where the director stood. Yes, it was all perfectly clear. He was quite capable of surveying what the director surveyed—the naked foot, the abandoned knife, the blood like a pattern spread beneath the body, the soft dismembered carcass fouling the torn shirt and crumpled pants. The remnants of significant male anatomy were still in hiding, dazed, anesthetized, but the pinched white hairy groin, still bleeding, was calling itself to his passive consciousness while beckoning the director to a long proud glance of disapproval, scorn, distaste.

Gongs rang, the ambulance came and went, he lay alone on the floor. Had the girls fled? Or were they simply backed against those dusty walls with legs crossed and thumbs hooked in leather belts, casually defying the man in the doorway? Or silent, sullen, knowing the worst was yet to come for them, perhaps they were simply trying to right the benches, repair the room. In any case he was too bruised to regret the hands that did not reach for him, the white ambulance that would forever pass him by.

"Sovrowsky, Coletta, Rivers, Fiume," said the director from his point of authority at the door. "Pick him up. Fix his pants. Follow me. You bitches."

In the otherwise empty room off the director's office was an old leather couch, there not merely for the girls' cramps but, more important, for the director's rest, a fact which he knew intuitively and immediately the moment he came awake and felt beneath him the pinched and puffy leather surface of the listing couch. And now the couch was bearing him down the dirty tide and he was conscious enough of adding new blood to fading stains.

Somebody was matter-of-factly brushing the cut above his eye with the flaming tip of a long and treacherous needle. And this same person, he discovered in the next moment, was pouring a hot and humiliating syrup into the wounds in his groin.

"Look at him," murmured the thin young woman, and made another stroke, another daub at the eye, "look at him, he's coming round."

Seeing the old emergency kit opened and breathing off ammonia on the young woman's knees pressed close together, and furthermore, seeing the tape and scissors in the young woman's bony hands and hearing the tape, seeing the long bite of the scissors, it was then that he did indeed come round, as his helpful young colleague had said, and rolled one gelatinous quarter-turn to the edge of the couch and vomited fully and heavily into the sluggish tide down which he still felt himself sailing, awake or not. His vomit missed the thin black-stockinged legs and narrow flat-heeled shoes of the young teacher seated beside him.

THE UNIVERSAL FEARS

"I warned you," the director was saying, "I told you they were dangerous. I told you they beat your predecessor nearly to death. How do you think we had your opening? And now it's not at all clear you can handle the job. You might have been killed. . . ."

"Next time they'll kill him, rightly enough," said the young woman, raising her brows and speaking through the cheap tin nasal funnel of her narrow mouth and laying on another foot-long strip of tape.

Slowly, lying half on his belly, sinking in the vast hurt of his depthless belly, he managed to lift his head and raise his eyes for one long dismal stare at the impassive face of the director.

"I can handle the job," he whispered, just as vomiting started up again from the pit of his life. From somewhere in the depths of the building he heard the rising screams of the girl with the thick lips, auburn hair, and broken nose.

He was most seriously injured, as it turned out, not in the groin or flanks or belly, but in the head. And the amateurish and careless ministrations of the cadaverous young female teacher were insufficient, as even the director recognized. So they recovered his cream and magenta tie, which he stuffed into his jacket pocket, helped to replace the missing shoe and sock, draped his shoulders in an old and hairy blanket, and together steadied him down to his own small ancient automobile in which the young female teacher drove him to the hospital. There he submitted himself to something under two hours of waiting and three at least of professional care, noting in the midst of fresh pain and the smells of antiseptic how the young teacher stood by to see the handiwork of her own first aid destroyed, the long strips of tape pulled off brusquely with the help of cotton swabs and a bottle of cold alcohol, and the head rather than chest or groin wrapped in endless footage of soft gauze and new strips of official tape. He felt the muffling of the ears, the thickening sensation of the gauze going round the top of his head and down his swollen cheeks, was aware of the care taken to leave stark minimal openings for the eyes, the nose, the battered mouth.

"Well," muttered the medical student entrusted with this operation of sculpting and binding the head in its helmet and face-mask of white bandages, "somebody did a job on you, all right."

No sooner had he entered the flat than his little dog Murphy, or Murph for short, glanced at the enormous white hive of antiseptic bandages and then scampered behind the conveniently open downstairs door of the china cabinet, making a thin and steady cry of uncommonly high pitch. He had frightened his own poor little dog, he with his great white head, and now he heard Murph clawing at the lower inside rear wall of the china cabinet and, leaning just inside his own doorway, became freshly nauseous, freshly weak.

"Come out, Murph," he tried to say, "it's me." But within its portable padded cell of bandage, his muffled voice was as wordless as Murphy's. From within the cabinet came the slow circular sounds of Murphy's claws, still accompanied by the steady shrill music of the little animal's panic, so that within the yet larger context of his own personal shock, he knew at once that he must devote himself to convincing the little dog that the man inside the bandages was familiar and unchanged. It could take days.

"Murphy," he meant to say, "shut your eyes, smell my hands, trust me, Murph." But even to his own steady ear the appeal sounded only like a faint wind trapped in the mouth of a mute.

It was dusk, his insulated and mummified head was floating, throbbing, while the rest of him, the masses of beaten and lacerated flesh beneath the disheveled clothes, cried out for sleep and small soft hands to press against him and slowly eliminate, by tender touch, these unfamiliar aches, these heavy pains. He wanted to lie forever on his iron bed, to sit swathed and protected in his broken-down padded chair with Murph on his lap. But the night was inimical, approaching, descending, filling space everywhere, and the flat no longer felt his own. The chair would be as hard as the bed, as unfamiliar, and even Murphy's latest hectic guilt-ridden trail of constraint and relief appeared to have been laid down by somebody else's uncontrollable household pet. Why did the window of his flat give onto the same dockyard scene, though further away and at a different angle, as the window of the schoolroom in which he had all but died? Why didn't he switch on a light, prepare his usual tea, put water in Murphy's bowl? A few minutes later, on hands and knees and with his heavy white head ready to sink to the floor, he suddenly realized that injury attacks identity, which was why, he now knew, that assault was a crime.

He did his clean-up job on hands and knees, he made no further effort to entice his dog from the china cabinet, he found himself wondering why the young teacher had allowed him to climb to the waiting and faintly kennelish-smelling flat alone. When he had dropped the last of poor little bewhiskered Murphy's fallen fruit into a paper sack now puffy with air and unavoidable waste, and in pain and darkness had sealed the sack and disposed of it in the tin pail beneath the sink, he slowly dragged himself to the side of the iron bed and then, more slowly still, hauled himself up and over. Shoes and all. Jacket and torn shirt and pants and all. Nausea and all. And lay on his side. And for the first time allowed the fingers of one hand to settle gently on the bandages that bound his head, and slowly and gently to touch, poke, caress, explore. Then at last, and with the same hand, he groped and drew to his chin the old yellow comforter that still exhaled the delicate scent of his dead mother.

SHORT FICTION

Teacher Assaulted at
Training School for Girls

Mr. Walter Jones, newly appointed to the staff of
St. Dunster's Training School for Girls, received
emergency treatment today at St. Dunster's Hospital for multiple bruises which, as Mr. Jones
admitted and Dr. Smyth-Jones, director of the
school, confirmed, were inflicted by the young
female students in Mr. Jones's first class at the
school. Mr. Jones's predecessor, Mr. William
Smyth, was so severely injured by these same
students November last that he has been forced
into early and permanent retirement. Dr. Smyth-
Jones expressed regret for both incidents, but
indicated that Mr. Jones's place on the staff would
be awaiting him upon his full and, it is to be hoped,
early recovery. "The public," he commented,
"little appreciates the obstacles faced by educa-
tors at a school such as St. Dunster's. After all,
within the system for the rehabilitation of crimi-
nally inclined female minors, St. Dunster's has
been singled out to receive only the most intractable of girls. Occasional injury to our staff and
to the girls themselves is clearly unavoidable."

With both hands on the wheel and Murph on his lap and a
large soft-brimmed felt hat covering a good half of the
offending white head, in this condition and full into the sun
he slowly and cautiously drove the tortuous cobbled route
toward Rose and Thyme, that brutally distended low-pitted
slab of tenements into which his father, Old Jack, as he was
known by all, had long since cut his filthy niche. The sun on
the roof of the small old coffin of a car was warm, the narrow
and dusty interior was filled with the hovering aroma of fresh
petrol, and Murph, with his nose raised just to the level of the
glass on the driver's side, was bobbing and squirming gently
to the rhythm first of the footbrake and then the clutch. As
for himself, and aside from the welcome heat of the little dog

and the ice and glitter of the new day, it gave him special pleasure to be driving cautiously along with a lighted cigarette protruding from the mouth-slit in the bandages and, now and again, his entire head turning to give some timorous old woman the whole shock full in the face. He was only too conscious that he could move, that he could drive the car, that he filled the roaring but slowly moving vehicle with his bulk and age, that Murph's tiny pointed salt-and-pepper ears rose just above the edge of the window, and then was only too conscious, suddenly, of the forgotten girls.

Why, he asked himself, had he forgotten the girls? Why had he forced from his mind so simply, so unintentionally, the very girls whose entry into his life had been so briefly welcome, so briefly violent? Would he give up? Would he see them again? But why had he applied for that job in the first place? Surely he had not been going his own way, finally, after what his nimble old Dad called the juicy rough. All this pain and confusion for easy sex? Not a bit of it.

And then, making a difficult turn and drawing up behind a narrow flat-bedded lorry loaded down with stone and chugging, crawling, suddenly he saw it all, saw himself standing in Old Jack's doorway with Murph in his arms, saw his nimble Dad spring back, small and sallow face already contorted into the familiar look of alarm, and duck and turn, and from somewhere in the uncharted litter of that filthy room whip out his trench knife and standing there against the peeling wall with his knees knocking and weapon high and face contorted into that expression of fear and grievous pride common to most of those who lived in the ruin and desolation of Rose and Thyme. Then he heard the silent voices as the little old man threw down the trench knife and wiped his little beak and small square toothless mouth down the length of his bare arm.

It's you, is it?

Just me, Dad. Come to visit.

You might know better than to be stalking up here like some telly monster with that head of yours and that dead dog in your arms.

Murph's all right, Jack. Aren't you, Murph?

It's that school, that fucking school. My own son beaten near to death by a bunch of girls and written up in the papers. I read it, the whole sad story. And then stalking up here like a murderous monster.

They're very strong girls. And there were a lot of them. Twenty-seven actually.

Why were you there? Tell me why, eh? Oh, the Good Samaritan. . . .

Yes, the Good Samaritan.

Or were you really after a little juicy rough?

Mere sex? Not a bit of it. Of course I wouldn't rule out possibilities, but there's more than that.

Juicy rough. Walter, juicy rough. Don't lie.

I believe I want to know how those girls exist without romance. Or do they?

Use the glove, Walter! Let me give you the old fur glove. It does a lovely job. You can borrow it. . . .

"Yes," he heard himself musing aloud from within the bundle of antiseptic stuffing that was his head, and pressing first the brake and then the accelerator, "yes, I want to be at the bottom where those girls are. Without romance."

At a faster pace now and passing the lorry, he headed the little blue car once more in the direction from which he and Murphy had started out in the first place. Occasionally it was preferable to meet Old Jack not in the flesh but in the mind, he told himself, and this very moment was a case in point.

"No," said the young female teacher in the otherwise empty corridor, "it's you! And still in bandages."

"On the stroke of eight," he heard himself saying through the mouth-slit, which he had enlarged progressively with his fingers. "I'm always punctual."

"But you're not ready to come back. Just look at you."

"Ready enough. They couldn't keep me away."

"Wait," she said then, her voice jumping at him and her face full of alarm, "don't go in there . . . !"

"Must," he said, and shook her off, reached out, opened the door.

The same room. The same grilled and dusty windows. The same machinery in spidery operation in the vista beyond. Yes, it might have been his first day, his first morning, except that he recognized them and picked them out one by one from the silent rows—the narrow slant-eyed face, the girl with tuberculosis of the bone, the auburn-haired ringleader who had held the knife. Yes, all the same, except that the ringleader was wearing a large piece of sticking plaster across her nose. Even a name or two came back to him and for an instant these names evoked the shadowy partial poem of the forgotten rest. But named or unnamed their eyes were on him, as before, and though they could not know it, he was smiling in the same old suit and flaming tie and dusty pointed shoes. Yes, they knew who he was, and he in turn knew all about their silence game and actually was counting on the ugliness, the surprise, of the fully bandaged head to put them off, to serve as a measure of what they had done and all he had forgiven even before they had struck, to serve them as the first sign of courage and trust.

"Now, girls," he said in a voice they could not hear, "if you'll take out pencils and paper and listen attentively, we'll just begin." Across the room the pointer was lying on the old familiar desk like a sword in the light.

The Assassination

from THE CANNIBAL (1949)

My earliest pertinent recollections are of childhood and of lying awake wheezing in my nightly asthma attacks and listening to the thumping and snorting of the horses in the riding stable that adjoined our yard back then in Old Greenwich, Connecticut. The worst thing about asthma is the sound—as of bees packed and buzzing in the chest. Yet sweating in those nightly attacks, somehow I confounded the hated noise of my breathing with the comforting, somnambulant sounds of the horses, and even grew to enjoy those long hours in the dark. During the day, my mother practiced her skills with hypodermic syringe and needle on an orange (she relieved my worst attacks with shots of adrenaline) while I worked in the gardens of the stable for fifty cents an hour in order to pay for the infrequent riding lessons I so dearly loved. I was allowed to ride an enormous box-like donkey free of charge, but I despised him for the ugly parody of a horse that he was. One afternoon, while squatting in a little plot of dusty ground beside the barn, I looked up at the sound of hooves and watched as a trim young girl trotted by on a large and handsome chestnut mare. She did not see me of course, where I squatted at the age of six or so in my humiliation, admiration, and envy. It was a very impossible love at first sight, and I think that my writing has always depended in one way or another on those first configurations of suffocation, faint stirrings of desire, and horses.

My formative years of 1935–40, from the ages of ten to fifteen, were spent in Juneau, Alaska, where my father, a tall and adventurous man somewhat like Uncle Ben in *Death of a Salesman*, searched vainly for the riches he thought were due him after the stock market collapse of 1929. By then I was clearly established as "the important one" (as E. M. Forster, another only child, was called). My mother, with her artistic temperament, wanted only to spend her life studying music in New York City, but made the best of her imprisonment in Juneau, at the time reachable only by ship from Seattle. Those were years of being hemmed in and oppressed by grim mountains, black waters smelling of dead fish, eighty-mile-an-hour winds. The local papers often reported my father as missing; my mother's anxiety was constant; and yet when we accompanied my father on one of his abortive expeditions aboard a hulking, unseaworthy boat named "The Prince of Wales," my mother heroically did the cooking in the tiny galley while I lay wheezing in the smoky fo'c'sle. What I remember of Alaska is like what can be dug from the unconscious, and our five years up there helped to determine not explicitly but psychologically the future cast of my fiction.

Our attic apartment in Juneau overlooked Gastineau Channel and its flanking mountains, and in 1939 my mother and I used to watch the carbon lamps of the miners coming down at night like fireflies from the mountain they were tunneling for the Alaska-Juneau Gold Mine, and then, on an archaic radio, we used to listen to Hitler making his violent, incomprehensible speeches. When the Japanese were about to invade the Aleutian Islands in 1940, my father sent my mother and me back to the east coast for safety.

In New York City I went to Trinity School for about eighteen months. There I learned to fence in its cold corridors and was embarrassed by young boys miming the strip-teasers they had discovered in downtown burlesque houses. In time I joined a ragged drum and bugle corps that practiced in a church basement. Those tough young drummers and buglers were an ugly lot, and I still remember the night when one of the boys bragged about a game of kicking a dead baby in a gunny sack along a side street off Amsterdam Avenue.

My mother began to fear that New York City would be bombed and devastated, so decided that we should move again and to some rural and hence safer place. Randomly she stuck a pin into a map of New York state: chance yielded the little upstate farming town of Pawling where we settled. I went to the local high school and spent my time as an outcast in "The Sweet Shop," the neighborhood ice cream parlor, or sitting on a rock at the edge of town and writing morbid verse on the backs of envelopes. I wanted to be a poet; I loved Poe; I was proud of a snapshot that was taken of me wearing a homburg, and a checked waistcoat, and carrying a copy of the Bible in one hand and a bottle of whiskey in the other.

Somehow I was admitted to Harvard in 1943, and that summer made my way to Cambridge where the poet Robert Hillyer encouraged me to continue writing, and a young Polish count ridiculed my country ways and brown and white saddle shoes. By Christmas, having failed a considerable number of courses, I found myself dismissed from Harvard and lying in a hospital at Fort Devens, in Ayer, Massachusetts; six weeks later, a disgusted lieutenant told me I was then and there discharged from the Army because of my chronic asthma.

Then came the experience that outdid my Alaskan boyhood and became the background of my first novel, *The Cannibal*. I joined the American Field Service, a group of volunteer ambulance drivers attached to British units in Burma and the European Theater. In the summer of 1944, without knowing how to drive a car, I arrived in Naples with a remarkable group of men and boys including a midget, an epileptic, and a seventy-year-old artist. For me, the last nine months of the war were not so much horrific as bizarre. In the Apennines we drove at night without lights, following another driver who walked ahead carrying a white handkerchief. One afternoon, in an abandoned farmhouse, I pulled the head from a very much alive chicken, which helped me, much later, to read "The Rime of the Ancient Mariner" with a guilty shock of personal understanding. For hours I would study rows of burn victims lying swathed in cocoons of gauze on stretchers set up on saw-horses in an abandoned winery. One time we were billeted in a still partially occupied mental institution in Louvain, Belgium; outside our village near Bremen, Germany, were mile-long lines of pajamaed inmates who had just been liberated from Belsen concentration camp. Victory in Europe was a night of green flares and shouts in the dark. When finally a group of us disembarked from a freighter tied up to a pier on Staten Island in the summer of 1945,

THE CANNIBAL

I knew well the value of anxiety and just how much I owed to my months in the American Field Service.

It took me two years to return to Harvard. But in the fall of 1947 I was again in Cambridge. Now I was married, and had been admitted into the fiction writing class of a great teacher and mentor, the novelist Albert J. Guerard. Suddenly it no longer mattered to me that I had failed German so many times; the kindness of Harvard deans had prevailed; I had given up writing bad poetry for writing fiction. My joy was immense, and I found my newly acquired confidence a kind of shocking wonder. My wife and I lived in Somerville, just beyond the edge of Cambridge, in a two-room apartment; I sat in a golden Empire chair and wrote on my lap. Sophie and I fashioned splendid meals of overcooked spaghetti on a hot plate, and she was able to teach me the rudiments of required French. Every Tuesday we took the trolley to Harvard Square and went to Albert's class, where the spouses of veterans were welcome. I read aloud pages from *The Cannibal*, and Sophie, who had already graduated from Radcliffe and had found a job at the Harvard Press, argued spectacularly with the wife of my keenest rival. In other classes I wrote out paragraphs of fiction instead of taking notes; I spent my time in a large lecture course on the eighteenth-century novel reading and re-reading letters from J. Laughlin, who had already agreed to publish *The Cannibal* at New Directions. This novel was all but finished, and J. had by then become my second mentor. The sense of well-being that was mine that fall was exceeded only twelve years later when I was writing *Second Skin* on a tropical island in the Caribbean.

The Cannibal had its immediate source in H. R. Trevor-Roper's *The Last Days of Hitler*, which I had read, to my everlasting good fortune, just before entering Albert's class. In the Trevor-Roper's description of Hitler committing suicide in his bunker that suddenly made me think of trying to render my own version of total destruction, total nightmare, by writing about a defeated "mythical" Germany from the German point of view. I saw it all: a neo-Nazi narrator named Zizendorf; Germany reduced to the little town of Spitzen-on-the-Dein (my revenge on the failed

German courses); a murdered school teacher who played the tuba; the single American motorcycle rider, Leevey, appointed by the Allies as the overseer of Zizendorf's conquered country. In the course of the novel, the "history" of Germany in 1914 is alternated with Zizendorf's plot in 1945 to assassinate Leevey and hence to liberate Germany from the invaders. The assassination is successful, and the novel culminates with an old aristocrat killing a child and joining Madame Snow, the landlady of Zizendorf's boarding house, in the cannibalistic meal of the novel's title. Finally Zizendorf sends forth his proclamation of freedom and his new Germany arises. In *The Cannibal* I discovered an impulse toward comedy and a love of prose.

In "The Assassination," American soldiers execute Pastor Miller, who preached against God and church in Spitzen-on-the-Dein, and Zizendorf, with his cohorts Stumpfegel and Fegelein, finally manages to murder Leevey, the American overseer, when he returns at night on his puttering motorcycle.

The Assassination

All during the day the villagers had been burning out the pits of excrement, burning the fresh trenches of latrines where wads of wet newspapers were scattered, burning the dark round holes in the back stone huts where moisture traveled upwards and stained the privy seats, where pools of water became foul with waste that was as ugly as the aged squatter. These earthen pots were still breathing off their odor of burned flesh and hair and biddy, and this strange odor of gas and black cheese was wafted across the roads, over the fields, and collected on the damp leaves and in the bare night fog along the embankment of the *Autobahn*. This smell not only rested over the mud, but moved, and with every small breath of air, the gas of mustard, soft goat pellets and human liquid became more intimate, more strong and visible in reddening piles. One's own odor could always be sifted out and recognized, a disturbingly fresh stream in the turning ash, a personal mark that could be sniffed and known after midnight, sometimes as if the tongue were poking in the incinerator and the warm air curling about the hewn seat.

The three of us waited by the side of the road, stockingless feet burning and itching in our unlaced shoes, plucking at nostrils, listening to a wasted mongrel paw the leaves, hearing an occasional tile slide from a roof and fall to the mud with the swishing of a tail. The flats turned away before us, unpeopled, dark, an occasional shell-case filling with seepage, the fingers of a lost glove curling with dew. Behind us the ghosts left the stalled tank and filed downward toward the canal.

"He's late," said Fegelein.

"Yes."

"No sleep for us then."

"Wait, have patience," I answered.

We crowded invisibly together with the road high over-head that extended far beyond this edge of town, and there were no precision transits or plumb lines to point the kilometers of travel or show the curve on the map where the blank spot of this town would be. We never ventured away, though we still wore the grey shirts and had signed our way to the outside world.

"It's a good machine he's riding," said Fegelein.

"Don't worry. I won't shoot at it."

"Good."

"Remember, no talking. Stintz would be sure to say some-thing when the next rider comes through in a month looking for this one." I constantly had to give commands.

"In a month we'll be ready."

"Yes."

"And the motorbike will be useful."

"Yes." I had to humor them.

In every town there are a few who, though they don't remember how it came about, or how they returned, or when they went away, or what the enemy expects, gather together in the night to rise again, despite the obstacle of their own people or the swarming invader. Behind us the town grew smaller; the sleepers were cold and numberless.

"No one will see?"

"No," I answered.

"I don't want to go forward tonight; you mustn't make me . . ."

"Stop that. You know there isn't any forward."

"I'm sorry."

The cold night air quickened my hunger, and I put the

thought out of mind, concentrated on the hunched man in goggles and helmet. Once the old horse clattered by above our ears and then moved off as if he smelled nothing, neither fresh grass nor humans nearby.

The three of us leaning against the clay bank were all that remained of the shadows of sentries, were primal, unordered, unposted sentries, lounging against the earth without password, rifles or relief. The sharp foreign voice had disappeared from the dark road and unlighted doorway, the rolls of wire, the angry tones, the organized guards were gone. Though unmistakable signs remained, a trampled package of woodbines, a tossed-off canteen, a piece of white webbing, these scraps still littered the floors of sheds or hung in the room corners where white women lay. The keepers, who had asked for papers, swore only with one word, lighted the night with red, and confiscated bicycles, and had moved on to the hunting ground of rodents. And we, the three shadows who remained, gaunt for the great land, dependent on the enemy's tin cans to squat in, waiting in our black unbuttoned coats and peaked caps, were sentries of the civilians, unemployed during the day, plotting for the greatest good by night.

The American on the motorcycle knew no more of the country that his eagle-colonels scourged, than did his free-eyed sergeants, roving in their green work clothes. He traveled along hypothetical lines of communication that chased miles beyond the end of the war and he had beer at each stopover. Desperation was not for this plains-rider, bouncing over once endless roads with his sack filled with unintelligible military scrawl, columns of figures, personal resentments, not for this oblivious traveler whose only communication was silence to the dark countrymen and "hi-ya, Mac" to his listless fellows. From the littered fields and overhanging branches, from the town library charred and unpurged, from the punctured rubber rafts plugging the canal, to the hanging mouths, to the enemy colors, to the unexploded traps, to the drunk official, it was an unrecognized, unadmitted, unnamed desperation that persisted beyond the tied prostitute and enemy news, beyond the cadaverous houses and American outposts, to give strength to us, the hovering sentries, to bring words to the lolling historians. Poison their camps, if only in a quip or solitary act.

I thought of it during each day in the newspaper office and thought of it against the mud-bank; life is not the remarkable, the precious, or necessary thing we think it is. The naked dark pawing of that eternal old horse who lingered on through no fault of his own, bereaved and unquiet in the night, told me that. And with the hoarded, secret sailor's black rum running through my mind, heaped about by past years' correspondence, dead letters, by fragments of broken type, I knew that the tenant was the law.

You can ask no man to give up his civilization, which is his nation. The old must go, stagger over the failing drawbridge, fall down before the last coat of arms. I thought Madame Snow too old to understand, I thought she should wither away and die, with her long, false, flaxen hair, because I thought she would run rattle-tattle through the night for preservation. Here I was wrong, since she was the very hangman, the eater, the greatest leader of us all. Death is as unimportant as life; but the struggle, the piling of bricks, the desperate attempts of the tenant; that is the man of youth, the old woman of calm, the nation of certainty.

". . . It is you who will die," said the Priest to the Mayor. That had been the day when the motorcycle rider and the rest of the Allies had first passed through *Spitzen-on-the-Dein.* The convoy crept up the long bright highway through the snow, through the handful of silent watchers, down the main street like a centipede with the motorcycle first, followed by the jeep, ending with proud band of four riflemen. An American colonel and two corporals rode in the jeep, an automatic rifle propped in the back seat, their canteens filled with rum, and the dispatch-rider in the lead wobbled from side to side and waved the children off, flurries of snow shooting up behind him.

"So this is Germany," said the Colonel, and leaning out from behind the cold wheel he blew his whistle and the convoy stopped. Before the eyes of the crowd he got out and fastened a slender wirecutter to the smoking radiator, then with a final quick word to the motorcycle man they made their way to the center of town, pulling on their mufflers, eyes frozen ahead. On the floor of the jeep beneath the jutting rifle, they carried their black robes and a few sealed envelopes. The foot-soldiers alternately ran and walked to keep warm.

By the middle of the afternoon they had stripped Madame Snow's apartment and established a headquarters, of three maps, a table and chair, temporary seat of American representation in the evil zone. The jeep was under a tarpaulin in the rear garden in the shed, the four troops billeted in the hall, and the dispatch rider was standing guard over his still warm machine. Through the uncurtained window, glancing for a moment from the red envelopes, the Colonel saw the sky darken for snow, and worried, he peered at his highly secret route through the nation, studied the undecipherable diagram and code. Satisfied, he signaled the corporal who quickly brought forth the three robes. The Colonel, short, heavyset, graduate of a technical institute, a brilliant engineer, thought in dotted parabolas, considered in fine red lines, and while lonely, overworked, and short in the knees, directed the spreading occupation. Except for the silver eagle sewn above the pocket of his black robe, he might have been the foreman of a jury pointed out to speak before the supreme law. Once more he carefully read the letter of instruction, tapped his pen on the bare wood, then dropped the paper into the heater in the corner, an open can of flaming petrol. The Mayor, Herr Stintz and myself stood in a corner, as there was no anteroom, watching these preparations, while out in the cold alone, walking up and down, waited Miller, the prisoner, thinking of the sweet children and his fair wife.

The robed men muttered together at the far end of the room behind the table, and we three, the witnesses, waited while a thin soot from the burning can settled over the floor, the walls, collected on the Colonel's two musette bags and on the neat small row of cracking army boots. The maps, freshly tacked to the wall, grew darker and the chill in the air grew worse with the promise of snow, soot speckled the grease on the Colonel's mess tins tied to the bedroll. Once one of the corporals turned, "No talking there," and we did not understand, for only the Colonel spoke German. Then, after a short silence, the Colonel seemed to remember. "My God, Corporal, get my pistol—and you might bring my pipe." The young man, holding the black hem above his boots, scowled once at us, the witnesses, and searched in one of the small dirty bags. Then a pause while they fumbled under his gown to arm him and he lit the pipe, his black cassock skirt and tough hands stiff with cold. The motorcycle rider's white helmet moved back and forth across the window, scattered flakes of snow dropped on his jacket.

"Mayor," the corporal called, and the frightened old man stepped into the dock, tensed for a dangerous question.

The Colonel took his place and spoke:

"How old are you?"

"Eh, what's that?"

"Your age, age."

"I'm sixty-one." His paper collar wilted, the official sash sagged on his waist, and he was afraid.

"Where were you born?"

"Right here, here in this very place."

"I understand you keep some sort of civil records?"

"I did, quite true, very fine writing. But they're gone, burned up, shells hit my house, zip, zip, and in the fallen glass the flames spread, so my papers are all gone."

"Well, I want to know something about," the Colonel looked at his notes, "a man named Miller."

"I've known him for years, his wife, children."

"Now, is it true he was a pastor?"

"Pastor? Ah, yes, pastor."

· "But now he no longer is?"

"No longer? Well, not actively, the war, I don't think there were many people to listen . . ."

"Did he *want* to stop being a pastor?"

"Well, there was a good deal of trouble in this town, we suffered . . ."

I called from the corner, "He *is* a pastor."

"Silence, keep quiet, there."

Then Herr Stintz came forward, a primer under his arm, smiling, and he edged himself in front of the Mayor.

"If you'll permit me," he said.

"Well, what is it?"

Stintz stepped closer, glasses pinching over his nose. "Herr Colonel, I think perhaps you should take into account that there was, you know, a new gospel, the war made a change in what a man might want to preach to the dumb people—other ears heard, the new gospel was a very strong thing, even his wife could do nothing with Miller."

The Colonel looked for a long moment at the Mayor.

"Is this true? Was there a change in Miller?"

"Well, everyone, the war was a hard thing but," the old man found himself staring at the eagle on the Colonel's chest, and it seemed to glow with a phosphorescent sheen, "but

I'm alone, I don't know him that well, he was away . . ."
The eagle grew bright and the old man wiped his chin,
tried to fasten the sash tighter, "but I think, maybe, he did
change . . ."

"He did not," I said.

"He's a tough one," whispered the officer to the corporal,
pointing at me, and the judges retired. The snow fell harder,
the rider covered his bike with a gunnysack. "I think," said
the Colonel, "that the case is closed, but we better be just, it
will be excellent to impress them with our thoroughness." So
for the rest of the afternoon, while the snow became thick and
we waited in the corner, while one of the corporals took notes
and the can ran out of fuel, a long line of civilians was formed
and one by one each citizen of the town passed into the dark
room, was questioned, and was returned to the raw cold
evening. At last the entire population had come and gone,
steel slats had been driven across the cellar window where
Miller waited, and the Colonel undid his bedroll and lay
down in the deep rich fur to sleep out the night. Long after-
wards the Mayor blamed everything on the shining eagle, "It
had frightful curled claws and a sharp hooked nose with red
terrifying eyes. That's what it did to me."

The Colonel shook himself awake before dawn, five o'clock
by his wrist watch accurate as a micrometer, and in only his
grey underwear donned a long sheepskin field coat and stumbled into the day's work. Moving about in the dark hallway
where his riflemen lay, he left a bright blank cartridge by each
man and emptied each weapon of its live ammunition, in-
specting each oiled chamber and silver whirling bore. Back in
the long bare living room he filled the petrol tin and, hunched
in the great curling coat, made himself a pot of black coffee,
warming, the while, his hands over the small flame. The
Mayor, Stintz and I slept together in the corner, the corporals
were buried deep in their cots, and in the basement, trapped

amid the piles of debris, Miller waited to see the morning through the narrow slats. The Colonel busied himself with a worn grammar, put his mess kit aside to be cleaned, and let his men sleep for another hour. Finally, ten minutes before six, he dug into his gear and pulled forth his best garrison cap, polished the badge with a rag, left it ready for the important hour and then padded out of doors. His were the first prints through the snow in the back yard; he was the first to break the air still heavy as with waiting flakes. The canal smelled strongly of vermin and slapping rubber, a broken rake handle and emery wheel jutted up through the damp snow, no smoke came from the chimneys on the other bank. Plough handles, shafts of wood, caked earthenware, the jaws of a wooden vice, old scraps of leather filled the slanting shed where the jeep was garaged under the tarpaulin, and a spot of thick green oil spread over the dirt floor. Two planks, nailed along one thin wall that was once a work bench, were bare— for all pieces of metal, tools, iron wheels had been melted down for shells—bare except for a pair of faded pink pants left on one end, shriveled to the size of a fist. The door swung shut behind the Colonel, he rummaged about the shed, thought of the Fraulein who owned the pants, caught with long braids and bright smile, then he reached into the jeep and pulled out another rifle, bright and clean. The odor of chickens, old herbs, mold, mixed with the oil, and he heard the slapping of low water in the canal, trickling over layers and shreds of thin ice. He checked the tires, looked once more about the shed, then walked back to his headquarters across the unkempt white garden.

By six o'clock he had waked the men, decided that the roads were passable and had loaded the new rifle with a live cartridge.

"Here now, Leevey," he called out the window to the still-walking dispatch rider, "you handle the prisoner this morning." Then, while the three of us sat up and blinked, the Colonel shaved, peering into a mechanical mirror that had crooked collapsible legs. After he was dressed, one of the corporals brushed his uniform, helped him bundle back into the heavy coat, and handed him the cap with the bright badge.

By six-thirty the whole town had been raised and stood crammed together in the garden and the motorcycle rider fastened the red cloth about Miller's eyes while, he, the prisoner, stood rigidly on the edge of the canal. The Colonel hurried out, followed by the Mayor, Stintz, and me, and his troop, hurried to see that Miller was placed correctly, checked the time. Though the sky was heavy, he was sure it would not snow, and if they got an early start should be able to cover two hundred miles at least. "Come," he said turning to me, "I need another rifleman. You just take this gun and fall in line with my men." He handed me the new weapon, the fifth, well greased, light, loaded, then arranged our squad in good order. "Mayor," he called, "Mayor, come here." The old man trembled and came forward, his nose gray with the cold, his chest hollow. The Colonel reached into a woollen pocket and brought forth a large white handkerchief, thrust it upon the shivering leader. "Now you hold this over your head, and when you see me nod, drop it. All right, Leevey," called the Colonel, "come away from the prisoner." The water slid by in the canal. Stintz watched carefully, eager for justice, the Census-Taker, drunk, leaned on Madame Snow's arm and held Jutta's hand, watched the white cloth drooping in the dull morning.

"Leevey," said the Colonel when they were abreast, speaking in a lowered voice, "you might see about loading the jeep, we have a long way to go today."

The crowd grew restless, a thin sickly pink began to stain the clouds, the four men and myself raised our short barrels while the two bow ends of the Pastor's red bandanna flapped in a light breeze.

His upraised arm began to pain, and the Mayor felt his legs knocking together, backwards and forwards, and he thought he would perish with the cold. Then he caught the glance from the man with the big eagle on his cap and his fingers opened. "It is you who will die," called the Pastor, and the Mayor shut his eyes.

The noise of the rifles sounded small and muffled, padded in the heavy air, and his fingers still felt as if they held the cloth. Miller fell back, dropped through the film of ice and floated jerkily down over the shoals, catching against rocks, dragging over pieces of wood, bumping the flabby rafts, the red cloth flashing for a moment.

"You're a good shot," the Colonel said to me, "that's the gun that did it." The Census-Taker had to be carried back to the house.

A half-hour later the convoy rolled out onto the highway, jeep coughing, the Colonel carefully driving, leaving behind the several posters and proclamations that the motorcycle-rider had pasted up to the peeling walls: "The Government of the United States . . ." For the most part, they were un-readable.

"My God, he's not coming at all!" said Fegelein.

"Don't be a fool, it's almost time." Sometimes I had to be harsh.

"You don't think he'll see the log and stop?"

"Of course not."

I myself began to wish that the *Schmutz* on the little motor-cycle would hurry up, morning would soon come and the newspaper office would be waiting, the old women with their bright eyes would be out watching in the streets, the dumb children would be snooping. The land is important, not the

Geist; the bronx-mongolians, the fat men, the orators, must be struck down. The three of us, the sentries, drew closer together in the low fog.

A hundred miles from *Spitzen-on-the-Dein* in the early morning of the day when the killing occurred, the intended victim, Leevey, lay wearied and injured beside a laughing slut who was covered with invisible red clap. All through the darkness they had struggled, barring each other with the point of a knee, angry and calling each other *schmuck*, and she had struck his face so that the eyes bled. She raised her white legs above the sheets, then grimaced and threw him off, jabbing with her fists as he fell against the wall. Over and over she said, "My house, you come to *my* house," but Leevey was afraid that if he left the safety of his room she would shellac him, cut with the scissors, and finally leave him dead with a pin through his neck. For he had heard the stories, stories of murder in the empty lot, the special deaths, the vaginae packed with deadly poison. He clung to her, "You stay here," and her sharp wooden sandals sliced at his shins and her unwashed hair fell over his aching shoulder. His white helmet, goggles, and gauntlets lay beside the bunk, his tunic and trousers the girl used as a pillow. "Candy," she said, pinching and poking with her strong fingers. "Go to hell," he whined and the forearm crushed down on his nose and mouth, bruising and dull. Finally, unsuccessful, Leevey tried to sleep, but she scratched and pushed, whistled in his ear, squeezed, cried, jammed with her feet, and just as he dozed would slap with all her strength.

The sun gradually brightened the gray walls, the girl's white laughing eyes never left his face, a quick pinch. The heavy tiredness and pain swept over him and he wished he was back in the delicatessen, his long nose pushed among the cheeses.

THE CANNIBAL

When she reached the door she turned, leaned her shoulder against the jamb, thrust out her hip and smiled at the feeble one, also filmed now with red invisible clap, tousled and unprotesting, sick in the bunk:

"*Auf Wiedersehen, Amerikaner,*" she said, "*Amerikaner!*"

Leevey doused his face in the basin, slicked down his black hair. "That's life," he said, "that's life," and as the sun rose clear and cold he slung the Sten-gun on his back, polished his boots, fastened the gauntlets, climbed on his rusty motorcycle, and began the tour of his district.

He traveled ninety miles with his palms shivering on the steerhorn handlebars, the white cold air glazed endlessly ahead, his insides smacking against the broad cowhide saddle. He stopped a few times beside an abandoned farm or misturned sign or unburied Allied corpse to take a few notes, laying the machine on its side in the mud, and he sweated over the smeared pad and stubby pencil. He was overseer for a sector of land that was one-third of the nation and he frowned with the responsibility, sped along thinking of the letters he would write home, traveled like a gnome behind a searchlight when the sun finally set and the foreign shadows settled. He saw the bare spire rising less than a mile beyond, and crouching down, spattered with grease, he speeded up, to go past *Spitzen-on-the-Dein* with a roar. The late night and crowded broken road twisted around him, flames shot up from the exhaust.

Leevey was killed outright when his motorcycle crashed into the log. He was pitched forward and down into an empty stretch of concrete. The Sten-gun, helmet, and boots clattered a moment, canvas and cloth and leather tore and rubbed; then he lay quiet, goggles still over his eyes, pencil, pad, whistle and knife strewn ahead. The three of us quickly leaped upward over the embankment, crouched in the darkness a moment, and then eagerly went to work. I was the first to reach the motorcycle and I cut the ignition, guided it over the bank. We picked up Leevey and carried him down to his machine, lost none of his trinkets, then together rolled the log until it slid down the muddy slope and settled in silence in a shallow stream of silt.

"It's not smashed badly," said Fegelein and ran his fingers over the bent front rim, felt broken spokes brushing against his sleeve, felt that the tank was slightly caved-in and petrol covered his hand. "You'll be riding it in a month."

I put my ear to the thin chest but could hear nothing . . . The night had reached its darkest and most silent hour, just before dawn comes. Still there were no stars, the mist grew more dense overhead and even the dogs no longer howled. My fingers brushed the stiffening wrist.

"Are you ready?" asked my comrade by the machine.

I felt closer, more quickly, pulled away the cuff of the jacket, tore as quietly as possible at the cloth over the wrist.

"What's the matter with you? What are you doing anyway?" The voice was close; Stumpfegle also drew closer to my side.

"Eh, what's up?" The hoarse whispers were sharp.

I pulled at the strap, carefully, faster, and finally spoke, "He's got a watch." I leaned closer to the corpse.

"Well, give it here, you can't keep it just like that . . ."

I brought the pistol dimly into sight again, shoved the watch into my pocket, "I'm the leader and don't forget it. It's only right that I have the watch. Take the sacks off the machine and leave them here. We'll share what we can find, but not the watch."

Fegelein was already back tinkering with the engine. I listened to the watch and heard its methodical beat and could see the intricate clean dials rotating in precise fractions. The tongue was now sucked firmly and definitely into the back of Leevey's throat and his knees had cracked upwards and grown rigid. "We had better get him out of here." We picked him up and with the body between us stepped into the shallow ooze of the stream and headed out beyond the wall of fog towards the center of the lowlands.

"My God, the fog is thick."
"We're almost there," I replied.
"Which way?"
"A little to the right, I think."

The formless white puddles of fog moved, shifted among the stunted trees, rose, fell, trailed away in the areas of sunken swampwood where once tense and cowed scouting parties had dared to walk into the bayonet on guard, or to walk on a trigger of a grenade that had blown up waist high. An axle of a gun carriage stuck up from the mud like a log, a British helmet, rusted, old, hung by a threadbare strap from a broken branch.

"He's heavy."
"They feed the Americans well, you know," I answered.
"Well, he's going where they all belong."

Several times we stopped to rest, sitting the body upright in the silt that rose over his waist. A shred of cloth was caught about a dead trunk, the fog dampened our skin. Each time we stopped, the white air moved more than ever in and out of the low trees, bearing with it an overpowering odor, the odor of the ones who had eaten well. More of the trees were shattered and we, the pallbearers, stumbled with each step over half-buried pieces of steel.

"Let's leave him here."
"You know we cannot. Follow the plan."

Past the next tree, past the next stone of a gun breech blasted open like a mushroom, we saw a boot, half a wall, and just beyond, the swamp was filled with bodies that slowly appeared one by one from the black foliage, from the mud, from behind a broken wheel. A slight skirmish had developed here and when the flare had risen over this precise spot, glowed red and died in the sky, some twenty or thirty dead men were left, and they never disappeared. The fog passed over them most thickly here, in relentless circles, and since it was easier to breathe closer to the mud, we stooped and dragged the body forward.

"You see, no one could ever find him among these. No one would ever look for him here." My idea for disposing of the body was excellent.

After searching the body once more, we left it and found our way again to the roadside. We took the machine and its valuable saddlebags silently through the town to the newspaper office.

"It's time we had our meeting," I said, "I'll be back." Fegelein began to work on the engine; Stumpfegle broke the head from a bottle.

Even though the print was smeared quite badly, and some of the pamphlets were unreadable, the decree spread quickly and most people, except the Station-Master who didn't see the white paper, heard the news and whispered about it in the early morning light, trying to understand this new salvation, readjusting themselves to the strange day. The decree was carried, faithfully, by Stumpfegle and Fegelein who walked in ever widening circles about the countryside. They walked farther and farther, growing tired, until even the spire, struck with sunlight, was no longer visible.

In Winter Death steals through the doorway searching for both young and old and plays for them in his court of law. But when Spring's men are beating their fingers on the cold earth and bringing the news, Death travels away and becomes only a passer-by. The two criers passed him on his way and were lost in an unbounded field.

Ma's Wedding

from THE BEETLE LEG (1954)

In the summer of 1947 I discovered a landscape as shocking,
sterile, and paradoxically beautiful as the ruined Italian and German
terrains that had served as the fictional world of *The Cannibal*.
That summer I followed Sophie to Fort Peck, Montana, where
thanks to her father, then in the Army Corps of Engineers, I became
a guide on the longest earth-filled dam in the world. Each dawn
I would drive my pickup truck to the observation parking lot on
top of the dam that was a mile wide at its base and four miles long.
There were spectacular sunrises over "badlands" that I took to be
the bedrock of Dante's *Inferno*; behind me, on the western side of
the dam, was backed up a man-made lake 150 miles long beneath
which lay countless farms and ranches abandoned for the sake of
water. Visitors to the dam included, incongruously, an Indian chief
and his daughter on one occasion, and a philosopher from Columbia
on another. On the flats below the dam lay the remnants of makeshift huts that had housed the ten thousand workers employed at
the height of the construction of the Fort Peck Dam. And somewhere inside that immense quantity of earth there was buried a
single man, a worker rumored to have slipped and fallen into the
depths of the then unfinished government project. I became
obsessed with the dead man and the vastness of his grave, which
I took to be not only the dam itself but the surrounding plains and
buttes. Visitors were few, so in the cab of my truck, wearing a pair
of secondhand cowboy boots that gave me a splendid case of
athlete's foot, I had the chance to try my hand at writing fiction.

By the end of the summer Sophie and I were married by an
army chaplain in a little church that rises from the prairie town, in
memory, like a citadel of plywood walls with windows painted
to resemble stained glass. That very afternoon we fled Montana

THE BEETLE LEG

forever on a Great Northern Railway train that came swinging into our whistle stop like a bullet.

The Beetle Leg is a mock and sometimes surrealistic "western" about Mulge Lampson, a sinister cowboy buried in an earth-filled dam, and about his survivors: a brother, Luke, who tends the "grave"; Mulge's wife who is known as Ma; the mother of the two brothers, Hattie, herself dead and buried by the time of the story; an orphaned Mandan Indian girl, adopted daughter of the family, whose latent sexuality is a constant affront to Ma's stalwart purity. The action of the novel concerns the violent appearance of a third brother, Cap Leech, an itinerant dentist, and a band of motorcycle riders, the Red Devils, who harrass the Lampson family and the whole town of Mistletoe, Government City.

The following excerpt dramatizes Ma's wedding and the betrayal of her purity in the sexless apathy of the American West.

Ma's Wedding

A man lay buried just below the water level of the dam. He was embedded in the earth and entangled with a caterpillar, pump engine and a hundred feet of hose, somewhere inside the mountain that was protected from the lake on one side by rock and gravel and kept from erosion on its southward slope by partially grown rows of yellow grass. This man—he was remembered in Mistletoe, Government City, and would be as long as the Great Slide came to mind with every ale case struck open—was the brother of one who still hung on, having a place in the fields southwest of the official lines of the town. Boundaries were still marked with transit stakes ten years old.

In the sunset the survivor of the two, who had not taken part in the battle of the river and who had been on the range when the Slide occurred, drove his team of four horses across the sand of the southward slope, the machine under his seat spitting out seeds, grinding its unaligned rods. His voice carried all the way to the town on the bluff. He rode the boards holding the dry lines in one hand and a flattened cigarette pinched in the other, one knee cocked up and his hat pulled low over blackened cheeks and chin. Six days a week he nursed the animals across the sunward, dry side of the dam for twenty-five dollars a day, and the wind blew sand in his ears and blew the horses' manes the wrong way. A few hundred yards above his head, from the sharp-rocked track across the top of the dam, the dark, rarely fished miles of water narrowed into a cone through the hills of the badlands. Below him, in the middle of the mosquito flat and at the edge of the man-made delta and surrounded by piles of iron pipe and small, corrugated iron huts, red lead painted sections of the half completed turbine tower rose among steel girders spiked with insulators and weighted with hundreds of high tension, lead-in wires.

The day shift of the Metal and Lumber Company had stopped work an hour ago, and now the cowboy drove his team without the firing of the riveters or torches blasting sand from the air. For a moment the sun touched the black mounds of earth behind the tower and drifted off, down the almost dry channel as far as he could see, where once the wide river would have lost its mud color and changed to orange, then purple, in the days before Mistletoe even existed and when the fishing was good any place he sat down to cast.

When he heard a shrill faraway whistle in Clare, twenty miles away, he climbed down, unhitched the team, left the old machine for the night still dropping a few seeds, and let the horses tug him easily toward home on the end of the reins. For a whole day he had been sowing flowers, back and forth, on the mile long stretch of his brother's grave, and now the horses were tired and he was thirsty. Man and animals cut down from the crest of the dam to the high weeded plateau, basined in the rear by the long gravel approach and fronting on the filled in section of the horseshoe town. Soon the crest would be topped with a macadam road and the street lamps, if ever wired and the last switches installed, would be lit against the horizon.

The four brown dray horses chomped slowly across the dry track, swaying in the rear but shaking their round noses and twitching their ears in excitement, stumbling now and then in a hole by the road so heavily that it seemed they must fall. Passing one prong of the few hundred brown houses of Mistletoe, Luke Lampson waved to the Finn, a crippled ex-bronc rider hammering on a stoop with two white canes.

Then, digging his long heels into the turf, he pulled the

horses as a station wagon swung close, raising the dust. He waved again, this time at the tin helmeted Metal and Lumber night shift men, setting off to throw sparks from the tower until dawn. He followed the thin sticks hung from a string of barbed wire through the darkening fields, slapping at the mosquitoes that bit through his pants, until, after once more placing a few light logs across the gate, he could look down on the plank and tar paper buildings of his ranch. He turned the horses loose and they trotted downhill, for all their age like young dogs.

"Slow down there," he called, afraid that they would hit the wire in the darkness and skin open their broad two-sided chests. He splashed water on his face at the washstand by the house and looked over the bare country toward Mistletoe. He could see the light of fine sparks from the tower; they were at work already.

Only a few mile twists of wire sheared the damp land into fields and made it claim to a farm, a ranch, a fallen barn. Phosphorescent clumps of weed and sage rolled airily in sight, but lone animals moved invisibly though a hoof click on stone carried for miles through the warm evening.

Mosquitoes beat against the inside and outside of the windows and Luke Lampson's horses thudded out of range of the house and, motionless, hung their heads over the furthest stretch of wire. Luke stomped up the steps, two potato sacks filled with sand, pushed open the door wobbling on leather hinges, and walked across the leaning floor to the bunk on his bowed, tightly denimed, tired legs.

"Evening, Ma," he said and pulled off the cracked, square-toed, lady-size cowboy boots. And, more tiredly, under his breath:

"Evening, Maverick," and he glanced once at the Mandan who squatted by the dusty blanket hanging from the foot of the bunk. The black hair hung over her face.

The woman at the wood stove shook the skillet and it spit on the red iron.

"What's the matter, Ma, you out of sorts?"

"Not so's anybody'd see."

Luke lay back on the pile of covers and, lighting a short end of cigarette, flipped the wooden match to a tin can of water on the far side of the room. A pair of antlers, patches of hair and dried skin stuck to the yellow bone chip of skull, hung crookedly on the wall above the can. An old branch lay cradled in the horns. Luke rubbed his feet together—even in summer he wore thick-woven socks—and, with the toes of one foot sticking through a long raveling hole, scratched. The Mandan, crouching out of sight and never smiling, reached up one dark arm and with a long stem of hay tickled at the bare toes. But the black little feet, tough with rocks and hot with sand, did not feel it. He went on smoking.

"At least you could make her help. Me doing all this heavy work."

"Go on, Maverick, give her a hand."

The Indian climbed slowly to her feet, pulled down her red sweater, smoothed her faded, straw covered plaid skirt and padding to the open shelves, reached for thick lipped cups and plates. Her charm bracelets jangled as each piece of china was set heavily on the dark planks of the table. She kept out of the stove woman's way.

"That's the one job I like doing myself." Ma splattered onions in the pan. "Light work. And I never get to do it."

"Go fetch some water," Luke said to the girl. "Shut the door," he called. It remained open and mosquitoes hummed in and out.

"I ain't here the whole day long," Luke swung his feet to the floor. "I don't see what's to keep you from sprawling right here on this bunk from sunup to dark. If you want." Luke's face, black with the sun, would fit a palm of the woman's hand and when he rocked across the floor it caught the fire from the stove. He rolled like a child playing sailor, loosening his neckerchief.

Ma shook her head. "That's where she sneaks off to. I couldn't do it." The Mandan returned with the load of water; she carried the bucket almost as lightly as the older woman, who could lug six brimming gallons the whole mile long trail as easily as two pint jars of honey. Reaching under the bunk, the Indian pulled out her dusty, high heeled, patent leather store shoes. She squeezed them onto bare feet and sat down to table. She ate from the edge of the knife, her black sides of hair falling into the bowl of food. Now and then she watched the cowboy scowling into his mug behind the hurricane lamp.

Ma never sat to any meal. She kept her back to the world and her face toward the red range, toward the cartons of matches, the row of pans and long handled forks. Sometimes she pushed the lid off the skillet and stole a bite on a long blackened prong or a sip from a wooden spoon. She refilled their plates without turning around. But the Mandan had to pour the coffee.

The deep dish skillet, as big around as a butter tub, was never off the stove and the flames were never allowed to die from under it. The fat was rarely changed and it boiled and snapped from one month to the next. Whether it was a piece of fish dropped into it or a slab of beef pulled out, it tasted of the black countryside. Tempered by the heat of wood coals, warming the room itself in winter, the skillet was slated over with layer on layer of charred mineral, encrusted with drippings, accumulating from the inside out fragments of every meal. Not a night went by but what Ma, quickly awakened in the darkness, got up to feed the fire and make sure the skillet burned. It was Ma's pot, the iron of her life, to which came the pickings of her garden, the produce of her monthly shopping trips to Clare, the eggs she got each morning from the

coop and whatever Luke might bring home at night—rhu-
barb, apples or a quarter head of cabbage. She kept it steaming.

Ma was not Luke Lampson's mother. Hattie Lampson
now lay buried on the bluff where once the tents were pitched.
Ma had married, to the south in Clare and when the project
was first conceived, Luke's older brother, the Lampson incarcerated in the dam. Sometimes, rarely, wearing rubber boots
and a shawl and carrying an egg basket, she would walk the
high shoulder of mud, rock and gravel, and look down the
water toward the badlands.

"You never knew nothing about it," she told Luke, "you
were out where it was dry. You never even saw the Great
Slide." She moved the skillet a little off the fire.

Luke got up from the table and looked at the Mandan.
"You do those dishes for Ma. You hear?" She leaned on the
boards, hid her face behind her hands and went on eating.

"She never says anything when I'm around." Ma licked at
the edge of the spoon and opened the draft a notch.

"You just don't understand how she speaks, that's all."
Luke undid his belt and shuffled among a pile of men and
women's clothing until he found a fresh black and white
checked shirt. He pulled on his best pair of boots and polished
the toes with the blanket tip.

Smelling of hair oil—the Mandan groomed herself from the
same bottle—he rolled the brim of his hat, wiped at the
sweatband, and drew it sharply over his eyes. He hopped to
the ground over the potato sacks with the same jump and
spring with which he used to run across the barn dance floor
when the river was still indefinitely harnessed and the proposed streets on the bluff were not approved by the central
office. He stood in the light of the hurricane lamp and ahead,
above the rise in the darkness where his own place ended, he
saw the small glow in the sky, as if far into the plains a few
branders crouched by embers and sets of cooling irons.

"Them boys are flaring up tonight for sure," he said and, whistling through his teeth, stepped out of sight. The night shift men were on the scaffold welding and below, by an iron hut, Harry Bohn put a pot of coffee back on the fire and prepared to return to Mistletoe.

Ma turned from her skillet and called out. "Don't you say anything against Mulge. I won't have it!"

Ma was old already when she married the dead Lampson in the dam. And the Mandan was but a child.

She prepared herself in the morning, lasted and traveled the entire day to the wedding at dusk far south in Clare. In those days Ma had friends. They helped her, though they did not arrive until after sunrise. But, carrying her bundle out to the darkness, Ma filled her heart with the family rolled asleep behind, and knowing that wagonloads would find her, except for death or accident, thought not of friends but only of her tentative husband's mother.

"There's just one thing I got to ask. That is for Hattie Lampson to come. For her to watch it."

Ma put her clothes by the basin, filled it, and between the house wall and the roost, plunged thin tough arms and face into the water and after rinsing raised her eyes to twenty miles of dripping clouded sand across which lay the town where weddings were announced nearly once a month. She had heard of them. The pulse beat in the hollow of her elbow.

"It's too late for her," Luke's mother said the night before, "I won't go."

But Ma dashed herself with water and in the hour before dawn—she had lain awake to see a matronly night die down —she put a bounty on her own voice and expected, as if the very day could change her, to be persuasive in the ways of women. She shook out her hair. She soaked it. And the only thing she wanted she was sure of. The night before a wedding, perhaps then they spat and hard things were said against her; but on the very day of compliments, then the fires were set and the lock was on the door.

"She'll come around," thought Ma.

There were no holes from which wagons might appear, no hump to cross, no turning to bring them into sight. For miles of white land lay open and fallow on all sides of the ranch. But if they had to ride three days and nights and drive hard teams themselves, Ma would be surrounded by women married longer at her age than she could ever be. She patted her cheeks to draw up the color of the blood.

"I guess I can have my way. This once." Quickly Ma picked up the basin, flung it wide, and a shower of water splashed easily through the darkness.

In the open air, squatting in the sand for half an hour before the day of marriage, the woman sorted her clothes. She bit off a piece of thread. The gray hair dripped and slightly wet her shoulders. She tried not to listen for the stirring of the brothers and their old mother and now and then, wiping her mouth carefully, she raised her head and peered over the slight curve of the earth to the south where it would happen.

"If the sun don't come up soon," she thought, "I'll damp the pillow on our first night." And then: "I'll make Hattie Lampson dry it."

On all the days of the week, Ma never saw the sunrise though she awoke as early; for her the clearness of the day was noticed late and the first heat, which killed the very cry of the chickens, only wore her down by noon. But this morning she saw it gather, roll up and melt the east. The fire of the small, perfectly round sun was suddenly stretched, banded, across the entire horizon. She saw the thin red arms actually wrenched across the back of the earth.

"That's a bad light. But I don't care."

Luke found her hunched in a sun ray, head forward, hair laid flat on her knees.

"You ain't very energetic for a woman who's almost married." He picked up the basin. "You used the water."

"I'm entitled." Ma spread the strands. "But you ain't supposed to talk to me like this. You can't look at me, like he was out here watching what I do himself—before it's time."

"There'll be fuss enough," said Luke. "Just let me wash."

The head of hair grumbled. The cowboy took off his shirt.

"It's hard enough for me to keep my spirits collected without you around." Ma turned her back and drew the flowered satchel near.

"You aiming to carry something from the house?"

"I'm traveling, ain't I?"

"Right back to here. That's all." Luke blew into the water. "What's in it?"

"You don't watch me now! This finery ain't for men to see—except in the dark." She pulled wide the mouth of the bag and under spreading hair, arms deep, looked into the dust and flowers. For a moment, as the sun drew her scalp tight and turned the silver metal of her hair into powder, she slept and hands hung gently. Then, eyes closed, she straightened the layers and before tying shut the bag, stroked and settled whatever filled the bottom.

"People gave me these things. I'll keep it with me." On the other side of the wood and paper wall the old mother and her elder son were quiet. Ma listened for the splash of bare feet on the floor. The heat began to rack her shoulders and she heard only the scraping of the cowboy's fingers in the basin. He filled it again, trailing slowly down the sand and back.

"He's washing twice," thought Ma. She waited, thinking suddenly that she could have had it done in the cabin with the right man driven out from town and her own friends packed into the doorway. The sun brought it to mind, but the feeling passed as she thought of entering those streets that lead to church. She knew that in a moment she would want a long space to cover, a good many miles before sundown.

"Listen," the water dried on the cowboy's cheek, "you ain't aiming to take my mother to this wedding?"

"Yes, I've none to turn to."

Luke tilted the basin, poured, then stopped. He looked up—sky and desert shone tearless, clear, white—and rubbed his eyes. He dropped the bar of soap into the water and swept out the razor. He honed it once or twice against the sun, held it to a side of dry whisker, flourished and pulled. His young face had the acid smell of skin drawn under ingressive heat rays and his fist—it could pull a horse twice round on startled hoofs—was tightly fastened on the crook of the razor. After each stroke he held it outstretched vertically between his eyes. He aimed. The bright scroll on the blade that could twist the trickle of blood, turned white against his cheek.

Placing the razor on the wash box, careful to keep the steel edge free of the wood, he went into the cabin with shoulders hardly moving as he walked.

Before he came back, Ma saw the Indian child, too small to be a maiden, spying around the corner of the milk hut. The fingers of one hand spread stark and wild against the sod.

Ma colored, "You keep away from me today."

Luke returned with a towel. He rubbed on a fresh spot of soap. "No. She don't think she'll dress this morning." His mouth was hidden by a stiff arm. "I guess she better stay behind."

"I guess you shouldn't use his things! On a day like this."

Luke turned. He saw the hair which was fluffed out and starting to rise, the walnut ears, the fat shadow on the sand.

"He won't be shaving anymore. Not him."

Ma rose, laid aside the bag ready for loading, filled a bucket, and started for the coop.

"Don't wake him," she said. "Yet."

That was the day Ma sang. She carried a tune on dry nostrils and the Lampson ranch, by the sound of a woman's voice, livened in its bed of star thistle. Ma's song was louder when she passed the cabin, she raised it to leaning walls and the hidden flower of a man culled from the desert.

"My mother says it's time to start. If you're going to."

"I'll take her in my wagon. You tell her not to bother herself."

"She says she'll try to have a meal done when you get back."

"She can sit by me."

Three wagons rattled to the edge of the shell, as if they had been camped out of sight until the moment of noon, and slowly continued forward on salty flutes across the sand. Bravely three loads of women in gown and bonnet hymned together; Luke turned to locate the sound of women's voices, faint, from mouths already closed. He climbed on top of the sod milk hut and under brimmed hands watched the approach of old wives in the dust.

"I'm glad for you. They'll get here safely."

Ma smiled.

The desert filled with women. They swarmed within sideboards of beaten wagons, staring ahead for sign of well or a shade in which to dismount and shake. Three cartloads plied the desert. Banded warm members, they traveled free of the farmer and cattle driver, chopped to the roots stray outcroppings of slate colored grass. These were women who rode unwatched on the dry bottom of the lake with empty breasts and nameless horses, and even the oldest unsnapped heavy collars and soured the passing miles from the tail boards where they sat and dangled their weak legs. They nodded to the thrust, the side slapping of the wheels.

"But I believe there's trouble." Again Luke climbed to his sod post and waited. Narrowly he glanced at Ma. "Yes, sir. Them women don't have no water. Not a drop."

"That's all right." Ma passed quickly with the basket.

"You don't draw such things to my attention."

"Well," Luke pulled on his hat, "I reckon they'd survive about anything." He walked away, sat down and watched her.

And those women were roughly able to sing songs of the skewered lamb and waters driven back by faith or oath. They were dry. The boards on which they sat, scraped of fodder, might have burst aflame if the sun were caught briefly in the eye of a watch glass. They traveled in three lifeless dories with dead oarlocks and rotted sails; they sang stiffly, managed to hold the reins. They backtracked, chewed the sand and made their way over weary, salty miles to see one woman their own age brought to bed.

Every one of them made the trip. There was not a woman in the desert who had not left the animal pens, truck garden patch and particular gully of the home to sit all day in the sun, to breathe the air of ancient lying in and love. For hours, under a never swaying skirt, a bare ankle remained chocked against brake iron or plank. The desert gave them up and they advanced; they might have died of thirst. But open-jawed and black, with matted and twisted cuts of hair, they crowded wagons taken from the farm.

They drew near, and Luke for the first time saw women's faces. Once again on the sod hut, a thin scout in the sunlight, a bent marker limp though standing, his own face worked, pursed and dripping as he watched. Bonnets, ribbons but no curls, skull-blackened and thirsty they stared back above the slick fronts of horses plodding low, stepping singly, flat and without wind away from wheels that were nearly locked. Instead of three wagon loads he would have liked to have seen just one face cleansed of the sun and that had not been formed and set long ago to the sudden bloody impression of a coffin bone. A few could not hear the meek but steady notes of their sisters' hymns and pushed their ears with hands that had been raised trembling three days and nights. "I want to see one," he searched among the tucked and tired wives, "before she's learned to keep shut. And outlive a man."

He did not wave.

"Smile," said Ma, "when you're welcoming." The sounds of iron pleased her. She would rise and accommodate them too when they actually arrived, not sooner. But once she paused, "Go get her," Ma hissed, "bring her here."

Higher than the sod hut or cabin, outnumbering the buildings of the ranch, they broke down in the Lampson yard. They drove across and settled on the ground where Luke had shaved. With spikes and nails working out of the wood, reared loosely above dead wheels, they hid the cabin from corral, cut off the roost. Only two front animals found room to emerge and hang toward the south and open plains on the other side. All those women and a dozen horses mauled in the first enclosure they had found since setting forth. Luke climbed and stepped among them. Little spars, a few carrying flimsy woven heads of sage, balanced with the slack, tipped and dug into the ground. The air was filled, below voices and slowly slobbering bits, with the steady descending sounds of rope and shroud, skirt and ringlet.

Ma, too late, suddenly cried out: "Don't get down!" Carrying the satchel with both hands, smiling, snapping her eyes, she darted from wagon to wagon. "Keep your seats!"

Luke hid among the horses; he unbuckled them. Bits slipped in and all the way out of crooked mouths, away from square, flat, slanted teeth. Breast collars were hung loose and low and the weight of wagons dragged against forelegs instead of chests. Tight cruppers wrenched the raw high ends of tails, bristling and gray, pink and choked, straight above the mounded rumps and to one side.

"They must have last had this gear on cows."

A few big ears were pinned back against manes under headbands that had ridden up, and as they stood like burned men dumbly waiting for cindered clothes to fall away, the harness slipped aside from cuts and abrasions. Steam rags had been ironed to their sides and stripped off. Large hoofs, one before the other as if to step, were planted—unpared blocks of chalk—on loose ends of leather that had dragged the miles of the journey. Blister beetles sat on the brass terrets or suddenly still, fell dryly to the ground.

"Ma," he caught her arm while she continued to hasten, to urge and push them up again, "we can't reach Clare today."

"You load this bag. And fetch me Hattie Lampson."

"Don't listen," answered a small, steadily nodding voice, "don't pay none of this family heed."

They swept back, made room and left Luke Lampson's mother her own bright place to stand. She waited, then spoke no louder:

"You're all welcome." She nodded, this little woman darkly turned out of the house, this last and oldest divulged by the desert. "I'll see you off." She looked at her younger son, but took no step. Ma caught her arm.

"Hattie," Ma moved her, "can you get up on that seat alone?"

They stood her by the wheel. They stepped back and the old woman shortly swayed, a stalk snapped upwards from the sand by the iron, mud colored rim, a length of wire coiled and motionless in the spokes. The great pinwheel might have ground her cleanly into the dust and she would have crawled away with skin unbruised, with dry pulmonary parts intact. She and the wheel—its tapered bars, sanded rays, were longer than her two arms fully spread—looked as if they would never move again; one, the original means of carrying them from Boonville to the bloody plow handle, the other, that which was originally carried and turned to love in the night's wagon ring around the fire. But had it turned, and had she fallen, her kerchief caught in the spokes nearest the ground, she would have hung before her feet once more touched the settling, noisy track. And when the wheel did turn, smoke hung thinly about its tin bucket nave where wood burned against wood and miles wound in carbon around the axle.

"You ride in the one behind mine. Mulge comes last."

The animals awoke. Amid the scraping of slowly prodded hoofs, the slight sway of warty food buckets and rope ends under the wooden bodies, Ma remained at the front of the train holding his mother.

"Put Hattie right up there. That's it, by me."

Luke in the second wagon and his brother in the third did not join the singing. The horses, as large as they were, crouched down to pull, their legs spraddled outwards like the flappers of young and panting dogs. Each wagon carried not only its own sounds of travel, the tug, twist and strain of the wooden windlass, but was loaded with the clatter of the other two and moved—one wagon could never make such noise—across the plains like a house athwart rollers.

High on the first prow, wedding bag under the backless seat and the sun softening the wool of her dress, Ma leaned in front of Hattie Lampson and spoke to the driver. The ranch, with no men left behind and guarded only by the Indian child, had disappeared down its faraway indentation in the glazed sand.

"Swing us a little to the other way. I sense it more to the right."

The woman sawed the reins.

Thus they traveled a dog's pace on an enormous field that once, perhaps, had been cultivated with shrub, tree and herb, now extinct, which swelled before their eyes at moments with a few head of cattle, with larvae that clustered and disappeared. Not another rider or wagon train crossed their path.

Ma held her hand clasped to her eyes and peered through the thin red line between her fingers. She sat high, a gunman who had crossed the route for forty years on a rocking coach.

"A mighty lot of you turned up."

"Yep," said the driver.

"Hattie," Ma spoke louder, "I'm much obliged. Since you changed your mind."

The mother of the Lampson boys said nothing, seated in the open heat between a woman almost married to her own son and another still married after rearing five grown men. For Hattie Lampson was taken during the trip to town. Her flat, boneless nose was cold. She nodded.

"Clare by dark," said Ma to the driver, "maybe sooner." She shifted. Her long skirts pulled, and she changed her chin to the other hand.

Hattie Lampson began to mumble on top of the hymn singing and turn of the wheels.

"I'm indebted to you ever," said Ma and put her arm around the dwarfed shoulders. "You been here to give me courage." Ma rattled, looked at her quickly and gave the cold little woman a rigorous and sudden hug. She snapped free. Ma eased her again under a brown arm and widely ruffled sleeve.

"Hattie. You ain't going to be doggish. Not on a wedding day."

They rode unmolested over the flat pan—fifty miles away there might have been a mountain range to seal them perfectly within the white disk passable and clear—and looking way to the ground Ma watched the last of the hoofs, so slowly dropped, switch and explode in dust. She felt under the seat for her finery.

"He's probably thinking just like me. Now," said Ma and fanned herself.

Hattie Lampson spoke: "He wasn't brung up for such. Not to be handed straight over. Naked. He'll work some now. There ain't no family. There ain't even any boys, men neither. You can't pass them all out. They're supposed to laze around home. Take care of their own farmyard, they was told.

"They get no pardon. It ain't just any hound can go out shorn and keep his head up. I say they're done. My younger has gone just like him. Bringing that Indian into the house is about as bad. Neither one can hold himself straight. They was behind my back.

"Around their age they start feeling worms inside and nothing I say will change it. Why, he's been walking you sideways for two years steady. And when he won't touch no food, there's enough to kill him right there.

"Some just worm themselves in. I ain't going to be touched now the way you do. You ain't going to get me to help you mix no water in his meal. Just to lie spread in the dish. I got to watch for him and keep him quiet. But I'm not sure he'll make much noise anyway. Folks forget. They'll forget the whole family.

"They won't even remember what month it was. And he won't, for sure. No one knows mine neither. You ain't going to live long enough with my boy to get the yellow off his teeth or bleach out what I learned him. You're too old.

"It wasn't much. About when to come inside or out, is all. And if he's found presumption to do more—and be offensive to some for the time being—I guess you ain't going to get any good of it. Least to your face.

"I ain't a person to have stood up for either one of them. I don't like to see a man worrying about whether his hat is on to front or back. And taken to traveling around on foot, tucking at his shirt and leaning down to loose his shoes. But as of now I cut them off, the two of them.

"Maybe a woman ain't fit to make something of them in the first place. Maybe I done wrong. And mine is even worse than most. Wherever them worms come from, that's part the trouble.

"If you can be like me, and I ain't ready to admit that, your trouble might not be more than mine. But a bad dog just gets worse. I ain't sure what you'll do to him; I won't thank you for it."

"Hattie," Ma dropped her arm, "you better draw breath."

The begrimed driver shook the reins, wiped her face and looked at the old woman. "Mrs. Lampson, you shouldn't question so. It ain't right for you to hold out so harsh. This girl's pure as snow." She drove again.

"Hattie just ain't feeling well," said Ma. "We got to overlook it. She come along for the sake of Mulge and me. That's enough. And she's going to stand right up there in front of all them people whether she's sick or not. So we got to make allowance. She'll be nicer when it's done. Won't you, Hattie?"

For the last time his mother spoke and stopped mumbling. "I don't know anything about snow. I ain't ever seen none."

They rode without wagon-headed sails. Lava and a few skull halves cracked beneath the wheels. Toward dusk a wind from the surface of the sun swept their path and blew against them live, lightly running bunches of gray wire and weed which sang against the sides of the wagons, across the burning bush, caught in the spokes and harness, stuck like burrs in the horses' manes. The storm passed, hardly ruffling the discomfort of so many old and rigid women.

Clare was nothing but a spot on the plain where the sand thinly billowed, kicked up by someone crossing the street, stirred by the closing of a swinging door. The women sat straight and smoothed themselves when they saw the small constant geyser raised by the mere presence of a few men. The horses suddenly began to pull, as if they too, heads to the ground, could see the camp town—Mistletoe was less than that at the time—and the hitching rail near the bare wood church.

They were stopped by a shout from the Sheriff.

"You can't bring all them people in here. No, sir, not without a license!"

Luke, not his brother, climbed down. He beat his hat against a sore unlimbered leg. He tucked in his shirt, loosening the muscles of his arms and back, drawing up his chest, and walked the length of the wagon train to the Sheriff.

"Howdy." The man in khaki pants, knee high boots and Stetson, never left the barroom porch.

"I don't see how you can keep us out," said Luke.

The Sheriff leaned back against the post and again put the knife blade to his fingernails.

"All's I got to do is call my boys. Of course, if you scatter, it'll take us a little longer to round you up. But I wouldn't." The Sheriff brushed the parings from his vest, leaned forward and pushed the blade down a patent leather boot top to scratch his calf. The uncut nails on his red hands were longer than the manicured.

"But this here is a wedding!"

"Don't matter. I don't care if the whole pack aims to rut. You the man?"

"No, sir. I ain't the one. That's sure."

The Sheriff raised his head and slowly scanned the wagons, looked at the quiet and waiting eyes of the women who stared back. In a low voice he muttered to the boy who stepped closer and listened with his back to the train. Then louder: "But that don't make much difference. This town's got a law. My men would be here in fifteen minutes, if I called."

Luke heard the knocking of the horses. He smelled molasses and rubber gum, gun grease and a handful of browned leaves loose in a hot pants pocket. And suddenly he jumped onto the porch, two short steps loud on the swaydown boards.

"Well, now!" The Sheriff squinted.

Luke whispered in his ear. He spoke softly, using all his breath, against wax and smile, his own forehead near thick temples, his boy's chin low to the bulging collar. He broke out as he felt the air fall from his throat, not caring that he was unable to see the other's eyes. The pistol butt pressed upward against his thin stomach. The head bent slightly forward, looking for a damp match dropped in the dust. Luke spoke into it with haste, perhaps asking how many cartridges the gun would hold. The ear was yellow since the squat man, in jest when drunk, bragged and fixed into it the moist end of a smoking cigarette. Luke shut his eyes.

"All right," the Sheriff gently stopped him, "let them by."

The Clare geyser churned and climbed suddenly higher as they rolled.

Ma married, by bonfire light and to the music of a borrowed and portable celesta, in a roped-off lot behind the church which, at the last moment, she refused to enter. At some time, after food was found, and away from the crowd of women, Luke spread out his neckerchief and said to the Sheriff, "This here pie's for Maverick. She ain't never seen a wedding."

Throughout the night, Luke's first in town, and until the middle of the morning when the trip home was attempted, Ma sat alone by the stretched, flat, feverish body of her husband's mother. Ma's chair faced the open window—it was a short jump from the strange and empty room to the ground —and at her feet lay the satchel, tightly closed, and the old woman who cried out, in the racking of her shoulders and occasional thump of her hand against the floor, for sleep. Ma sat straight and listened for the sound of returning footsteps. Now and then she leaned down to dry the darkening forehead or touch the plaited hair already wild.

"You did come. And I've married me a torment. I deserve to sit here on a folding chair, not even able to ease you off to sleep. I nagged you the whole day. And all's I got is a bare finger which, had a ring been set on it—and you was right to keep it back—would have been yours, since he had none to give. It wasn't mine to take. Nor was he. I guess it ain't just me he's shown he's got no feeling for. And I can't make it up to you. Since he's left us both."

Rock Castle

from THE LIME TWIG (1961)

The sources of *The Lime Twig* are few, elusive, and disparate. Early in the summer of 1956, after spending my first year teaching writing at Harvard, I found myself obsessed by what was nearly a waking vision: of an empty room which was unlike any I had ever seen in actuality yet was also totally familiar. I still see it—the rough wooden floors, the darkly painted walls, the green light that came from a single shaded window. I wanted to know what had happened in that room, or what would in fact happen in it; who had lived in it, dreamt in it, suffered violence in it, or was going to. For some reason I thought that this rather sinister room existed in London, though at the time I had never been to England. And for some reason the room reminded me of my father's story of a famous horse that had been buried on the grounds of his parents' place in Ireland. As the story went, a young woman, who was a competition rider and a person of daring, had the remains of this horse secretly dug up so that she could carry the skull back to America, where she had it mounted on a silver plaque. It was a lark that horrified her Irish relatives but made her a legend in Connecticut.

Then, inexplicably, I thought of Michael Banks, child hero of the Mary Poppins books, and associated him with the violated Irish horse of my father's anecdote. From horse and innocent hero came the idea for a novel about two young married Londoners, Michael and Margaret Banks, whose lives are destroyed when Michael Banks is lured by an underworld gang into helping to steal a racehorse named Rock Castle. The dream that the gang holds out to Michael Banks is of mystery, riches, illicit sex in the context of an England impoverished at the end of World War II. In the course of the story Margaret is beaten to death on the orders of Larry, the leader of the gang, while Michael succumbs to Sybilline, another member of the gang. In the end, Michael tries to redeem his innocence by throwing himself in front of Rock Castle and thus preventing this mythical horse from winning the race at Aldington.

I spent the rest of that summer writing a first draft, and the next four years tinkering with it, revising it, attempting to discover its final shape. When *The Lime Twig* was completed at last, I recognized that the room I had originally envisioned was in fact an attic in the house we were renting in 1956; that I had gotten my England and English "voice" from the British soldiers I had known during the war; and that *The Lime Twig* also owed its beginnings to my admiration for Graham Greene's *Brighton Rock*.

In the following pages, Hencher, a fat and insignificant member of Larry's gang, leads Michael Banks to a wharf where he has his first sight of Rock Castle, recently stolen and brought down the Thames in a barge.

Rock Castle

And now the dawn was gone, the morning hours too were gone. He had found the crabbed address and come upon the doorway in which Hencher waited; had walked with him down all those streets until the squat ship, unseaworthy, just for pleasure, lay ahead of them in a berth between two tankers; had already seen the rigging, the smokestacks, the flesh-colored masts and rusty sirens and whistles in a blue sky above the rotting roof of the cargo sheds; had boarded the *Artemis*, which smelled of coke and rank canvas and sea animals and beer and boys looking for sport.

"We'll just have some drink and a little talk on this ship before she sails, Mr. Banks. . . ."

He leaned toward Hencher. His elbows were on the table and his wet glass was touching Hencher's frothy glass in the center of the table. Someone had dropped a mustard pot and beneath his shoe he felt the fragments of smashed china, the shape of a wooden spoon, the slick of the mustard on the dirty spoon. A woman with lunch packed in a box pushed through the crowd and bumped against him, paused and rested the box upon their table. Protruding from the top of the box and sealed with a string and paper was a tall jar filled with black bottled tea. The woman carried her own folding chair.

"Bloody slow in putting to sea, mates," she said, and laughed. She wore an old sweater, a man's muffler was knotted round her throat. "I could do with a breath of that sea air right now, I could."

Hencher lifted his glass. "Go on," he said, "have a sip. Been on the *Artemis* before?"

"Not me."

"I'll tell you then. Find a place for yourself in the bows. You get the breeze there, you see everything best from there."

She put her mouth to the foam, drank long, and when she took the glass away she was breathing quickly and a canker at the edge of her lip was wet. "Join me," she said. "Why don't you join me, mates?"

"We'll see you in the bows," said Hencher.

"Really?"

"Good as my word."

It was all noise of people wanting a look at the world and a smell of the sea, and the woman was midships with her basket; soon in the shadow of the bow anchor she would be trying to find a safe spot for her folding chair. Hencher was winking. A boy in a black suit danced by their table, and in his arms was a girl of about fourteen. Banks watched the way she held him and watched her hands in the white gloves shrunk small and tight below the girl's thin wrists. Music, laughter, smells of deck paint and tide and mustard, sight of the boy pulled along by the fierce white childish hands. And he himself was listening, touching his tongue to the beer, leaning close as he dared to Hencher, beginning to think of the black water widening between the sides of the holiday ship and the quay.

"What's that, Hencher? What's that you say?"

Hencher was looking him full in the face: ". . . to Rock Castle, here's to Rock Castle, Mr. Banks!"

He heard his own voice beneath the whistles and plash of bilge coming out of a pipe, "To Rock Castle, then. . . ."

The glasses touched, were empty, and the girl's leg was only the leg of a child and the woman would drink her black tea alone. He stood, moved his chair so that he sat not across from Hencher but beside him.

"He's old, Mr. Banks. Rock Castle has his age, he has. And what's his age? Why, it's the evolution of his bloody name, that's what it is. Just the evolution of a name—Apprentice out of Lithograph by Cobbler, Emperor's Hand by Apprentice out of Hand Maiden by Lord of the Land, Draftsman by Emperor's Hand out of Shallow Draft by Amulet, Castle Churl by Draftsman out of Likely Castle by Cold Masonry, Rock Castle by Castle Churl out of Words on Rock by Plebeian—and what's this name if not the very evolution of his life? You want to think of the life, Mr. Banks, think of the breeding. Consider the fiver bets, the cheers, the wreaths. Then forgotten, because he's taken off the turf and turned out into the gorse, far from the paddock, the swirl of torn ticket stubs, the soothing nights after a good win, far from the serpentine eyes and bowler hats. Do you see it, Mr. Banks? Do you see how it was for Rock Castle?"

He could only nod, but once again—the *Artemis* was rolling—once again he saw the silver jaw, the enormous sheet, the upright body of the horse that was crashing in the floor of the Dreary Station flat. And he could only keep his eyes down, clasp his hands.

". . . Back sways a little, you see, the color of the coat hardens and the legs grow stiff. Months, years, it's only the blue sky for him, occasionally put to stud and then back he goes to his shelter under an old oak at the edge of a field. Useless, you see. Do you see it? Until tonight when he's ours—yours—until tonight when we get our hands on him and tie him up in the van and drive him to stables I know of in Highland Green. Yours, you see, and he's got no recollection of the wreaths or seconds of speed, no knowledge at all of the prime younger horses sprung from his blood. But he'll run all right, on a long track he'll run better than the young ones good for nothing except a spring. Power, endurance, a forgotten name—do you see it, Mr. Banks? He's ancient, Rock

Castle is, an ancient horse and he's bloody well run beyond memory itself. . . ."

Flimsy frocks, dancing children, a boy with the face of a man, a girl whose body was still awkward; they were all about him and taking their pleasure while the feet tramped and the whistle tooted. But Hencher was talking, holding him by the brown coat just beneath the ribs, then fumbling and cupping in front of his eyes a tiny photograph and saying, "Go on, go on, take a gander at this lovely horse."

Then the pause, the voice less friendly and the question, and the sound of his own voice answering: "I'm game, Hencher. Naturally, I'm still game. . . ."

"Ah, like me you are. Good as your word. Well, come then, let's have a turn round the deck of this little tub. We've time yet for a turn at the rail."

He stood, trying to scrape the shards of the smashed mustard pot from his shoe, followed Hencher toward the white sea doors. The back of Hencher's neck was red, the checked cap was at an angle, they made their slow way together through the excursion crowd and the smells of soap and cotton underwear and scent behind the ears.

"We're going to do a polka," somebody called, "come dance with us. . . ."

"A bit of business first," Hencher said, and grinned over the heads at the woman. "A little business first—then we'll be the boys for you, never fear."

A broken bench with the name *Annie* carved into it, a bucket half-filled with sand, something made of brass and swinging, a discarded man's shirt snagged on the horn of a big cleat bolted to the deck and, overhead, high in a box on the wall of the pilot house, the running light flickering through the sea gloom. He felt the desertion, the wind, the coming of darkness as soon as he stepped from the saloon.

She's home now, she's thinking about her hubby now, she's asking the cat where's Michael off to, where's my Michael gone to?

He spat sharply over the rail, turned his jacket collar up, breathed on the dry bones of his hands.

Together, heads averted, going round the deck, coming abreast of the saloon and once more sheltered by a flapping canvas: Hencher lit a cigar while he himself stood grinning in through the lighted window at the crowd. He watched them kicking, twirling, holding hands, fitting their legs and feet to the steps of the dance; he grinned at the back of the girl too young to have a girdle to pull down, grinned at the boy in the black suit. He smelled the hot tobacco smell and Hencher was with him, Hencher who was fat and blowing smoke on the glass.

"You say you have a van, Hencher, a horse van. . . ."

"That's the ticket. Two streets over from this quay, parked in an alley by the ship-fitter's, as good a van as you'd want and with a full tank. And it's a van won't be recognized, I can tell you that. A little oil and sand over the name, you see. Like they did in the war. And we drive it wherever we please—you see—and no one's the wiser."

He nodded and for a moment, across the raven-blue and gold of the water, he saw the spires and smokestacks and tiny bridges of the city black as a row of needles burned and tipped with red. The tide had risen to its high mark and the gangway was nearly vertical; going down he burned his palm on the tarred rope, twice lost his footing. The engines were loud now. Except for Hencher and himself, except for the officer posted at the foot of the gangway and a seaman standing by each of the hawsers fore and aft, the quay was deserted, and when the sudden blasting of the ship's whistle commenced the timbers shook, the air was filled with steam, the noise of the whistle sounded through the quay's dark cargo shed. Then it stopped, except for the echoes in the shed and out on the water, and the man gave his head a shake as if he could not rid it of the whistling. He held up an unlighted cigarette and Hencher handed him the cigar.

"Oh," said the officer, "it's you two again. Find the lady in question all right?"

"We found her, Captain. She's comfy, thanks, good and comfy."

"Well, according to schedule we tie up here tomorrow morning at twenty past eight."

"My friend and me will come fetch her on the dot, Captain, good as my word. . . ."

Again the smothering whistle, again the sound of chain, and someone shouted through a megaphone and the gangway rose up on a cable; the seamen hoisted free the ropes, the bow of the *Artemis* began to swing, the officer stepped over the widening space between quay and ship and was gone.

"Come," said Hencher, and took hold of his arm, "we can watch from the shed."

They leaned against a crate under the low roof and there were rats and piles of dried shells and long dark empty spaces in the cargo shed. There were holes in the flooring: if he moved the toe of his shoe his foot would drop off into the water; if he moved his hand there would be the soft pinch of fur or the sudden burning of dirty teeth. Only Hencher and himself and the rats. Only scum, the greasy water and a punctured and sodden dory beneath them—filth for a man to fall into.

"There . . . she's got the current now. . . ."

He stared with Hencher toward the lights, small gallery of decks and silhouetted stacks that was the *Artemis* a quarter mile off on the river.

"They'll have their fun on that little ship tonight and with a moon, too, or I miss my guess. Another quarter hour," Hencher was twisting, trying for a look at his watch in the dark, "and I'll bring the lorry round."

Side by side, rigid against the packing crate, listening to the rats plop down, waiting, and all the while marking the disappearance of the excursion boat. Only the quay's single boom creaking in the wind and a view of the river across the now empty berth was left to them, while ahead of the *Artemis* lay a peaceful sea worn smooth by night and flotillas of landing boats forever beached. With beer and music in her saloon she was off there making for the short sea cliffs, for the moonlit coast and desolate windy promontories into which the batteries had once been built. At 3 A.M. her navigator discovering the cliffs, fixing location by sighting a flat tin helmet nailed to a stump on the tallest cliff's windy lip, and the *Artemis* would approach the shore, and all of them—boy, girl, lonely woman —would have a glimpse of ten miles of coast with an iron fleet half-sunk in the mud, a moonlit vision of windlasses, torpedo tubes, skein of rusted masts and the stripped hull of a destroyer rising stern first from that muddied coast under the cliffs. Beside the rail the lonely woman at least, and perhaps the rest of them, would see the ten white coastal miles, the wreckage safe from tides and storms and snowy nights, the destroyer's superstructure rising respectable as a lighthouse keeper's station. All won, all lost, all over, and for half a crown they could have it now, this seawreck and abandon and breeze of the ocean surrounding them. And the boy at least would hear the moist unjoyful voice of his girl while the *Artemis* remained off shore, would feel the claspknife in the pocket of her skirt and, down on the excursion boat's hard deck, would know the comfort to be taken with a young girl worn to thinness and wiry and tough as the titlings above the cliffs.

Michael stood rigid against the packing crate, alone. He waited deep within the shed and watched, sniffed something that was not of rats or cargo at all. Then he saw it drifting along the edges of the quay, rising up through the rat holes round his shoes: fog, the inevitable white hair strands which every night looped out across the river as if once each night the river must grow old, clammy, and in its age and during these late hours only, produce the thick miles of old woman's hair within whose heaps and strands it might then hide all bodies, tankers, or fat iron shapes nodding to themselves out there.

Fog of course and he should have expected it, should have carried a torch. Yet, whatever was to come his way would come, he knew, like this—slowly and out of a thick fog. Accidents, meetings unexpected, a figure emerging to put its arms about him: where to discover everything he dreamed of except in a fog. And, thinking of slippery corners, skin suddenly bruised, grappling hooks going blindly through the water: where to lose it all if not in the same white fog.

Alone he waited until the great wooden shed was filled with the fog that caused the rotting along the water's edge. His shirt was flat, wet against his chest. The forked iron boom on the quay was gone, and as for the two tankers that marked the vacated berth of the excursion boat, he knew they were there only by the dead sounds they made. All about him was the visible texture and density of the expanding fog. He was listening for the lorry's engine, with the back of a hand kept trying to wipe his cheek.

An engine was nearby suddenly, and despite the fog he knew that it was not Hencher's lorry but was the river barge approaching on the lifting tide. And he was alone, shivering, helpless to give a signal. He had no torch, no packet of matches. No one trusted a man's voice in a fog.

All the bells and whistles in mid-river were going at once, and hearing the tones change, the strokes change, listening to the metallic or compressed-air sounds of sloops or ocean-going vessels protesting their identities and their vague shifting locations on the whole of this treacherous and fog-bound river's surface—a horrible noise, a confused warning, a frightening celebration—he knew that only his own barge, of all this night's drifting or anchored traffic, would come without lights and making no sound except for the soft and faltering sound of the engine itself. This he heard—surely someone was tinkering with it, nursing it, trying to stop the loss of oil with a bare hand—and each moment he waited for even these illicit sounds to go dead. But in the fog the barge engine was turning over and, all at once, a man out there cleared his throat.

So he stood away from the packing crate and slowly went down to his hands and knees and discovered that he could see a little distance now, and began to crawl. He feared that the rats would get his hands; he ran his fingers round the crumbling edges of the holes; his creeping knee came down on fragments of a smashed bottle. There was an entire white sea-world floating and swirling in that enormous open door, and he crawled out to it.

"You couldn't do nothing about the bleeding fog!"

He had crossed the width of the quay, had got a grip on the iron joint of the boom and was trying to rise when the voice spoke up directly beneath him and he knew that if he fell it would not be into the greasy and squid-blackened water but onto the deck of the barge itself. He was unable to look down yet, but it was clear that the man who had spoken up at him had done so with a laugh, casually, without needing to cup his hands.

Before the man had time to say it again—"You couldn't do nothing about the bleeding fog, eh, Hencher? I wouldn't ordinarily step out of the house on a night like this"—the quay had already shaken beneath the van's tires and the headlamp had flicked on, suddenly, and hurt his eyes where he hung from the boom, one hand thrown out for balance and the other stuck like a dead man's to the iron. Hencher, carrying two bright lanterns by wire loops, had come between himself and the lorry's yellow headlamps—"Lively now, Mr. Banks," he was saying without a smile—and had thrust one of the lanterns upon him in time to reach out his freed hand and catch the end of wet moving rope on the instant it came lashing up from the barge. So that the barge was docked, held safely by the rope turned twice round a piling, when he himself was finally able to look straight down and see it, the long and blunt-nosed barge riding high in a smooth bowl scooped out of the fog. Someone had shut off the engine.

"Take a smoke now, Cowles—just a drag, mind you—and we'll get on with it."

She ought to see her hubby now. She ought to see me now.

He had got his arm through the fork of the boom and was holding the lantern properly, away from his body and down, and the glare from its reflector lighted the figure of the man Cowles below him and in cold wet rivulets drifted sternward down the length of the barge. Midships were three hatches, two battened permanently shut, the third covered by a sagging canvas. Beside this last hatch and on a bale of hay sat a boy naked from the waist up and wearing twill riding britches. In the stern was a small cabin. On its roof, short booted legs dangling over the edge, a jockey in full racing dress sat with a cigarette now between his lips and hands clasped round one of his tiny knees.

"Cowles! I want off . . . I want off this bloody coop!" he shouted.

The cigarette popped into his mouth then. It was a trick he had. The lips were pursed round the hidden cigarette and the little man was staring up not at Cowles or Hencher but at himself, and even while Cowles was ordering the two of them, boy and jockey, to get a hop on and drag the tarpaulin off the hold, the jockey kept looking up at him, toe of one little boot twitching left and right but the large bright eyes remaining fixed on his own—until the cigarette popped out again and the dwarfed man allowed himself to be helped from his seat on the cabin roof by the stableboy whose arms, in the lantern light, were upraised and spattered with oil to the elbows.

"Get a hop on now, we want no coppers or watchman or dock inspectors catching us at this bit of game. . . ."

The fog was breaking, drifting away, once more sinking into the river. Long shreds of it were wrapped like rotted sails or remnants of a wet wash round the buttresses and hand-railings of the bridges, and humped outpourings of fog came rolling from within the cargo shed as if all the fuels of this cold fire were at last consumed. The wind had started up again, and now the moon was low, just overhead.

"Here, use my bleeding knife, why don't you?"

The water was slimy with moonlight, the barge itself was slimy—all black and gold, dripping—and Cowles, having flung his own cigarette behind him and over the side, held the blade extended and moved down the slippery deck toward the boy and booted figure at the hatch with the slow embarrassed step of a man who at any moment expects to walk upon eel or starfish and trip, lose his footing, sprawl heavily on a deck as unknown to him as this.

"Here it is now, Mr. Banks!" He felt one of Hencher's putty hands quick and soft and excited on his arm. "Now you'll see what there is to see. . . ."

He looked down upon the naked back, the jockey's nodding cap, the big man Cowles and the knife stabbing at the ropes, until Cowles grunted and the three of them pulled off the tarpaulin and he was staring down at all the barge carried in its hold: the black space, the echo of bilge and, without movement, snort, or pawing of hoof, the single white marble shape of the horse, whose neck (from where he leaned over, trembling, on the quay) was the fluted and tapering neck of some serpent, while the head was an elongated white skull with nostrils, eye sockets, uplifted gracefully in the barge's hold—*Draftsman by Emperor's Hand out of Shallow Draft by Amulet, Castle Churl by Draftsman out of Likely Castle by Cold Masonry, Rock Castle by Castle Churl out of Words on Rock by Plebeian . . . until tonight when he's ours, until tonight when he's ours. . . .*

"Didn't I tell you, Mr. Banks? Didn't I? Good as his word, that's Hencher."

The whistles died one by one on the river and it was not Wednesday at all, only a time slipped off its cycle with hours and darkness never to be accounted for. There was water viscous and warm that lapped the sides of the barge; a faint up and down motion of the barge which he could gauge against the purple rings of a piling; and below him the still crouched figures of the men and, in its moist alien pit, the silver horse with its ancient head, round which there buzzed a single fly as large as his own thumb and molded of shining blue wax.

He stared down at the lantern-lit blue fly and at the animal whose two ears were delicate and unfeeling, as unlikely to twitch as two pointed fern leaves etched on glass, and whose silver coat gleamed with the colorless fluid of some ghostly libation and whose decorous drained head smelled of a violence that was his own.

Even when he dropped the lantern—"No harm done, no harm done," Hencher said quickly—the horse did not shy or throw itself against the ribs of the barge, but remained immobile, fixed in the same standing posture of rigorous sleep that they had found it in at the moment the tarpaulin was first torn away. Though Cowles made his awkward lunge to the rail, saw what it was—lantern with cracked glass half sunk, still burning on the water, then abruptly turning dark and sinking from sight—and laughed through his nose, looked up at them: "Bleeding lot of help he is. . . ."

"No harm done," said Hencher again, sweating and by light of the van's dim headlamps swinging out the arm of the boom until the cable and hook were correctly positioned above the barge's hold. "Just catch the hook, Cowles, guide it down."

Without a word, hand that had gripped the lantern still trembling, he took his place with Hencher at the iron bar which, given the weight of Hencher and himself, would barely operate the cable drum. He got his fingers round the bar; he tried to think of himself straining at such a bar, but it was worse for Hencher, whose heart was sunk in fat. Yet Hencher too was ready—in tight shirtsleeves, his jacket removed and hanging from the tiny silver figure of a winged man that adorned the van's radiator cap—so that he himself determined not to let go of the bar as he had dropped the lantern but, instead, to carry his share of the horse's weight, to stay at the bar and drum until the horse could suffer this last transport. There was no talking on the barge. Only sounds of their working, plash of the boy's feet in the bilge, the tinkle of buckles and strap ends as the webbed bands were slid round the animal's belly and secured.

Hencher was whispering: "Ever see them lift the bombs out of the craters? Two or three lads with a tripod, some lengths of chain, a few red flags and a rope to keep the children away . . . then cranking up the unexploded bomb that would have bits of debris and dirt sticking peacefully as you please to that filthy big cylinder . . . something to see, men at a job like that and fishing up a live bomb big enough to blow a cathedral to the ground." Then, feeling a quiver: "But here now, lay into it gently, Mr. Banks, that's the ticket."

He pushed—Hencher was pushing also—until after a moment the drum stopped and the cable that stretched from the tip of the boom's arm down to the ring swiveling above the animal's webbed harness was taut.

"O.K." It was Cowles kneeling at the hold's edge, speaking softly and clearly on the late night air, "O.K. now . . . up he goes."

The barge, which could support ten tons of coal or gravel on the river's oily and slop-sullied tide, was hardly lightened when the horse's hoofs swung a few inches free of that planking hidden and awash. But drum, boom, cable and arms could lift not a pound more than this, and lifted this—the weight of the horse—only with strain and heat, pressure and rusted rigidity. Though his eyes were closed he knew when the boom swayed, could feel the horse beginning to sway off plumb. He heard the drum rasping round, heard the loops of rusted cable wrapping about the hot drum one after another, slowly.

"Steady now, steady . . . he's bloody well high enough."

Then, as Hencher with burned hands grasped the wheel that would turn the boom its quarter circle and position the horse over quay, not over barge, he felt a fresh wind on his cheek and tilted his head, opened his eyes, and saw his second vision of the horse: up near the very tip of the iron arm, rigid and captive in the sling of two webbed bands, legs stiff beneath it, tail blown out straight on the wind and head lifted —they had wrapped a towel round the eyes—so that high in the air it became the moonlit spectacle of some giant weather vane. And seeing one of the front legs begin to move, to lift, and the hoof—that destructive hoof—rising up and dipping beneath the slick shoulder, seeing this slow gesture of the horse preparing to paw suddenly at the empty air, and feeling the tremor through his fingers still lightly on the bar: "Let him down, Hencher, let him down!" he cried, and waved both hands at the blinded and hanging horse even as it began to descend.

Until the boom regained its spring and balance like a tree spared from a gale; until the drum, released, clattered and in its rusty mechanism grew still; until the four sharp hoofs touched wood of the quay. Cowles—first up the ladder and followed by Jimmy Needles the jockey and Lovely the stable-boy—reached high and loosed the fluttering towel from round its eyes. The boy approached and snapped a lead-rope to the halter and the jockey, never glancing at the others or at the horse, stepped up behind him, whispering: "Got a fag for Needles, mister? Got a fag for Needles?" Not until this moment when he shouted, "Hencher, don't leave me, Hencher . . ." and saw the fat naked arm draw back and the second lantern sail in an arc over the water, and in a distance also saw the white hindquarters on the van's ramp and dark shapes running—not until this moment was he grateful for the little hard cleft of fingers round his arm and the touch of the bow-legged figure still begging for his fag but pulling and guiding him at last in the direction of the cab's half-open door. Cowles had turned the petcocks and behind them the barge was sinking.

These five rode crowded together on the broad seat, five white faces behind a rattling windscreen. Five men with elbows gnawing at elbows, hands and pairs of boots confused, men breathing hard and remaining silent except for Hencher who complained he hadn't room to drive. In labored first gear and with headlights off, they in the black van traveled the slow bumping distance down the length of the cargo shed, from plank to rotted plank moved slowly in the van burdened with their own weight and the weight of the horse until at the corner of the deserted building—straight ahead lay darkness that was water and all five, smelling sweat and river fumes and petrol, leaned forward together against the dim glass—they turned and drove through an old gate topped with a strand of barbed wire and felt at last hard rounded cobblestones beneath the tires.

"No one's the wiser now, lads," said Hencher, and laughed, shook the sweat from his eyes, took a hand off the wheel and slapped Cowles' knee. "We're just on a job if anyone wants to know," smiling, both fat hands once more white on the wheel. "So we've only to sit tight until we make Highland Green . . . eh, Cowles . . . eh, Needles . . . eh, Mr. Banks?"

But Michael himself, beneath the jockey and pressed between Cowles' thick flank and the unupholstered door, was tasting lime: smells of the men, smells of oil, lingering smells of the river and now, faint yet definite, seeping through the panel at his back, smells of the horse—all these mixed odors filled his mouth, his stomach, and some hard edge of heel or brake lever or metal that thrust down from the dash was cutting into his ankle, hurting the bone. Under his buttocks he felt the crooked shape of a spanner; from a shelf behind the thin cushions straw kept falling; already the motor was over-heated and they were driving too fast in the darkness of empty shopping districts and areas of cheap lodgings with doorways and windows black except for one window, seven or eight streets ahead of them, in which a single light would be burning. And each time this unidentified black shabby van went round a corner he felt the horse—his horse—thump against one metal side or the other. Each time the faint sound and feel of the thumping made him sick.

"Hencher. I think you had better leave me off at the flat."

Then trying to breathe, trying to explain, trying to argue with Hencher in the speeding overheated cab and twisting, seeing the fluted dark nostril at a little hole behind the driver's head. Until Hencher smiled his broad worried smile and in a loud voice said: "Oh well, Mr. Banks is a married man," speaking to Cowles, the jockey, the stableboy, nudging

Cowles in the ribs. "And you must always make allowance for a married man. . . ."

Cowles yawned, and, as best he could, rubbed his great coatsleeves still wet from the spray. "Leave him off, Hencher, if he gives us a gander at the wife."

The flat door is open and the cat sleeps. Just inside the door, posted on a straight chair, market bag at her feet and the cat at her feet, sitting with the coat wrapped round her shoulders and the felt hat still on her head: there she waits, waits up for him. The neighbor on the chair next to her is sleeping—like the cat—and the mouth is half-open with the breath hissing through, and the eyes are buried under curls. But her own eyes are level, the lids red, the face smooth and white and soft as soap. Waiting up for him.

Without moving, without taking her eyes from the door: "Where's Michael off to? Where's my Michael gone?" she asks the cat. Then down the outer hall, in the dark of the one lamp burning, she hears the click of the house key, the sound of the loose floor board, and she thinks to raise a hand and dry her cheek. With the same hand she touches her neighbor's arm.

"It's all right, Mrs. Stickley," she whispers, "he's home now."

The engine is boiling over when the van reaches Highland Green. Water flows down the dented black hood, the grille, and a jet of steam bursting up from the radiator scalds the wings of the tiny silver figure of the man which, in attitude of pursuit, flies from the silver cap. Directly before the machine and in the light of the headlamps Hencher stands shielding his face from the steam. Then moves quickly, throws his belly against the hot grille, catches the winged figure in a rag and gives it a twist.

"Come along, cock, we haven't got all the bleeding night," says Cowles.

It is dark in Highland Green, dark in this public stable which lies so close to the tanks and towers of the gasworks that a man, if he wished, might call out to the old watchman there. Dark at 3 A.M. and quiet; no one tends the stables at night and only a few spiritless horses for hire are drowsing in a few of the endless stalls. Hardly used now, dead at night, with stray dogs and little starved birds making use of the stalls, and weeds choking the yard. Refuse fills the well, there is a dry petrol pump near a loft building intended for hay.

Hencher steps out of the headlamp's beam, drops the radiator cap, throws the rag to the ground, soothes his hand with his lips. "You needn't tell me to hurry, Cowles," he says, and kicks the tiny winged man away from him into the dead potash and weeds.

Hencher hears the whistles then—two long, a short—and all at once straightens his cap, gives a last word to Cowles: "Leave the animal in the van until I return. And no noise now, mind you. . . ." From beneath the musty seat in the cab he takes a long torch and walks quickly across the rutted yard. Behind him the jockey is puffing on a fresh cigarette, the stableboy—thinking of a girl he once saw bare to the flesh—is resting his head against a side of the van, and Cowles in the dark is frowning and moving his stubby fingers across the watch chain that is a dull gold weight on his vest.

Once in the loft building Hencher lights the torch. Presses the switch with his thumb but keeps the torch down, is careful not to shine the beam toward the exact spot where he knows the man is standing. Rather lights himself with the torch and walks ahead into the dark. He is smiling though he feels sweat on his cheeks and in the folds of his neck. The loft building smells of creosote, the dead pollen of straw, and petrol. He cannot see it, but he knows that to his left there is a double door, closed, and beside it, hidden and waiting within the darkness, a passenger car stately with black lacquer and a radiator cap identical to that on the van. If he swings the torch, flashes it suddenly and recklessly to the left, he knows the light will be dashed back in his face from the car's thick squares of polished window glass. But he keeps the beam at his heel, walks more and more slowly until at last he stops.

"You managed to get here, Hencher," the man says.

"I thought I was on the dot, Larry . . . good as my word, you know."

"Yes, always good as your word. But you've forgotten to take off your cap."

Hencher takes it off, feels his whole head exposed and hot and ugly. At last he allows himself to look, and it is only the softest glow that his torch sheds on the man before him.

"We got the horse, right outside in the van . . . I told you, right outside."

"But you stopped. You did not come here directly."

"I did my best. I did my bloody best, but if he wants to knock it off, if he wants to stop at home and have a word with the wife, why that's just unfortunate . . . but no fault of mine, is it, Larry?"

And then, listening in the direction of the car, waiting for a sound—scratch of the ignition key, oiled suck of gear-lever— he sees the hand extended in front of him and is forced to take hold of it. One boot moves, the other moves, the trenchcoat makes a harsh rubbing noise. And the hand lets go of his, the man fades out of the light and yet—Hencher wipes his face and listens—once in the darkness the footsteps ring back to him like those of an officer on parade.

He keeps his own feet quiet until he reaches the yard and sees the open night sky beginning to change and grow milky like chemicals in a vat, and until he sniffs a faint odor of dung and tobacco smoke. Then he trudges loudly as he can and suddenly, calling the name, shines the bright torch on Cowles.

"Pissed off, was he," says Cowles, and does not blink.

But in the cab Hencher already braces the steering wheel against his belly; the driver's open door swings to the movement of the van. Cowles and the jockey and stableboy walk in slow procession behind the van, which is not too wide for the overgrown passage between the row of stalls, the long dark space between the low stable buildings, but which is high so that now and again the roof of the van brushes then scrapes against the rotted eaves. The tires are wet from the dampness of tangled and prickly weeds. Once, the van stops and Hencher climbs down, drags a bale of molded hay from its path. Then they move—horse van, walking men—and exhaust fumes fill empty bins, water troughs, empty stalls. In darkness they pass a shovel in an iron wheelbarrow, a saddle pad covered with inert black flies, a whip leaning against a whited post. Round a corner they come upon a red lantern burning beside an open and freshly whitewashed box stall. The hay rack has been mended, clean hard silken straw covers the floor, a red horse blanket lies folded on a weathered cane chair near the lantern.

"Lovely will fetch him down for you, Hencher," says Cowles.

"I will fetch him down myself, if you please."

And Lovely the stableboy grins and walks into the stall; the jockey pushes the horse blanket off the chair, sits down heavily; Cowles takes one end of the chain while Hencher works with the other.

They pry up the ends of the chain, allow it to fall link upon ringing link into bright iron pools at their feet until the raised and padded ramp swings loose, opens wider and wider from the top of the van as Cowles and Hencher lower it slowly down. Two gray men who stand with hands on hips and look up into the interior of the van. It is dark in there, steam of the horse drifts out; it appears that between the impacted bright silver flesh of the horse and padded walls no space exists for a man.

Hencher puts the unlighted cigar between his teeth and steps onto the ramp. Silent and nearly broad as the horse he climbs up the ramp, gets his footing, squeezes himself against the white and silver flesh—the toe of one boot striking a hoof on edge, both hands attempting to hold off the weight of the horse—then glances down at Cowles, tries to speak, and slides suddenly into the dark of the van.

And Cowles shouts, doubles over then as powerless as Hencher in the van. The ramp bounces, shakes on its hinges, and though the brake holds and the wheels remain locked, the chassis, cab, and high black sides all sway forward once at the moment they absorb that first unnatural motion of horse lunging at trapped man. Shakes, rattles, and the first loud sound of the hoof striking its short solid blow to metal fades. But not the commotion, the blind forward swaying of the van. While Cowles is shouting for help and dodging, leaping away, he somehow keeps his eyes on the visible rear hoofs and sees that, long as it lasts—the noise, the directionless pitching of the van—those rear hoofs never cease their dancing. The horse strikes a moment longer, but there is no metallic ringing, no sharp sound, and only the ramp drags a little more and the long torch falls from the cab.

Then Cowles is vomiting into the tall grass—he is a fat man and a man as fat as himself lies inside the van—and the grass is sour, the longest blades tickle his lips. On his knees he sweats, continues to be sick, and with large distracted hands keeps trying to fold the grass down upon the whiteness collecting in the hollow of bare roots.

Hencher, with fat lifeless arms still raised to the head kicked in, huddles yet on the van's narrow floor, though the horse is turning round and round in the whitewashed stall. The jockey has left his chair and, cigarette between his lips, dwarfed legs apart, stands holding the long torch in both his hands and aiming it—like a rifle aimed from the hip—at Cowles. While Lovely the stableboy is singing now in a young pure Irish voice to the horse.

"Give me a hand with the body, Cowles, and we'll drag it into the stall," the jockey says. "Can't move it alone, cock, can't move it alone."

The Kissing Bandits

From SECOND SKIN (1964)

The ten months in which I wrote *Second Skin* were the most intensely pleasurable and the most lyrically conducive to imaginative work of any other writing time in my life, before or since. I had taught at Brown for four years; our youngest of four children had reached the age of nine months, old enough to travel; I had received a Guggenheim Fellowship and so, in 1962–63, was free to write. That spring I had had pneumonia, a footnote to one of Providence's rusty iron winters, as I thought of them, and I longed for the sun, for some unimaginably exotic world, as different as possible from New England. That September—pallid, anxious, risking the safety of home for the sake of discovering an island paradise—Sophie and I flew with our children, the oldest of whom was ten, to Grenada, the Caribbean island closest to Trinidad and the coast of South America. In my mind, Grenada still remains an unspoiled paradise despite the American blighting of that island in 1983.

Only months before we left Providence, a close friend committed suicide, leaving behind an infant child. I took the pain of that event to our tropical island, and in a perfumed landscape of the purest sensuality, the fact of our friend's suicide became the dark seed of the novel I wanted to write. I had spent two years thinking about this projected novel: it was to be told in the first person; it was to be unmistakably comic; its protagonist was to be a middle-aged man struggling to help his daughter regain her emotional life. Originally the novel was to take place on a New England island (based on Vinalhaven, Maine, where Sophie and I had spent a few weeks the previous summer). But because of the abrupt death of our friend, and my chance witnessing of a cow artificially inseminated within days of our arrival on Grenada, the idea of *Second Skin* took a suddenly different turn. Now the novel was to be told in the first person by a fifty-nine-year-old ex-Navy Lieutenant, Junior Grade, called Skipper. Skipper would be an artificial inseminator of cows on a "wandering" tropical island of the imagination. There he and his former messboy, Sonny, would together father a black child (an impossibility that would be totally natural on such an island); there Skipper would write the "naked history" of his unsuccessful attempts to prevent the suicide of his daughter, Cassandra, on a cold and cruel New England island after Skipper's return from his tour of wartime duty in the South Pacific.

On Grenada our children attended a British school while Sophie and I picked frangipani blossoms, walked on shelves of barely submerged coral, swam from the crescent of white sand below our cottage, and searched for jewel-box shells in the clear depths of water as warm as the temperature of our own bodies. Every morning I went to my "office," an unused cinder-block room in a combination pigsty and dog kennel made available to me by our landlords, where I worked on *Second Skin*. The walls of my bare room were covered with small green lizards, the floor was carpeted with ants. There was a glassless window looking out to sea. From afternoons on the beach I had acquired great patches of superating sandfly bites on one shin, and every working day armies of ants climbed up to the rung of the wooden table where my feet were propped and, climbing further, feasted on my sandfly bites. A small bird always came to perch on the sill of the window and drank from a tin can that was as dry as a bone. Every morning a distant ship passed across the horizon behind the bird in its empty window. No conditions could have been so perfect for writing a novel that phrases birth against suicide and takes as its theme the idea that the rose is meaningless without its thorns.

In *Second Skin*, Skipper's father is a mortician who commits suicide; Skipper's wife is an alcoholic who commits suicide in a cheap motel called the U-Drive Inn; Skipper's daughter is the cold object of his incestuous devotion, the mother of a little girl named Pixie, and the abandoned wife of a Peruvian guitar player named Fernandez, later perversely and brutally murdered. Cassandra revenges herself on both husband and father by leaping from an abandoned lighthouse on the New England island. But Skipper survives to tell their story, to inseminate his great Brahmin cows, and to hold in his arms at last the black child.

In the following pages Skipper, Sonny, and Cassandra meet in San Francisco at the end of the war and begin their journey to the cold Atlantic island.

The Kissing Bandits

She was in my arms and lifeless, nearly lifeless. Together
we stood: the girl, young mother, war bride in her crumpled
frock, and I in my cap and crumpled uniform of white duck—
it was damp and beginning to soil after these nights awake,
was bunched at the knees and down the front spotted with the
rum and Coca-Cola from poor Sonny's upset glass—I hardly
able to smile, perspiring, sporting on my breast the little
colorful ribbon of my Good Conduct Medal and on my
collar the tarnished insignia of my rank, and unshaven, tired,
burned slightly red and lost, thoroughly lost in this midnight
Chinatown at the end of my tour of duty and still wearing in
my forgetfulness the dark blue armband of the Shore Patrol,
and so protected, protecting, I holding the nearly lifeless hand
and feeling her waist growing smaller and smaller in the wet
curve of my arm, feeling even her cold hand diminishing,
disappearing from mine and wondering how to restore this
poor girl who would soon be gone. I looked around, trying
to catch sight of Sonny where he sat in the booth with Pixie.
And suddenly I was aware of the blind, meaningless, mo-
mentary presence of her little breast against my own and I,
regretting my sensitivity but regretting more the waste, the
impossibility of bringing her to life again—there in the small
fleshed locket of her heart—I wished all at once to abandon
rank, insignia, medal, bald head, good nature, everything, if
only I might become for a moment an anonymous seaman
second class, lanky and far from home and dancing with this
girl, but felt instead the loose sailors pressing against us, all of
them in their idiotic two-piece suits and laced up tight, each

one filling me with despair because she and I were dancing together, embracing, and there wasn't even someone to give her a kiss. Here then was our celebration, the start of adventure and beginning of misery—or perhaps its end—and I kept thinking that she was barelegged, had packed her only pair of stockings—black market, a present from me—in the small tattered canvas bag guarded now between Sonny's feet.

There should have been love in our dark and nameless Chinatown café. But there was only an hour to spare, only the shotglasses flung like jewels among the sailors—each provided with his pocket comb, French letters, gold watch and matching band—only the noise, the smoke, the poster of the old national goat-faced man over the bar, the sound of the record and torch singer, orchestra, a song called "Tangerine," only the young boys with their navy silk ties and Popeye hats, crowded elbows and bowls of boiled rice; only this night, the harbor plunging with battleships, the water front blacked-out, bloody with shore leave and sick with the bodies of young girls sticking to the walls of moist unlighted corridors; only our own café and its infestation of little waiters smiling their white-slave smiles and of sailors pulling down their middies, kicking their fresh white hornpipe legs; only ourselves—agitated eccentric naval officer, well-meaning man, and soft young woman, serious, downcast—only ourselves and in the middle of no romance.

So in the shame and longing of my paternal sentiment, flushed and bumbling, I felt her knee, her hip, once more her breasts—they were of a child in puberty though she was twenty-five—and touched the frock which I had found tossed over the back of the hotel sofa. I glanced down at her head, at the hair pinned up and her neck bare, at her face, the beautiful face which reminded me suddenly of a little death mask of Pascal. From one wrist she carried a dangling purse, and

when it swung against my ribs—dull metronome of our
constrained and hollow dance—I knew it was an empty purse.
No stockings, no handkerchief, no lipstick or keys; no love,
no mother, no Fernandez. There among all those sailors in
the smoke, the noise, I pulled her to me, wincing and lunging
both as I felt imprinted on my stomach the shape of hers, and
felt all the little sinews in her stomach banding together,
trembling. It was midnight—Pacific War Time—and I tried
to collect myself, tried to put on a show of strength in my
jaw.

"I've never been afraid of the seeds of death," I said,
tightening my arm, staring over her head at the litter of
crushed cherries and orange rind wet on the bar, "and if I
were you I wouldn't blame Gertrude for what she did." We
executed a fairly rakish turn, bumped from the rear, blocked
by the tall airy figure of a bosun's mate—the uniform was
stuffed against his partner in an aghast paralysis of love, bell-
bottoms wrapped tight around the woman's ankles, the man's
white face swaying in an effort to toss aside the black hair
drenched in rum—and I looked down into my own partner's
eyes which were lifted to mine at last and which were as clear
as sea shells, the pupils gray and hard, the irises suddenly
returning to sight like little cold musical instruments. I sighed
—my sigh was a hot breath on her dry lips—I blushed, I got
my wind again, and it was a mouthful of smoke, mouthful of
rum, fragrance of salty black sauce and yellow plague.

"As you know," I said, "I grew up very familiar with the
seeds of death; I had a special taste for them always. But when
I heard about Gertrude something happened. It was as if I had
struck a new variety. Her camel's-hair coat, her pink mules,
her cuticle sticks scattered on the floor, her dark glasses left
lying on the unmade bed in the U-Drive-Inn, I saw the whole
thing, for that moment understood her poor strangled solitude, understood exactly what it is like to be one of the

unwanted dead. Suddenly Gertrude and I were being washed together in the same warm tide. But in our grief we were casting up only a single shadow—you."

Quickly, artfully, I gave the bosun's mate a shove with my sea-going hip and, heavy as I was, stood hovering, sagging in front of Cassandra. I held her, with a moistened finger I touched her dry mouth, I raised her chin—unsmiling dimple, unblemished curve of her little proud motherhood—I watched her gray eyes and I waited, waited for the sound of the voice which was always a whisper and which I had never failed to hear. And now the eyes were tuned, the lips were unsealed—moving, opening wide enough to admit a straw—I was flooded with the sound of the whisper and sight of a tiny golden snake wriggling up the delicate cleft of her throat—still no smile, never a smile—and curling in a circle to pulse, to die, in the shallow white nest of her temple.

"I think you would like to know," she began, whispering, spacing the words, "you would like to know what I did with the guitar. Well, I burned it. Pixie and I burned it together." And in her whispered seriousness, the hush of her slow enunciation, I heard then the snapping of flames, the tortured singing of those red-hot strings. Even as I dropped her hand, let go of her waist, brought together my fat fingers where the Good Conduct Ribbon like a dazzling insect marked the spot of my heart in all that wrinkled and sullied field of white, even as I struggled with the tiny clasp—pinprick, drop of blood, another stain—and fastened the ribbon to the muslin of her square-collared rumpled frock, even while I admired my work and then took her into my arms again, hugging, kissing, protecting her always and always, and even while I gave her the Good Conduct Medal—she the one who deserved it; I, never—and shook long and happily in my relief: through all this hectic and fragile moment I distinctly heard the gray whisper continuing its small golden thread of intelligence exactly on the threshold of sound and as fine and formidable as the look in her eye.

"Pixie and I were alone, mother and daughter, and we did what we had to do. I think she disapproved at first, but once I got the kerosene out of the garage she began to enjoy the whole thing immensely. She even clapped her little hands. But you ought to have known," taking note of the ribbon, touching it with the tip of her pinky—no other sign than this—and all the while whispering, whispering those minimum formal cadences she had learned at school and gently moving, turning, arching her bare neck so I should see how she disciplined her sorrow, "you ought to have known the U-Drive-Inn was no place for a child. . . ."

I blushed again, I glanced down at the small bare feet in the strapless shoes—scuffed lemon shells—I welcomed even this briefest expression of her displeasure. "It was no place for you, no place for you, Cassandra," I said, and wished, as I had often wished, that she would submit to some small name of endearment, if only at such times as these when I loved her most and feared for her the most. A name of endearment would have helped. "You were too innocent for the U-Drive-Inn," I said. "I should have known how it would end. Your mother always told me she wanted to die surrounded by unmarried couples in a cheap motel, and I let her. But no more cheap motels for us, Cassandra. We won't even visit Gertrude in the cemetery."

She caught my spirit, she caught my gesturing hand: "Skipper?"—at least she allowed herself to whisper that name, mine, which Sonny had invented for me so long ago before we sailed—"Skipper? Will you do something nice for me? Something really nice?"

She was still unsmiling but was poised, half-turned, giving me a look of happiness, of life, in the pure agility of her body.

And hadn't she, wearing only the frock, only a few pins in the small classical lift of her hair, hadn't she come straight from a sluggish bath tub in the U-Drive-Inn to the most violent encounter ever faced by her poor little determined soul? Now she held before me the promise of her serious duplicity, watching and gauging—me, the big soft flower of fatherhood—until I heard myself saying, "Anything, anything, the bus doesn't leave for another hour and a half, Cassandra, and no one will ever say I faltered even one cumbersome step in loving you." I gripped her small ringless hand and fled with her, though she was only walking, walking, this child with the poise and color and muscle-shape of a woman, followed her through the drunken sailors to the door.

In the dark, whipped by pieces of paper—the torn and painted remnants of an old street dragon—a sailor stood rolling and moaning against the wall, holding his white cupcake-wrapper hat in one hand and with the other reaching into the sunken whiteness of his chest, the upturned face, the clutching hand, the bent legs spread and kicking to the unheard Latin rhythm of some furious carnival. But on flowed Cassandra, small, grave, heartless, a silvery water front adventuress, and led me straight into the crawling traffic—it was unlighted, rasping, a slow and blackened parade of taxicabs filled with moon-faced marines wearing white braid and puffing cherry-tipped cigars, parade of ominous jeeps each with its petty officer standing up in the rear, arms folded, popping white helmets strapped in place—led me on through admiring whistles and the rubbery sibilance of military tires to a dark shop which was only a rat's hole between a cabaret —girl ventriloquist, dummy in black trunks—and the fuming concrete bazaar of the Greyhound Bus Terminal—point of our imminent departure—drew me on carefully, deftly, until side by side we stood in the urine-colored haze of a guilty light bulb and breathed the dust, the iodine, the medicinal alcohol of a most vulgar art.

"But, Cassandra," I said in a low voice, flinching, trying to summon the dignity of my suffering smile, all at once aware that beneath my uniform my skin was an even and lively red, unbroken, unmarked by disfiguring scars or blemishes, "look at his teeth, smell his breath! My God, Cassandra!"

"Skipper," she said, and again it was the ghostly whisper, the terrifying sadistic calm of the school-trained voice, "don't be a child. Please." Then she whispered efficiently, calmly, to the oaf at the table—comatose eyes of the artist, the frustrated procurer, drinking her in—and naturally he was unable to hear even one word of her little succinct command, unable to make out her slow toy train of lovely sounds. He wore a tee-shirt, was covered—arms, neck, shoulders—with the sweaty peacock colors of his self-inflicted art.

"There's no need to whisper, lady," he said. Up and down went his eyes, up and down from where he fell in a mountain on his disreputable table, watching her, not bothering to listen, flexing his nightmare pictures as best he could, shifting and showing us, the two of us, the hair bunched and bristling in his armpits, and even that hair was electrical.

She continued to whisper—ludicrous pantomime—without stopping, without changing the faint and formal statement of her desires, when suddenly and inexplicably the man and I, allied in helpless and incongruous competition, both heard her at the same time.

"My boy friend is bashful," she was saying, "do you understand? Let me have a piece of writing paper and a pencil, please."

"You mean he's afraid? But I got you, lady," and I saw him move, saw his blue tattooed hand swim like a trained seal in the slime of a drawer which he had yanked all at once into his belly.

"Father, Cassandra, father!" I exclaimed, though softly, "Pixie's grandfather, Cassandra!"

"No need to worry, Skipper," said the man—his grin, his fiendish familiarity—"I'm a friend of Uncle Sam's."

Yellow and silver-tinted, prim, Cassandra was already sitting on the tattooer's stool, had placed her purse on the table beside her, had forced the man to withdraw his fat scalloped arms, was writing with the black stub of pencil on the back of a greasy envelope which still contained—how little she knew —its old-fashioned familiar cargo of prints the size of postage stamps, each one revealing, beneath a magnifying glass, its aspect of faded pubic area or instant of embarrassed love. Alone and celebrating, we were war orphans together and already I had forgiven her, wanted to put my hand on the curls pinned richly and hastily on the top of her head. I could see that she was writing something in large block letters across the envelope.

She stood up—anything but lifeless now—and between his thumb and finger the man took the envelope and rubbed it as if he were testing the sensual quality of gold laminated cloth or trying to smear her tiny fingerprints onto his own, and then the man and I, the oaf and I, were watching her together, listening:

"My boy friend," she said, and I was measuring her pauses, smelling the bludwurst on the tattooer's breath, was quivering to each whispered word of my child courtesan, "my boy friend would like to have this name printed indelibly on his chest. Print it over his heart, please."

"What color, lady?" And grinning, motioning me to the stool, "You got the colors of the rainbow to choose from, lady." So even the oaf, the brute artist was a sentimentalist and I sat down stiffly, heavily, seeing against my will his display of wet dripping rainbow, hating him for his infectious colors, and telling myself that I must not give him a single wince, not give him the pleasure of even one weak cry.

"Green," she said at once—had I heard her correctly?—and she took a step closer with one of her spun sugar shoes, "a nice bright green." Then she looked up at me and added, to my confusion, my mystification, "Like the guitar."

And the oaf, the marker of men, was grinning, shaking his head: "Green's a bad color"—more muscle-flexing now and the professional observation—"Green's going to hurt, lady. Hurt like hell."

But I had known it, somehow, deep in the tail of my spine, deep where I was tingling and trying to hide from myself, had known all along that now I was going to submit to an atrocious pain for Cassandra—only for Cassandra—had known it, that I who had once entertained the thought of a single permanent inscription in memory of my mother—gentle Mildred—but when it came to rolling up my sleeve had been unable to endure the shock of even a very small initial M, would now submit myself and expose the tender flesh of my breast letter by letter to the pain of that long exotic name my daughter had so carefully penciled out on that greasy envelope of endless lunchroom counters, endless lavatories in creaking burlesque theaters. So even before I heard the man's first order—voice full of German delicacies and broken teeth—I had forced my fingers to the first of my hard brass buttons, tarnished, unyielding—the tiny eagle was sharp to the touch —and even before he had taken the first sizzling stroke with his electric needle I was the wounded officer, collapsing, flinching, biting my lip in terror.

He worked with his tongue in his cheek while Cassandra stood by watching, waiting, true to her name. I hooked my scuffed regulation white shoes into the rungs of the stool; I allowed my white duck coat to swing open, loose, disheveled; I clung to the greasy edge of the table. My high stiff collar was unhooked, the cap was tilted to the back of my head, and sitting there on that wobbling stool I was a mass of pinched declivities, pockets of fat, strange white unexpected mounds, deep creases, ugly stains, secret little tunnels burrowing into all the quivering fortifications of the joints, and sweating, wrinkling, was either the wounded officer or the unhappy picture of some elderly third mate, sitting stock still in an Eastern den—alone except for the banana leaves, the evil hands—yet lunging, plunging into the center of his vicious fantasy. A few of us, a few good men with soft reproachful eyes, a few honor-bright men of imagination, a few poor devils, are destined to live out our fantasies, to live out even the sadistic fantasies of friends, children and possessive lovers.

But I heard him then and suddenly, and except for the fleeting thought that perhaps a smile would cause even this oaf, monster, skin-stitcher, to spare me a little, suddenly there was no escape, no time for reverie: "OK, Skipper, here we go."

Prolonged thorough casual rubbing with a dirty wet dis-integrating cotton swab. Merely to remove some of the skin, inflame the area. Corresponding vibration in the victim's jowls and holding of breath. Dry ice effect of the alcohol. Prolonged inspection of disintegrating cardboard box of little scabrous dusty bottles, none full, some empty. Bottles of dye. Chicken blood, ground betel nut, baby-blue irises of child's eye—brief flashing of the cursed rainbow. Tossing one par-ticular bottle up and down and grinning. Thick green. Then fondling the electric needle. Frayed cord, greasy case—like the envelope—point no more than a stiff hair but as hot as a dry frying pan white from the fire. Then he squints at the envelope. Then lights a butt, draws, settles it on the lip of a scummy brown-stained saucer. Then unstoppers the ancient clotted bottle of iodine. Skull and crossbones. Settles the butt between his teeth where it stays. Glances at Cassandra, starts the current, comes around and sits on the corner of the table, holding the needle away from his own face and flesh, pushing a fat leg against victim's. Scowls. Leans down. Tongue in position. Rainbow full of smoke and blood. Then the needle bites.

The scream—yes, I confess it, scream—that was clamped between my teeth was a strenuous black bat struggling, wrestling in my bloated mouth and with every puncture of the needle—fast as the stinging of artificial bees, this exquisite torture—I with my eyes squeezed tight, my lips squeezed tight, felt that at any moment it must thrust the slimy black tip of its archaic skeletal wing out into view of Cassandra and the working tattooer. But I was holding on. I longed to disgorge the bat, to sob, to be flung into the relief of freezing water like an old woman submerged and screaming in the wild balm of some dark baptismal rite in a roaring river. But I was holding on. While the punctures were marching across, burning their open pinprick way across my chest, I was bulging in every muscle, slick, strained, and the bat was peering into my mouth of pain, kicking, slick with my saliva, and in the stuffed interior of my brain I was resisting, jerking in outraged helplessness, blind and baffled, sick with the sudden recall of what Tremlow had done to me that night— helpless abomination—while Sonny lay sprawled on the bridge and the captain trembled on his cot behind the pilot-house. There were tiny fat glistening tears in the corners of my eyes. But they never fell. Never from the eyes of this heavy bald-headed once-handsome man. Victim. Courageous victim.

The buzzing stopped. I waited. But the fierce oaf was whistling and I heard the click, the clasp of Cassandra's purse—empty as I thought except for a worn ten dollar bill which she was drawing forth, handing across to him—and I found that the bat was dead, that I was able to see through the sad film over my eyes and that the pain was only a florid swelling already motionless, inactive, the mere receding welt of this operation. I could bear it. Marked and naked as I was, I smiled. I managed to stand.

Cassandra glanced at my chest—at what to me was still a mystery—glanced and nodded her small classical indomitable head. Then the tattooer took a square dirty mirror off the wall, held it in front of me:

"Have a look, Skipper," once more sitting on the edge of the table, eager, bulking, swinging a leg.

So I looked into the mirror, the dirty fairy tale glass he was about to snap in his two great hands, and saw myself. The pink was blistered, wet where he had scrubbed it again with the cooling and dizzying alcohol, but the raised letters of the name—upside down and backwards—were a thick bright green, a string of inflamed emeralds, a row of unnatural dots of jade. Slowly, trying to appear pleased, trying to smile, I read the large unhealed green name framed in the glass above the ashamed blind eye of my own nipple: *Fernandez.* And I could only try to steady my knees, control my breath, hide feebly this green lizard that lay exposed and crawling on my breast.

Finally I was able to speak to her, faintly, faintly: "Sonny and Pixie are waiting for us, Cassandra," as I saw with shame and alarm that her eyes were harder than ever and had turned a bright new triumphant color.

"Pixie and I been worried about you. You going to miss that bus if you two keep running off this way. But come on, Skipper, we got time for one more round of rum and coke!"

With fondness, a new white preening of the neck, an altered line at the mouth, a clear light of reserved motherhood in the eye, Cassandra glanced at the little girl on Sonny's lap and then smoothed her frock—this the most magical, envied, deferential gesture of the back of the tiny white hand that never moved, never came to life except to excite the whole ladylike sense of modesty—and slid with the composure of the young swan into the dark blistered booth opposite the black-skinned petty officer and platinum child. I took my place beside her, squeezing, sighing, worrying, aware of my burning chest and the new color of her eyes and feeling her withdrawing slightly, making unnecessary room for me, curving away from me in all the triumph and gentleness of her disdain. I fished into a tight pocket, wiped my brow. Once more there was the smoke, the noise, the sick heaviness of our water front café, our jumping-off night in Chinatown, once more the smell of whisky and the sticky surface of tin trays painted with pagodas and golden monsters, and now the four of us together—soon to part, three to take their leave of poor black faithful Sonny—and now the terrible mammalian concussion of Kate Smith singing to all the sailors.

Duty gave still greater clarity, power, persistence to the whisper: "Has she been crying, Sonny?"

"Pixie? My baby love? You know Pixie never cries when I croon to her, Miss Cassandra. And I been crooning about an hour and a half. But Miss Cassandra," lulling us with his most intimate voice—it was the voice he adopted in times of trouble, always most melodious at the approach of danger—lulling us and tightening the long black hand—shiny knuckles, long black bones and tendons, little pink hearts for fingertips —that spraddled Pixie's chest limply, gently, "Miss Cassandra, you look like you been cashing in your Daddy's Victory bonds. And Skipper," sitting across from us with the child, glancing first at Cassandra and then myself, "you've got a terrible blue look about you, terrible tired and blue." Then:

"No more cemetery business, Skipper? I trust there's no more of that cemetery stuff in the cards. That stuff's the devil!"

Cocked garrison cap and shiny visor; petty officer's navy blue coat, white shirt, black tie; two neat rows of rainbow ribbons on his breast; elongated bony skull and black velvet face—he called himself the skinny nigger—and sunglasses with enormous lenses coal-black and brightly polished; signet ring, little Windsor knot in the black tie, high plum-colored temples and white teeth of the happy cannibal; tall smart trembling figure of a man whose only arrogance was affection: he was sitting across from us—poor Sonny—and talking through the Chinese babble, the noise of the Arkansas sailors, the loud breasty volume of mother America's possessive war-time song. Poor Sonny.

"Skipper," once more the whisper of fashion, whisper of feminine cleanliness, cold love, "show Sonny, please."

"What's this? Games?" And casting quick razor looks from Cassandra to myself, shifting Pixie still further away from us and leaning forward, craning down: "What you two been up to anyway?"

I unhooked my stiff collar and worked loose the top brass button and then the next, gingerly, with chin to collar bone trying to see it again myself, through puckered lips trying to blow a cold breath on it, and leaned forward, held open the white duck in a V for Sonny, for Sonny who respected me, who was all bone and blackness and was the best mess boy the U.S.S. *Starfish* ever had.

He looked. He gave a long low Negro whistle: "So that's the trouble. Well now. You two both grieving not for the dead but for that halfpint Peruvian fella who run out on us. I understand. Well now. Husbands all ducked out on us, wives all dead and buried. So we got to do something fancy with *his* name, we got to do something to hurt Skipper. Got to turn a man's breast into a tombstone full of ache and pain. You better just take your baby girl and your bag of chicken salad sandwiches—I made you a two-days' supply—and get on the bus. This family of ours is about busted up."

But: "Hush," I said, done with the buttons and still watching Cassandra—chin tilted, lips tight in a crescent, spine straight—and reaching out for the black angle of his hand, "You know how we feel about Fernandez. But Sonny, you'll find a brown parcel in the back of the jeep. My snapshots of the boys on the *Starfish*. For you."

"That so, Skipper? Well now. Maybe we ain't so busted up after all."

He puffed on his signet ring—the teeth, the wrinkled nose, the fluttering lips, the twisted wide-open mouth of the good-natured mule—and shined it on his trousers and flashed it into sight again—bloodstone, gold-plated setting—and took off his cocked and rakish hat, slowly, carefully, since from the Filipino boys he had learned how to pomade his rich black opalescent hair, and fanned himself and Pixie three or four times with the hat—the inside of the band was lined with bright paper medallions of the Roman Church—and then treated the patent leather visor as he had the ring, puffing, polishing, arm's length examination of his work, and with his long slow burlesquing fingers tapped the starched hat into place again, saying, "OK, folks, old Sonny's bright as a dime again, or maybe a half dollar—nigger money of course. But, Skipper," dropping a bright black kiss as big as a mushmelon in Pixie's platinum hair and grinning, waving toward Cassandra's glass and mine—Coca-Cola like dark blood, little drowning buttons of melted ice—then frowning, long-jawed and serious: "whatever did happen to that Fernandez fella?"

I shifted, hot, desperate, broad rump stuck fast and uncomfortable to the wooden seat, I looked at her, I touched my stinging breast, tried to make a funny grandfather's face for

Pixie: "We don't know, Sonny. But he was a poor husband for Cassandra anyway." I used the handkerchief again, took hold of the glass. She was composed, unruffled, sat toying with a plastic swizzle stick—little queen—and one boudoir curl hung loose and I was afraid to touch it.

"Maybe he got hisself a job with a dance band. Maybe he run off with the USO—I never liked him, but he sure was a whizz with the guitar—or maybe," giving way to his black fancy, his affectionate concern, "maybe he got hisself kidnapped. Those South American fellas don't fool around, and maybe they decided it was time he did his hitch in the Peruvian Army. No, sir," taking a long self-satisfied optimistic drink, cupping the ice in his lip like a lump of sugar, "I bet he just couldn't help hisself!"

Then she was stirring the swizzle stick, raising it to the invisible tongue, touching the neckline of her wrinkled frock, once more whispering and informing us, tormenting us with the somber clarity of what she had to say: "Fernandez deserted his wife and child"—hairs leaping up on the backs of my hands, scalp tingling, heart struck with a hammer, fit of coughing—"deserted his wife and child for another person. Fernandez left his wife and child"—I clutched again the handkerchief, wishing I could extricate myself and climb out of the booth—"abandoned us, Pixie and me, for the love of another person. A man who was tall, dark-haired, sun-tanned and who wore civilian clothes. A gunner's mate named Harry. He had a scar. Also, he was tattooed," the whisper dying, dying, the mouth coming as close as it could to a smile, "like you, Skipper."

Then silence. Except for the shot glasses. Except for the tin trays. Except for the moaning sailor and the bay plunging and crashing somewhere in the night. Except for the torch song of our homeless millions. I slumped, Sonny shook his head, threw out suddenly a long fierce burnt-up hand and pure white dapper cuff: "Oh, that unfaithful stuff is the devil! Pure devil!"

The shaft goes to the breast, love shatters, whole troop trains of love are destroyed, the hero is the trumpet player twisted into a lone embrace with his sexless but mellow horn, the good-bys are near and I hear Cassandra whispering and I see the color in her eyes: "There aren't any husbands left in the world. Are there, Skipper?"

But Sonny answered, Sonny who took a shower in our cheap hotel, Sonny whose uniform was pressed dark blue and hard and crisp in a steaming mangle: "Dead or unfaithful, Miss Cassandra, that's a fact. Damn all them unfaithful lovers!"

Bereft. Cool. Grieved. Triumphant. The frozen bacchanal, the withered leaf. Taps in the desert. Taps at sea. Small woman, poor faithful friend, crying child—Pixie had begun to cry—and I the lawful guardian determined but still distressed and past fifty, nose packed with carbonated water, head fuming with rum, all of us wrecked together in a Chinatown café and waiting for the rising tide, another dark whim of the sea. But still I had my love of the future, my wounded pride.

"I think I told you, Sonny, that I'm taking Cassandra and Pixie to a gentle island. You won't need to worry about them."

"That's it, that's it, Skipper. These two little ladies are in good hands. Well now. Well, I understand. And I got a gentle island too if I can just find her. Wanders around some, true enough, but she sure is gentle and she sure just about accommodates an old black castaway like me. Oh, just let Sonny crawl up on that gentle shore!" He was nodding, smiling, with his long smoky five-gaited fingers was trying to turn Pixie on his lap, fondling, probing the fingers, gently feeling for the source of her tiny noise, and all the while kept the two great cold black lenses of his pink and white shell-rimmed sunglasses fixed in my direction. Nodding, at last beginning to croon through his nose—tight lips, menacing cheekbones —holding Pixie and shining all his black love into my heart.

But Pixie was crying. She was crying her loudest with tiny pug nose wrinkled, wet, tiny eyes bright and angry, tiny hands in fists, tiny arms swinging in spasms and doll's dress bunched around her middle, and her cry was only the faint turbulence of an insect trapped in a bottle. Amusing. Pitiful. A little bottle of grief like her mother.

"Pixie don't like this separation stuff," crooning, chucking her under the chin with the tip of his long black finger while Cassandra and I leaned forward to see, to hear: "Pixie don't approve of our family busting up this way." And she bent her rubbery knees, kicked, striking on the table the little dirty white calfskin shoe that was untied, unkempt, forlorn, and then she was suddenly quiet, appeased, and smiled at Sonny and caught his finger as if to bite it to the bone with all the delight and savagery of the tiny child spoiled and underfed— rancid baby bottles, thin chocolate bars—through all her dreary abandoned days in wartime transit.

"That's the sign, folks! Pixie's ready! Time to go!"

I sat still, I flung my face into the smell of the empty glass, Cassandra took up her purse. And then we were in single file and pushing through the crowd of sailors. First Sonny—flight bag, paper bag stuffed with chicken salad sandwiches, Pixie riding high on his shoulders and thumping his cap—and then Cassandra—small, proud, prisoner of lost love, mother of child, barelegged and desirable, in her own way widowed and silvery and slender, walking now through anchors and booze and the anonymous cross-country passion of the Infantry March—and then in the rear myself—more tired than ever, bald, confused, two hundred pounds of old junior-grade naval officer and close to tears. This our dismal procession with Sonny leading the way. "Step aside there, fella, you don't want to tangle with the Chief!" Pixie was blowing kisses to the sailors; Cassandra was wearing her invisible chains, invisible flowers; and I refused to see, to acknowledge the scampering white-slavers, refused to say good-by to all those little Chinese waiters. Then out the door.

Long steel body like a submarine. Giant black recapped tires. Driver—another mean nigger, as Sonny would say—already stiff and silhouetted behind his sheet of glass and wearing his dark slant-eyed driving glasses and his little Air Force style cap crushed and peaked, ready and waiting to take her up, to start the mission. Concrete pillars, iron doors, dollies heaped high with duffel bags, no lights, crowds of sailors, odor of low-lying diesel smoke, little dry blisters of chewing gum under our feet, and noise. Noise of sailors banging on the sides of the bus and singing and vomiting and crying out to their dead buddies. The terminal. Our point of departure. And the tickets were flying and the SP's were ferocious ghosts, leaping in pairs on victim, lunging slyly, swinging hard with the little wet oaken clubs.

So at last we were packed together in rude and shameless embrace and at last we were shouting: "You go on now, Skipper," tall dancer, black cannon mouth, blow in the ribs, weighing me down with child, provisions, canvas bag, "you go on and get you a nice seat. Take your ladies on off to your island—I'm going to be on mine—no unfaithful lovers on my island, Skipper, just me, now you keeps your island the same. Good-by now, and you remember, Skipper, I'm going to lie me down on my island and just look at them pictures and think of you and Pixie and Miss Cassandra. So long!"

"Sonny!" Crying aloud, crying, bumping against him, bumping and trying to shift the wretched child out of our way, then falling against his tall black twisting form—glint of the buttons, bones of a lean steer, glimpse of a fading smile—

then throwing myself and managing at last to kiss the two dark cheeks, warm, oddly soft and dry, affectionate long panther paws, kissing and calling out to him: "Good-by, Sonny. *Bon voyage!*" Then we were flowing on a rough stream toward the bus and he was gone. Poor Sonny.

But Sonny was not gone at all. Not yet. The three of us were carried backwards and up into the great dark steel cylinder of our reckless ten-wheeled transport. We joined that monstrous riot for seats—one hundred and three men, a woman, a child, swallowed up for numerous sins and petty crimes into this terrible nonstop belly of ours and fighting hopelessly for breath, for privacy—and were lucky enough to snatch two seats together and to crouch down with flight bag and sandwiches between our legs and my hat askew and the skirt of Cassandra's frock crumpled above her knees. They were slim knees, bare, slender, glistening, disregarded. It was dark, the aisle was heaped high with white duffel bags. And did each of those sagging white canvas shapes represent the dead body of a bantamweight buddy saved from the sea and stowed away in canvas, at last to be lugged or flung aboard Interstate Carrier Number twenty-seven, bound nonstop for the great navy yard of the east? I looked for only a moment at Cassandra's knees and then quickly lifted my grandaughter to the pitch-dark window at my side. Pixie was crying again—insect going berserk in his glass, little fists socking the window—and the sailors were flashing their Zippo lighters and slowly, slowly, we were beginning to move. And then three figures struggled out of the flat gray planes and cumbersome shadows of the concrete, and dashed toward the front of the bus. The tall drunk bosun's mate was waving, Sonny was waving, and between them the moaning sailor was rolling his head, dragging his feet. The tubular door sprang halfway open and, "That's it," helpful, officious, out of breath, "get these fellas inside there . . . that's it!" And then Sonny was alone in the dark and we were backing slowly from the terminal in a wake of oil and compressed air. I pressed my face to the window, against the glass, too tired to make a farewell sign with my hand.

Off to one side, puffing, straightening his coat, Sonny continued to follow us. I saw his imperious arm, saw his slow imperious stride and the long fingers pointing instructions to the driver. Sonny held up his flat hand and we stopped; Sonny began to swing his arm and we started forward, turned, paced his tall backward-stepping shadow—anxious glance over his shoulder, summoning gesture of the long thin arm and flashing cuff—and then he stood aside and waved us on. I smiled, lost him, but even in the blast of the diesel heard what he must have communicated to his mean black brother in the cockpit: "You're OK. Now just keep this thing on the road. . . ."

Then I leaned back heavily and, pain or no pain, shifted Pixie so that she stretched herself flat on my chest and slept immediately. I lay there watching the stars and feeling my hunger grow. The paper bag was between Cassandra's feet, not mine, yet I could see the crushed bulk of it, the waxed paper and wilted lettuce, the stubby wet slices of white meat Sonny had prepared for us on a wobbling card table squeezed into the dirty porcelain lavatory of our cheap hotel. I could taste the white bread—no crusts—I could taste the black market mayonnaise. How many miles behind us now? Five? Ten? The bus was accelerating, was slowly filling with the smell of whisky—thick nectar of lonely travelers—and filled with the sounds of the ukelele, the tuneless instrument of the American fleet, and in her sleep Pixie was sucking her fingers and overhead the stars were awash in the empty black fields of the night. I thought of empty dry docks, empty doorways, empty hotels, empty military camps, thought of him fixing the sandwiches while we slept—pepper, salt, tin spoon and knife—saw him drinking a can of beer on the fantail of the *Starfish* on a humid and windless night. I saw him prostrate on his island of brown flesh, heard the first sounds of returning love.

"Cassandra? Hungry, Cassandra?"

He had diced celery into cubes, had cut olives into tiny green half-moons, had used pimento. Even red pimento. The moonlight came through the window in a steady thin slipstream and in it Cassandra's face was a small luminous profile on a silver coin, the coin unearthed happily from an old ruin and the face expressionless, fixed, the wasted impression of some little long-forgotten queen. I looked at her, as large as I was I wriggled, settled myself still deeper into the journey— oh, the luxury of going limp!—and allowed my broad white knees to fall apart, to droop in their infinite sag, allowed my right arm, the arm that was flung across sleeping Pixie, to grow numb. I was an old child of the moon and lay sprawled on the night, musing and half-exposed in the suspended and public posture of all those night travelers who are without beds, those who sleep on public benches or curl into the corners of out-of-date railway coaches, all those who dream their uncovered dreams and try to sleep on their hands. Suspended. Awake and prone in my seat next to the window, all my body fat, still, spread solid in the curvature of my Greyhound seat. And yet in my back, elbows, neck, calves, buttocks, I felt the very motion of our adventure, the tremors of our cross-country speed. And I felt my hunger, the stomach hunger of the traveling child.

"A little picnic for the two of us, Cassandra?"

She moved—my daughter, my museum piece—and hoisted the sack onto her lap and opened it, the brown paper stained with the mysterious dark oil stains of mayonnaise and tearing, disintegrating beneath her tiny white efficient fingers. Brisk fingers, mushy brown paper sack, food for the journey. She unwrapped a sandwich, for a moment posed with it—delicate woman, ghostly morsel of white bread and meat—then put it into my free hand which was outstretched and waiting. The bread was cold, moist, crushed thin with the imprint of dear Sonny's palm; the lettuce was a wrinkled leaf of soft green skin, the bits of pimento were little gouts of jellied blood, the chicken was smooth, white, curved to the missing bone. I tasted it, sandwich smeared with moonlight, nibbled one wet edge—sweet art of the mess boy—then shoved the whole thing into my dry and smiling mouth and lay there chewing up Sonny's lifetime, swallowing, licking my fingers.

My daughter was safe beside me, Pixie was sleeping on, dreaming the little pink dreams of her spoiled life, my mouth was full, the sailor was moaning. And now the distance threw out the first white skirts of a desert, a patch of poisoned water and a few black rails of abandoned track. I saw the salt mounds, the winding gulch, far off a town—mere sprinkling of dirty mica chips in the desert—and in the pleasure of this destitute world I was eager to see, eager to eat, and reached for another sandwich, stuffed it in. For Sonny.

But then I noticed her folded hands, her silent throat, the sack near empty on her lap, and I stopped in mid-mouthful, paused, swallowed it all down in a spasm: "Cassandra? No appetite, Cassandra?"

She did not answer. She did not even nod. And yet her face was turned my way, her knees tight, elbows tight, on one side not to be touched by thigh of sprawling father, on the other not to be touched by the stenciled name of the seaman whose duffel bag stood as tall as her shoulder and threatened her with reprehensible lumps and concealed designs, and in the thrust and balance of that expression, the minted little lips and nose, the bright nested eye, she made herself clear enough. No appetite. No sensation in a dry stomach. No desire. No orchids sweet enough to taste. Not the sort of woman to eat sandwiches on a bus. At least not the sort of woman who would eat in the dark. Not any more.

But I was alarmed and I persisted: "Join me, Cassandra. Please. Just a bite?"

She waited. Then I heard the firmness of the dreaming voice, the breath control of the determined heart: "My life has been a long blind date with sad unfortunate boys in uniform. With high school boys in uniform. With Fernandez. With you. A long blind date in Schrafft's. A blind date and chicken salad sandwiches in Schrafft's. With little black sweet pickles, Skipper. Horrible sweet pickles. Your sandwiches," the whisper dying out for emphasis, secret, explanatory, defensive, then rising again in the hush of her greatest declamatory effort, "your sandwiches make me think of Gertrude. And Gertrude's dark glasses. And strawberry ice cream sodas. And Gertrude's gin. I can't eat them, Skipper. I can't. You see," now leaning her head back and away, small and serpentine in the moonlight, and watching me with her wary and injured eyes, "nothing comes of a blind date, Skipper. Nothing at all. And," moving her naked fingers, crushing the wax paper into a soft luminous ball, "this is my last blind date. A last blind date for Pixie and me. I know you won't jilt us, Skipper. I know you'll be kind."

I wriggled. I blushed. I took the sandwich. I heard the catgut notes of the ukelele—vision of French letters floating downstream in the moonlight—I heard the black turbine roaring of our diesel engine, beyond this metal and glass heard the high wind filled with thistle and the flat shoe leather bodies of dead prairie rodents. And I was wedged into the night, wedged firmly in my cheerful embarrassment, and chewing, frowning, hoping to keep her feathery voice alive.

Our picnic, our predawn hours together on this speeding bus, our cramped but intricate positions together at the start of this our journey between two distant cemeteries, the nearly physical glow that begins to warm the darkest hour at the end of the night watch—when sleep is only a bright immensity put off as long as possible and a man is filled with a greedy slack desire to recall even his most painful memories—in all the seductive shabbiness of the moment I felt that I knew myself, heart and stomach, as peaceful father of my own beautiful and unpredictable child, and that the disheveled traveler was safe, that both of us were safe. We too would have our candy bars when the sun rose. Sonny had provided the sandwiches but I myself had thought of the candy bars, had slipped them secretly into the flight bag with Cassandra's stockings and Pixie's little fluffy pinafore. We too would have our arrival and departure, our radio broadcast of victory and defeat. In the darkness the driver sounded his horn— triple-toned trumpet, inane orchestrated warning to weak-kneed straying cows and sleeping towns—and my lips rolled into the loose shape of a thoughtless murmur: "Happy, Cassandra?"

"I'm sleepy, Skipper. I would like to go to sleep. Will you try?"

I chuckled. And she smoothed down her frock, brushed the empty paper bag to the floor, pressed her hands together, palms and fingers straight and touching as the child prays, and without glancing at me lay her cheek on her clasped hands and shut her eyes. As if she had toileted, donned her negligee, turned with her face averted and drawn the shade. Modest Cassandra. While I chuckled again, grimaced, rolled my head back to the window, grunted under the weight of Pixie—bad dreams, little pig sounds—then sighed and swung away and dropped to my army of desperate visions that leapt about in the darkness. But safe. Sleeping. Outward bound.

But wasn't Cassandra still my teen-age bomb? Wasn't she? Even though she was a war bride, a mother, a young responsible woman of twenty-five? At least I thought so when at last I awoke to the desert sunburst and a giant sea-green grandfather cactus stabbed to death by its own needles and to the sight of Cassandra begging Pixie to drink down a little more of the canned milk two days old now and pellucid. And wasn't this precisely what I loved? That the young-old figure of my Cassandra—sweet queenly head on an old coin, yet flesh and blood—did in fact conceal the rounded high-stepping baby fat and spangles and shoulder-length hair and dimples of the beautiful and wised-up drum majorette, that little bomb who is all hot dogs and Egyptian beads? Wasn't this also my Cassandra? I thought so and for the rest of the day the emotions and problems of this intensive fantasy saved me from the oppressive desert with its raw and bleeding buttes and its panorama of pastel colors as outrageous and myriad as the colors that flashed in the suburban kitchen of some gold-star mother. Saved me too from our acrobatic Pixie who at lunchtime added smears, little doll-finger tracks and blunt smudges of Nestlé's chocolate to my white naval breast already so crumpled and so badly stained. Smelling the chocolate, glancing at the unshapely humps and amputated spines, thorns, of miles of crippled cacti, I only smiled and told myself that the flesh of the cheerleader was still embedded in the flesh of Pixie's mother and so soothed myself with various new visions of this double anatomy, this schizophrenic flesh. And toward sundown—more chocolate, more smearing, end of a hot and untalkative and disagreeable day—when I was squinting between my fingers at the last purple upheaval of the pastel riot, I struggled a moment—it was a sudden cold sickening speculation—with the question of which was the greater threat to her life, the recklessness of the teen-age bomb or the demure determination of the green-eyed and diamond-brained young matron who was silvery, small, lovable with bare legs and coronet? It was too soon for me to know. But I would love them both, scrutinize them both, then at the right moment fling myself in the way of the ascendant and destructive image. I was still scowling and loving her, suspecting her, when the desert fireworks suddenly ended and the second night came sweeping up like a dark velvet wind in our faces.

"And we don't even have sandwiches tonight, Cassandra. Not one."

I felt the child's tiny knee in my groin—determined and unerring step—I felt her tiny hand return again and again to tantalize and wound itself against my unwashed cheek, absently I picked at the chocolate that had dried like blood on the old sailcloth or cotton or white drill of my uniform. And finding a plugged-up nipple secreted like a rubber talisman or ill omen in my pocket; watching Cassandra stuff a pair of Pixie's underpants into the flight bag; discovering that between my two white shoes there was another, the foot and naked ankle and scuffed black shoe of some long-legged sailor who had stretched himself out at last—in orgasm? in extreme discomfort?—and seeing Cassandra's face dead white and realizing that finally she had scraped the bottom of the cardboard face powder box which I had saved along with her stockings: all of it reminded me of the waxworks museum we had visited with Sonny, reminded me of a statue of Popeye the Sailor, naked except for his cap and pipe, which we had assumed to be molded of rubber until we read the caption and learned that it was made of eight pounds and five different brands of chewed-up chewing gum, and reminded me too that I could fail and that the teen-age bomb could kill the queen or the queen the bomb. The beginnings of a hot and hungry night.

But I must have lain there musing and grumbling for hours, for several hours at least, before the tire exploded.

"Oh!" came Cassandra's whispered shriek, her call for help, and I pinioned Pixie's rump, I sank down, my knees were heaved into flight, Cassandra was floating, reaching out helplessly for her child. In the next instant the rear half of the bus was off the road and sailing out, I could feel, in a seventy-eight-mile-an-hour dive into the thick of the night. Air brakes in full emergency operation. Accidental blow to the horn followed by ghastly and idiotic trill on the trumpet. Diving rear end of the bus beginning to describe an enormous arc—fluid blind path of greatest destruction—and forward portion lurching, hammering, banging driver's black head against invisible wall. Now, O Christopher . . . and then the crash.

Then: "Be calm, Cassandra," I said, and kept my hold on the agitated Pixie but uncovered my face.

And she, whispering, breathing deeply: "What is it, Skipper? What is it?"

"Blowout," I said, and opened my eyes. We were standing still. We were upright. Somehow we had failed to overturn though I saw her naked legs with the knees caught up to her chin and though everywhere I looked I saw the duffel bags lying like the bodies of white clowns prostrate after a spree of tumbling. And in this abrupt cessation of our sentimental journey, becoming aware of moonlight in the window and of the thin black line of the empty highway stretching away out there, and feeling a heavy deadness in my shoulder—twisted muscles? severed nerves?—I was able to glance at my free hand, to study it, to order flexing of my numerous and isolated fingers. I watched them. One by one they wiggled. Bones OK.

"Are you all right, Cassandra? Can you move your toes?"

"Yes, Skipper. But give Pixie to her mother, please."

So we disembarked. We joined the slow white procession of hatless sailors. In the dark and among the angular seventeen-year-olds with ties askew and tops askew, among all the boys red-eyed and damp from cat-napping and too baffled, too bruised to talk, we felt our way up the canted aisle until we reached the listing door, the puckered aluminum steps, the open night. I took her in my arms and swung her down, and out there we stood together, close together, frock and uniform both body-tight in the wind, ankles twisting and shoes filling with sand. The bus was a dark blue dusty shadow, deceptive wreck; our skid-marks were long black treacherous curves in the desert; the highway was a dead snake in the distance; the wind was strong. We stood there with the unfamiliar desert beneath our feet, stood with our heads thrown back to the open night sky which was filled with the tiny brief threads of performing meteors.

The wind. The hot wind. Out there it warmed the skin but chilled the flesh, left the body cold, and though we lifted our faces like startled sun-tanned travelers, we were shivering in that endless night and in the wind that set the long dry cactus needles scraping and made a rasping noise of all the debris of the desert: tiny cellular spines, dead beetles, the discarded translucent tissue of wandering snakes, the offal of embryonic lizards and fields of dead dry locusts. All this rasping and humming; all the night listening; and underfoot all the smooth pebbles knocking together in the hot-cold night. And she, Cassandra, stood there swaying and clasping Pixie awkwardly against her breast, swaying and trying to catch her breath behind Pixie's head; and the pale little fissure of Cassandra's mouth, the pale wind-chapped tissue of the tiny lips made me think of cold kisses and of goose flesh and of a thin dust of salt and of lipstick smeared helplessly on the white cheek. I took her elbow; I put a hand on her back and steadied her; I was surprised to feel the broad band of muscle trembling in her back; I thought of the two of us alone with a hundred and one sailors cut down and left for dead by a pack of roving and mindless Mexicans. Then in our roller-skating stance—hand to elbow, hand to waist—we began to move together, to stagger together in the moonlight, and over my shoulder and flung to either side of the harsh black visible track of our flight from the road I saw the prostrate silhouettes of a dozen fat giant cacti that had been struck head on by the bus and sent sailing. For a moment I saw them, these bloated shapes of scattered tackling dummies that marked the long wild curve of our reckless detour into the dark and milky night. Abandoned. As we were abandoned.

And then the lee of the bus. Clumps of squatting white shivering sailors. A pea jacket for Pixie. Another pea jacket for Cassandra. A taste of whisky for me. Little pharmacist mates clever in first aid and rushing to the sounds of chattering teeth or tidelands obscenity. While the black-faced driver hauls out his hydraulic jack and drags it toward the mutilated tire which has come to rest in a natural rock garden of crimson desert flowers and tiny bulbs and a tangle of prickly parasitic leaves. All crushed to a pulp. Mere pustules beneath that ruined tire.

It was the dead center of some nightmare accident but here at least, crouching and squatting together in the lee of the bus, there was no wind. Only the empty windows, shadows, scorched paint of the crippled monster. Only the flare burning where we had left the road and now the scent of a lone cigarette, the flick of a match, the flash of a slick comb through bay rum and black waves of hair, persistent disappointed sounds of the ukelele—devilish hinting for a community sing—only the cooling sand of the high embankment against which Cassandra and Pixie and I huddled while the sailors grew restless and the driver—puttees, goggles, snappy cap and movements of ex-fighter-pilot, fierce nigger carefully trained by the Greyhound line—bustled about the enormous sulphuric round of the tire. Refusing assistance, removing peak-shouldered military jacket, retaining cap, strutting in riding britches, fingering the jack, clucking at long rubber ribbons of the burst tire: "Why don't you fellows sing a little and pass the time?" But only more performing meteors and this hell's nigger greasing both arms and whistling, tossing high into the air his bright wrenches. In the middle of the desert only this American nigger changing a tire, winning the war.

I unlaced my dirty white buckskin shoes and emptied them. I glanced at Cassandra. I glanced at Pixie who, even though cloaked in her pea jacket, was beginning to play in the sand; I tried to smile but the driver cavorting in the moonlight dispirited me and I wondered where we were and what had become of poor dear Sonny. I hooked one foot onto the opposite knee, gripped the ankle, brushed the sand from the sole of my white sock, repeated the process. I glanced again at the night sky—unmoved by celestial side show—and for some reason, scowling into the salt and pepper stars, gritting my teeth at that silent chaos, the myriad motes of the unconsciousness, I found myself thinking of Tremlow, once more saw him as he looked when he bore down upon me during the height of the *Starfish* mutiny. Again I lived the moment of my degradation. Then just as suddenly I was spared the sight of it all.

Because I had heard a sound. Cassandra's sleeping head lay in my lap—high upturned navy blue collar of the pea jacket revealing only the briefest profile of her worn and lovely little deathmask face—because I was awake and had heard a sound and recognized it. And because suddenly that impossible sound established place, established the hour, explained the tangled bright loops of barbed wire that apparently ran for miles atop the steep rise of our protective sand embankment. I listened, gently pressed the rough collar to her cheek, shivered as I understood suddenly that the wire was not for Indians, not to imprison cows. Listened. And still the impossible sound came to me over the wastes and distant reaches of the blue desert.

Bugle. This mournful barely audible precision of the instrument held rigidly in only a single hand. An Army bugle. Taps. Across the desert the faint and stately and ludicrous sound of taps. Insane song of the forties. And slow, precise, each silvery dim note dragged all the way to the next, the various notes weaving and wafting the sentimental messages into the night air. End of the day—who's listening? who?—and of course lights out. But I listened to the far-away musical moon-howling of that benediction into a dusty P.A. system built on the sands, with a few stomach convulsions heard the final drawn-out bars of that impersonal cinematic burial song meant for me, for every bald-headed indoctrinated man my age. Taps for another bad dream. Brass bugle blown in the desert, a little spit shaken out on the bugler's sleeve.

So I knew that it was eleven o'clock of a hot-cold desert night and that we had come to stop not in the middle of nowhere but at the edge of some sort of military reservation —cavalry post of black horses that would explain the odor of dung on the wind? basic training camp with tequila in the PX and live ammunition on maneuvers? naval boot camp for special instruction in flying the blimp and dirigible?—and knew that whatever I had to guard Cassandra against it was not the Mexicans.

But now I was awake, alert, ready for anything. Hunching over my own daughter and my own granddaughter—outlandish bundles of pea jackets, flesh of my flesh—I became the solitary sentry with quick eyes for every shadow and a mass of moonlit veins scurrying across my naked scalp like worms. Fear and preparedness. Aching joints. Lap beginning to complain. But on the tail of the bugle and also miles away, several unmistakable bursts from a rapid-fire weapon. And I looked for a glow in the sky and tried to imagine the targets— cardboard silhouettes of men? gophers? antiquated armored vehicles?—and I listened and wondered when they would begin to shoot in our direction. Army camp, disabled bus, poor nomad strangers wandering through days and nights and hours that could be located on any cheap drugstore calendar: I took a deep breath, I stiffened my heavy jaw, I waited. In anger I heard a few more snorts of machine gun fire, in anger I nodded once more at the image of Tremlow the mutineer, in anger snapped myself awake.

"Cassandra," whispering, leaning close to her, lifting enormous collar away from her ear, touching the cold cheek, sweating and whispering, "wake up, Cassandra. We've got company. . . ."

Her open eyes, her rigid face and body, the quiver in the breasts and hips, and the outstretched rumpled figure was suddenly alert, half sitting up. And then she had thrust Pixie away, had hidden Pixie in a shadow on the sand. And then side by side Cassandra and I were kneeling together on our hands and knees, waiting with heads raised and red-rimmed eyes fixed on the barbed wire barricade directly above us.

"Men traveling on their bellies," I whispered. "Three of them. Crawling up the embankment to reconnoiter!" We heard the swishing sound of men pressed flat to the desert and, like children making angels in snow, swimming up the steep embankment through loose sand and pebbles and low-lying dried and prickling vines. We heard their concentrated breathing and the tinkling sound of equipment. I recognized the flat fall of carbine with each swing of invisible arm, recognized the uneven sound of a bayonet drumming on empty canteen with each dragging motion of invisible haunch. Then a grunt. Then squeal and scurry of little desert animal diving for cover. Then silence.

And then the heads. Three black silhouettes of helmeted heads suddenly there behind the wire where before there had been only the barbs, the loops, the tight strands and the velvet space and salt and pepper heavens of the whole night sky. But now the heads. All at once the three of them in a row. Unmoving. Pop-ups in a shooting gallery.

And as Cassandra and I knelt side by side in the sand, stiff and exposed and red-eyed in our animal positions, together and quiet but vulnerable, the three heads began to move in unison, turned slowly, imperceptibly, to the right and then to the left, in unison scanning the horizon and measuring the potential of the scene before them. The tops of the heavy helmets and the tips of the chin cups reflected the moon; in the sharp little faces the eyes were white. Soldiers. Raiders. Pleased with the scene. Their whispers were high, dry, choked with sand.

"Lucky, lucky, lucky! Ain't that a sweet sight?"

"Navy to the rescue!"

"Free ride on a Greyhound bus!"

The three of them looked straight ahead—intuitively I knew the driver was still throwing his wrenches into the air, still trying to boss the tire into place, and I groaned—and then in slow motion they began to shift. The heads sank down until the men were only turtle shells and hardly visible on the embankment; the muzzles of two carbines popped into view; the man in the center raised his helmeted head and his white hand and a pair of wire cutters, slipped and tugged and twisted while the wire sang past his face and curled into tight thorny balls. Until they could crawl through. Until they were free.

And then with heads down, shoulders down, rifles balanced horizontally in their hanging hands, they swung in a silent dark green trio over the embankment and down, down, like baseball players hitting the sand and landing not on top of Cassandra and myself but in front of us and to either side. Three sand geysers and Cassandra and I were trapped.

"Company C," panting, whispering, "Company C for

Cain," panting and aiming his gun and whispering, "Don't
you make a peep, you hear? Either one of you!"

Three small soldiers in full battle pack and sprawled in the
sand, gasping, leaning on their elbows, cradling the carbines,
staring us down with their white eyes. Web belts and straps,
brass buckles, cactus-green fatigue uniforms—name tags
ripped off the pockets—paratrooper boots dark brown with
oil; they lay there like three deadly lizards waiting to strike,
and all of their vicious, yet somehow timorous, white eyes
began blinking at once. The middle soldier, the leader, wore
a coal-black fingernail mustache and carried his bayonet
fixed in place on the end of his carbine. All little tight tendons
and daggers and hand grenades and flashing bright points and
lizard eyes. Unscrupulous. Disguised in soot. Not to be
trusted in a charge.

"Company C for Cain, like I said. But we been in that place
for twenty-eight weeks and now we're AWOL. The three of
us here are called the Kissin' Bandits and we're AWOL.
Understand?"

And the smallest, young and innocent except for his big
broken Brooklyn nose—my ghetto Pinocchio—and except
for the foam which he kept licking from the corners of his
mouth and swallowing, the smallest twitching there in the
sand and prodding each word with his carbine and with his
nose: "So on your feet, on your feet. No talking, and don't
forget the kid."

Slowly, laboriously, indignantly I stood up, helped Cassandra, brushed the seat of my trousers, jerked the creases out
of my uniform as best I could, indifferently picked off the
cactus burrs, and took little Pixie into my arms.

They marched us to the cactus, in single file herded us
thirty or forty feet into the shadow of that old fat prickly man
of the desert and out of sight of the bus, the leader at the head
of the column and swinging the carbine, slouching along

lightly in the lazy walk of the infantryman saving himself, feeling his way with his feet, straggling all the distance of his night patrol—easy gait, eyes down watching for the enemy, back and shoulders loose and buttocks hard, fierce, insepara- ble, complementary, all his walking done with the buttocks alone—and in the middle Cassandra and myself and Pixie, and in the rear the tinkling dragging sounds of the boys with their cocked carbines and darting tongues and eyes. Raiders. Captives. Firing squad with the cactus for a blank wall.

"Now get rid of your eggs," said the one with the glisten- ing mustache. "Dig your holes deep and bury them."

And there in the safety and shadow of the giant ruptured cactus, while Cassandra and I stood side by side and held hands under cover of her pea jacket, there and in unison the three of them unhooked their rows of dangling hand grenades, helped each other out of their packs and harnesses, freed each other of webbing and canteens and canvas pouches—watching us, watching us all the while—and then with unsheathed and flashing trench knives or bayonets held point down they squatted, dug their three black holes until at last they flung themselves back once more into sitting position and unfastened their boots, unbuttoned their green fatigues and then standing, facing us, watching us, suddenly stripped them off.

So the naked soldiers. White shoulder blades, white arms, white shanks, white strips of skin, white flesh, and in the loins and between the ribs and on the inside of the legs soft shadow. But white and thin and half-starved and glistening like watery sardines hacked from a tin. Naked. Still wearing their steel helmets, chin straps still dangling in unison, and still holding the carbines at ready arms. But otherwise naked. And now they were lined up in front of Cassandra, patiently and in close file, while I stood there trembling, smiling, sweating, squeezing her hand, squeezing Cassandra's hand for dear life and in all my protective reassurance and slack alarm.

"Leader's last," came the unhurried voice, "Baby Face goes first."

Lined up by height, by age and height, and each one nudging the next and shuffling, grinning, each one ready to have his turn, all set to go, and one of them hanging back.

"Drag ass, Bud . . . and make it count!"

His round young head was sweating inside the steel helmet, his freckled breast was heaving. I squeezed her hand—be brave, be brave—but Cassandra was only a silvery blue Madonna in the desert, only a woman dressed in the outlandish ill-fitting pea jacket of an anonymous sailor and in a worn frock belonging to tea tray, flowers and some forgotten summer house covered with vines. And in her hand there was no response, nothing. And yet her green eyes were searching him and waiting.

Then he leaned forward, eyes slowly sinking out of focus, tears bright on his cheeks, moon-face growing rounder and rounder under its rim of steel, and caught her behind the neck with a rough childish hand and drove his round and running and fluted mouth against the pale line of her lips. And sucked once, gulped once, gave her one chubby kiss, backed away step by step until suddenly Pinocchio made a wrenching clawlike gesture and threw him aside.

And Pinocchio's kiss: foam, foam, foam! On Cassandra's lips. Down the front of her frock. Snuffling action of the Brooklyn nose. But he couldn't fool Skipper, couldn't fool old Papa Cue Ball. So I squeezed again—brave? brave, Cassandra?—and felt what I thought was a tremor of irritation, small sign of impatience in her cold hand.

And then the third and last, the tallest, and the helmet tilting rakishly, the lips pulsing over the front teeth in silent appeal, the bare arm sliding inside the pea jacket and around her waist, and now the cumbersome jacket beginning to fall, to fall away, and now Cassandra's head beginning to yield, it seemed to me, as I felt her little hand leave mine and saw her returning his kiss—white shoe slightly raised behind her, pale mouth touching, asking some question of the slick black fingernail of hair on his upper lip—and saw my Cassandra raise a finger to his naked underdeveloped chest and heard her, distinctly heard her, whispering into all the shadowed cavities of that thin grisly chest: "Give me your gun, please," hanging her head, whispering, finger tracing meditative circles through the hair on his chest, "please show me how to work your gun. . . ."

But he was gone. All three were gone. They had whirled each to his hole, had flung on boots, carbines, helmets and fatigues, and had refilled the holes. Done with their separate burials they had fled from us in the direction of the unsuspecting sailors and the waiting bus, had run off with their stolen kisses and their crafty plans for travel. At the bus they used judo and guerrilla tactics on the bosun's mate, the moaning sailor and the noxious driver, and dressed like sailors they lost themselves in a busload of young sailors.

I turned and held out my free arm: "Cassandra, Cassandra!" I beckoned her with my fingers, with my whole curving arm, beckoned and wanted to tell her what a bad brush we had had with them, and that they were gone and we were safe at last. And she must have read my smile and my thoughts, I think, because she drew the pea jacket into place once more, thrust her hands carefully into the pockets, glanced soberly across the waste of the desert. And then she looked at me and slowly, clamly, whispered, "Nobody wants to kiss you, Skipper."

From that time forward our driver was dead white and licked a little patch of untweezered mustache all the while he drove. And so we recommenced our non-stop journey, rode with a fine strong tail wind until at last we reached our midnight (Eastern War Time) destination, found ourselves at last on the fourteenth floor of another cheap hotel. Here we stayed two days. Here I lived through my final shore patrol. And here I found Fernandez in this wartime capital of the world.

Be brave! Be brave!

The Chastity Belt

from THE BLOOD ORANGES (1971)

In the four years between the time I finished *Second Skin*
and finally began to write *The Blood Oranges* (in the fall of 1967),
I continued teaching at Brown, served on a panel on educational
innovation, tried playwriting with the Actors' Workshop in San
Francisco for a year, worked on an experimental writing project
at Stanford for another year—did everything, that is, except write
fiction, and had little to show for my efforts except a book of short
plays and the satisfaction of having tried some new kinds of
teaching. I was exhausted and wanted to return to writing; another
grant made possible a recuperative free year. So Sophie and I
decided to try to find a European Grenada, and, again with our
four children, fled from Palo Alto to the south of France, alighting,
by pure accident, in Vence, which is near Nice on the Côte d'Azur.

We lived outside town at the edge of a high gorge in a farmhouse
with a Moroccan flavor. There were roses, lemon trees, a grape
arbor, and views of terraced vineyards across the gorge. Far below
us in the other direction lay the Mediterranean, ten miles away.
We hauled water and tried to smother the fumes of sewage. We
discovered *vin de table*, Brie cheese, fish soup, lamb seasoned with
the thyme we gathered from the steep hillsides around us. We heard
our first nightingales. We read about the Ligurians who had lived
on the site of Vence in the Neolithic age.

The timelessness and sensuality we had once known in Grenada
were, in Vence, suffused with history and the art of Matisse and
Picasso; Vence was if anything more exotic than Grenada, more
idyllic, and in its pressures of tranquility, as I thought of them,
suddenly I found myself thinking of *Twelfth Night* and remembering Ford Madox Ford's *The Good Soldier*. As with *The Lime Twig*,
I "saw" another inexplicable scene: two men and two women,

accompanied by some children, carrying a small coffin through a wood and, though this episode has only a small place in the finished novel, still I had a starting place for *The Blood Oranges*.

In *The Blood Oranges* (the title comes from the succulent, partially purple blood oranges we found in the markets of Vence), Cyril, a self-styled "sex-singer," tells the story of how he and his wife Fiona seduced another couple in a barren village in a hot "mythical" Mediterranean world known by Cyril as Illyria. Hugh, a one-armed photographer of what he calls "peasant nudes," is a comic and bitter Malvolio who refuses until too late the advances of Fiona; Catherine, the fourth member of this quaternion, and Hugh's wife, is the bovine mother of their three children. In the course of the novel, Hugh dies in an accident caused by his New England puritanism, Catherine has a breakdown, and Fiona flees Illyria with Catherine's children, while Cyril, struck impotent by this series of comic catastrophes, stays behind to regain his powers, win back Catherine's love, and tell their tale.

"The Chastity Belt" describes Hugh's efforts to destroy the sexual idyll of the foursome. The chastity belt—a loathsome little sharp-toothed medieval device that appears in the scene—is no doubt still preserved in its museum case in Venice where Sophie and I saw it on a short tour from Vence into Italy.

The Chastity Belt

Steady wind, hard clear light, the four of us holding hands on the rocks that faced the squat ominous remains of the fortress across the narrow crescent of dark water now harboring only four or five half-sunken wooden boats with high prows, broken oars, red chains. Moody, we were bound together by wind and light and hands. All eyes were on the ruined penitential structure just across the water that was apparently unchanged, unnourished by the sea crashing on three sides of us. All eyes were on the gutted shape of history, as if the clearly visible iron base and broken stones and streaks of lichen were portentous, related in some way to our own presently idyllic lives. But I for one was conscious of bodies, hands, squinting eyes, positions in line, was well aware that Fiona stood on my left and Catherine on my right and that Hugh was doomed forever to the extreme left and could never share my privilege of standing, so to speak, between two opposite and yet equally desirable women. Even on our promontory of sharp wet rocks it amused me to think that, thanks to Hugh, our sacred circle would remain forever metaphysical. Nothing more.

But what was he saying?

"That fort, boy . . . soon . . ."

"Good idea," I shouted and, nodding my head up and down, again I was struck with the perception that he was black while I was gold. But a ruined fortress was not a safe place for a man like Hugh, and though I did not yet understand the basis for so much oblivious intensity, still I admired his courage and was beginning to share his eagerness to undertake the expedition to that unwholesome place of bone, charred wood, seaweed.

Suddenly I felt the pre-emptory childish tugging on my left hand and the cold lips against my ear. Fiona's words seemed to lodge immediately and permanently in the still room of my brain.

"Do you know where we are, baby? Tell me quick."

Surprised at her sudden and atypical desperation, but laughing and aiming my mouth toward the hint of white cartilage buried like an arrow in the now violent cream- and sable-colored hair: "Sure," I shouted, "we're in Illyria. Like it?"

"I like you, baby. You."

"What's the matter," I called, "getting old?"

Though we had started out together and with every intention of remaining together throughout a day this timeless and bright and clear, nonetheless we had once again drifted into pairs and begun to separate, to pull apart long before reaching the commencement of the breakwater. By the time Catherine and I first set foot on the breakwater and moved out from the shore, Hugh had already swept himself and Fiona far ahead, the two of them long-legged and impetuous and receding, growing smaller, flaunting their eagerness and similarity of temperament until, flanked on either side by sun and sea, they had all but disappeared. Yet midway on the breakwater between shore, village, beached fishing boats and at the other extreme, the ruined fortress, suddenly the two of them, Hugh and Fiona, had seated themselves on a couple of flat white rocks where now they waited for Catherine and me, the slow strollers, to close the long clear empty space between us.

"Not as old as you are," Hugh shouted back through the silence, and planted his single elbow, I saw, in Fiona's lap.

"There's no hurry," I said to Catherine, and squeezed her hand. "Let's take our time."

"Why does he want to explore that ugly place?"

"God knows."

But now that the village lay at our backs, there was no-where to walk except forward across the high narrow break-water into the open sea and toward the squat and ominous pile of dark stones that revealed in the midst of its wreckage the shape of the former fortress. How strong, I asked myself, was my empathy with Hugh's present eagerness? What could account for the rather special quality of desolation that appeared to characterize the abandoned structure now await-ing the sound of our four voices, the cautious tread of our feet? When did an ordinary stroll become a compulsive quest? And why did I now identify that unspectacular and es-sentially uninteresting ruin with the dark caves of the heart? Self-imprisonment, which was what we appeared to be heading for, was hardly my own idea of pleasure. And yet I was beginning to feel something of Hugh's elation. Today of all days my empathy with Hugh, I decided, was fairly strong.

"Does Fiona really want to climb around in there?"

"I suppose she does."

"Well, I don't."

"We could have stayed with the children."

"I'd never let him take Fiona in there alone."

"Jealous?"

"If she goes, I have to go. That's all."

"Fiona might fool us both. You never know."

"How?"

"But then," I said more to myself than to Catherine, "it's Hugh's expedition. We'll just have to wait and see where it leads."

One glance backward, and I knew what I would see: dark hills, brief and distant panorama of tiled roofs and white-washed walls, black little boats ranged on the gray beach and, far to the south, the fragile landmarks of the funeral cypresses. And yet all this was gone and for us there was only severance, isolation, the sensation of proceeding outward from the familiar shore and into the uninhibited world of blue sky, black sea, penitential fortress. We might have been walking down a country road, Catherine and I, except that the rutted track we followed across the high surface of the breakwater was white, not brown, and was composed of rock and crushed shells, rather than of dusty earth, and carried us not safely among the olive trees but precariously across deep salty water and into the light that had no source. We shaded our eyes, looked out to sea. No wonder Hugh had insisted that the four of us wear rubber-soled shoes. No wonder he had packed his enormous khaki-colored rucksack with rope, torch, knife, rolls of bandage and bottles of disinfectant. But was this clear vista of peace and treachery, space and confinement, reason enough for Hugh's excitement? I suspected not.

"Hey there," Hugh called, "what do you think of it?"

"Interesting," I called back, "but let's stay together."

"Graffiti, you two. Come look!"

"Can you read them, boy?"

"Sure can."

"Oh, baby, what do they say?"

No doubt the large and indecipherable signs were the work of passing fishermen who in their crafty loneliness had used pieces of soft and chalky masonry to inscribe their private sex legends on these dead walls. Appeals to big-boned virginal women said to inhabit small green islands lying somewhere beyond the horizon? Songs to a young girl of our own village? Ribald declarations of one grizzled fisherman's love for another and much younger fisherman? Whatever the content and whoever the lovers, for us these public testimonials remained no more than secret and unreal scrawls, since no sooner had I begun to gather Fiona and Catherine close to my sides, no sooner begun to scan the massive walls for clues to the specific sense of the abandoned messages, than Hugh was already shouting from the interior of this impressively dismal place and urging us to forget the graffiti and to follow him inside.

"Are they all about the singing phallus, baby?"

"I guess they are."

"Don't you know, for God's sake?"

"I'll read them to you another time, Fiona. OK?"

"Hurry," Catherine said then, "Hugh's alone in there."

"Well," I said, gripping Fiona's hand and Catherine's elbow, "it's too bad we can't all share Hugh's rather boyish interest in old fortresses and so forth. But on we go."

"I love these old masculine places," Fiona said. "You know I do."

Still I hung back, surveying the light that shone only at sea, the incongruous mustard-colored stone walls which on three sides descended at a steep angle into the dark random tide, the entrance that was low and rounded and deep. And I noted what I suspected Hugh had failed to note in his characteristic haste and determination to see it all at a glance and to find his own lean shadow wherever he looked: the briars clotting the entrance way, the ringbolts and fallen rock, the iron bars driven into the rounded arch and now bent aside. Yes, I thought, herding Fiona and Catherine into the dark mouth of the fortress, yes, the gates were gone and the marble monsters no longer stood on their sunken pedestals. But nonetheless the mouth of the fortress remained guarded, oddly protected, within its own matter-of-fact condition of disuse, and only a man like Hugh could rush through this brief tunnel unaware of ancient armaments and present obstacles to passage. Catherine stumbled, I gripped her arm, Fiona's uncertain voice echoed down the wet walls.

"Look," Hugh shouted then, "burned!"

Chin high, legs far apart, rucksack lying brown and lumpy in the weeds at his feet, there stood Hugh waving us into the hot and empty courtyard and at the same time indicating with his long good arm the high walls, the blackened doorways, the cracked tower, the vacant blue sky overhead. I saw immediately that he was right, because all four walls had been deeply and viciously scorched by some devastating blaze so that they were streaked and seared with enormous swatches of unnatural color—intestinal pink, lurid orange, great blistering sheets of lifeless purple. And everywhere the weeds and fallen pediments were encrusted with the droppings of long departed gulls.

"Burned clean, boy. There's nothing left."

"No juice of the growing fruit," I murmured, "that's for sure."

"Don't be cryptic, baby. Please."

"You can't even smell it, boy. No ashes. No smoke. Nothing. It's just a reflection—a reflection of some fiery nightmare. Don't you see?"

"Sure," I said and laughed, "if that's what you want. But I prefer a little more than weeds and discoloration. How about it, Catherine?"

"Oh, Cyril, stop arguing."

Everywhere I turned I could see that these burned walls were punctured with small charred doorless entrances leading no doubt into a labyrinth of pits and tunnels, cells and niches for birdlike archers. Never had the four of us been so starkly confined, starkly exposed. Hugh and Catherine and I were dressed appropriately for whatever ordeals might come our way (Hugh in his castoff Navy denims, Catherine wearing her gray slacks with the patches, I dressed in sweatshirt and chocolate-colored corduroys), whereas Fiona had disregarded Hugh's instructions and was wearing only her eggshell sandals and mid-thigh tennis dress of shocking white. Stark, alone together, exposed, self-conscious. But despite my predisposition in favor of the lyrical landscape or any of those places conducive to my own warmer inclinations, and despite my conversational reluctance of only a few moments past, nonetheless I too was beginning to understand Hugh's feeling for the condemned courtyard and gutted fortress, was already partially willing to forego my kind of pleasure for his.

"Well," I said, and picked up Hugh's rucksack, "what now? The tower?"

"No, boy, the dungeons."

"Treasure," Fiona said. "What fun."

"OK," I heard myself saying pleasantly, "I guess you know what you're doing. Let's go."

So I slung Hugh's clumsy burden from an easy shoulder, commiserated with Catherine in a long good-humored meeting of eyes, grinned at Fiona, trudged off across the courtyard toward the most distant and least inviting doorway in the northeast wall. Hugh leapt gaunt and spiderlike into that charred darkness, Fiona ducked after Hugh, Catherine entered head down and heavily, I whistled softly to myself and then pushed my way out of the sunlight and through the cold, tight, irregular doorless opening. There followed the typical moment of disorganization, confusion, pretended panic, while the four of us stood in single file and bumped together, enjoyed the last noisy sounds of indecision before starting down. I attempted to rummage inside the rucksack and dig out the torch, and discovered without surprise that Hugh's torch was a nickel-plated, long-handled affair that was obviously filled with greenish and partially corroded batteries. I flicked on the weak beam and passed the torch from hand to hand to Hugh. Catherine had turned her back to me and appeared ready, now, to undergo Hugh's childish adventure to the end.

"Cyril? Are you there?"

"Sure I am."

"Steps, boy. They're pretty steep. Careful now."

The darkness was like the water in a cold well, the roof of the narrow corridor became the sounding board for Hugh's loud voice. With slow shoulders and spread hands we felt our way along the slick invisible walls and occasional gritty patches of leprous masonry. In single file and breathing audibly, on we crept toward the diffused beam of Hugh's torch which he was flashing in all directions now to indicate, as he said, the beginning of the steps. Above Fiona's strong jasmine scent and the smell of the throbbing seaweed there drifted the unmistakable smell of human excrement—an undeniable fresh smell that could hardly help the tone of our quest, could not help but make Catherine uncomfortable and Fiona displeased. For a moment I allowed myself to muse on the odor of human offal, thinking that men inevitably relieved their bowels in all the ruined crypts of the world and that the smell struck some kind of chord in other men but to women was merely distasteful. What then of Fiona's earlier assertion of her love for the places of masculinity? Was that particular love of hers unqualified? The smell of the offal and Fiona's sudden silences were the first indications that it was not.

"Well," I heard myself saying, "we're like a bunch of kids."

"Speak for yourself, boy."

"At least you could shine the light this way once in a while. Might help, don't you think?"

"I'm cold, Cyril. What'll I do?"

"There are a couple of sweaters in the rucksack, boy. Why don't you pull one out?"

"No," I said. "We'll wait until we reach the bottom."

I heard our three pairs of spongy rubber-soled shoes making soft contact with the first half dozen steps, distinguished the hard leathery sound of Fiona's tissue-thin sandals on the stone. I saw Hugh's haste registered in the jerky disappearance and reappearance of the light of the torch. I hoped that

Hugh would find something to make this expedition of his worthwhile, I hoped that whatever he found would please Fiona and prove to be of interest, at least, to Catherine and me. I hoped that the last hours of the day would find Catherine and me alone together in one of those dense harmonious places of my choosing rather than Hugh's, and would find Fiona once again running free and nestling with a more appreciative and agreeable Hugh.

"If there's nothing down there," I called, "what then?"

"It's there, all right. I dreamed about it."

"Stop him," Catherine whispered in a flat voice. "Can't you do something?"

"Too late," I whispered back. "Besides, he's enjoying himself."

"Why can't we all hold hands?"

"Wouldn't do much good. It'll be over soon."

"Hugh," Fiona said. "Tell us the dream."

But even the timbre of Fiona's voice was oddly diminished, and the restraint and poignancy of this second brief appeal made it only too clear that even Fiona was beginning to have reservations about the intensity of Hugh's descent. And treading the dark air, sinking, fumbling, following each other down, once again it occurred to me that Hugh was somehow more than oblivious to Catherine's fear and resignation, more than insensitive to Fiona's now obvious misgivings and disappointment, more than indifferent to my quiet presence behind him at the end of the line. Perhaps our very compatibility was at last at stake. In all the thoughtlessness of his clearly secret self, perhaps his true interest was simply to bury our love in the bottom of this dismal place and in some cul-de-sac, so to speak, of his own regressive nature. Perhaps he was as indifferent to the male principle as he was to me, and was not searching for some sexual totem that would excite a little admiration in his wife and mine, but was instead determined to subject all four of us to the dead breath of denial. Who could tell?

"Oh, baby, look at the view."

Suddenly we paused, leaning against each other, and crowded together at a high narrow aperture cut with beveled edge through the dark thick mass of what we now understood to be the outside wall, so that in the sudden funnel of clear light and with our heads close and hands on shoulders, arms about familiar waists, the rucksack pressing against Catherine's hip as well as mine, suddenly we found ourselves sharing relief from the darkness and uncertainty of our now interrupted downward progress into this stone shaft. Silent, subdued and yet attentive, relieved and yet immobile, unemotional, touching each other and yet unmotivated by our usual feelings of mutual affection—for one brief somber moment we stared out toward the vacancy, the sheer distance, the brilliant timeless expanse of sea and air. Hugh had hiked himself as best he could into one corner of the empty aperture and was a grainy and rigid silhouette leering seaward. The scantness of Fiona's tennis dress was pressing against the stiffness of Hugh's denims, the breadth of my chest was partially straddling Fiona's left shoulder blade and Catherine's right arm, Catherine's waist was soft and comfortable beneath the casual pressure of my left hand. There were no boats on the horizon, no birds in the air. Only the four of us, the silence, the fortress heavier than ever above our heads, the stones larger and darker and more imprisoning, only the constricted view of the inaccessible water with its all-too-real surface of white transparencies and maroon-colored undulations.

"Hugh," Fiona said then, "why don't we just climb back up and go swimming? I feel like a little swim. Right now."

"I hate this place," Catherine said. "I want to leave."

"It's just not much fun. I want us to have fun, that's all."

"Hugh knows about my claustrophobia, don't you, Hugh? But at least you could listen to Fiona if you won't listen to me."

"The view's attractive, but the rest of it just isn't turning out as I thought it would."

"Hugh's selfish, that's all."

"Don't you want to go swimming with me, baby?"

"Of course he does. But Hugh's not about to change his mind. He'll deny us the same way he denies the children."

"But Hugh, we can't even have a little hugging and kissing down there. Don't you see?"

"He doesn't care. He won't listen to either one of us."

"Help me, Cyril. Tell Hugh I always mean what I say."

Laughing, leaning into both Catherine and Fiona and squinting heavily for another look at the gently shifting dark sea: "Don't pay any attention to them," I heard myself saying, "our wives don't want to admit how much they like this little dangerous hunt of yours."

"You'll be sorry, baby."

"No threats, Fiona."

"I'm bored. I'm not going to say it again."

"How about it, Hugh? Ready?"

Yes, I thought, my empathy was real enough, the tone of the position I had decided to take could not be missed. But did Hugh care? Had he been listening? Or was he more than ever oblivious, as I had at first suspected? Did it matter to Hugh that I had chosen sides—I who could always absorb the little resistances of his wife and mine, after all, with nothing to lose? Or was my support merely one more irritant that somehow enhanced Hugh's feelings of remoteness in this our first small disagreement?

It was then that I recalled the morning's trivial domestic incident described to me by Catherine in one long breath of privacy before we had assembled into our usual foursome—I leaving, Hugh returning, Hugh lunging into his rightful bed, Hugh appealing in hypnotic whispers for Catherine's nakedness, Dolores entering that room of circular love, Hugh bounding up and striking his head against the rotten shutter which I myself had opened only moments before. But had Hugh sensed my intervention in both Catherine's nakedness and the state of the shutter? Or had he simply viewed the unwitting appearance of the sleepy child along with the crack on his head as somehow deserved or as a deliberate manifestation of the dream he was still keeping to himself? Had the interruption accounted perversely for his morning's cheer? But if all this were true, as suddenly I thought it was, and if the day's expedition had in fact begun for Hugh with this misadventure, then of course the invisible lump on his head in some way accounted for his present leering confidence and refusal to talk. Surely the lump on his head fit in with his plans.

Still saying nothing, Hugh merely turned and once more started down. We followed, of course, and the light was gone, the vista of the bright sea was gone, a sudden vacuum in the dark air told me that Fiona was hurrying to catch up with Hugh in spite of herself. Catherine was doing her best, the walls were wet, the steps were steeper and the passage more narrow than before. From somewhere far below, the sound of Hugh's creaking denims drifted up to us. And suddenly from those depths below us came Fiona's faint cry along with an abrupt rush of pattering sounds that could only mean that one of them had fallen.

"What's that?"

"Accident."

"You better come on down here, boy. Your wife's in trouble."

"Keep going," I said to Catherine, "but don't try to hurry. Be careful."

Fiona was sure-footed. Fiona was not one of those women who convert minor injury into an instrument of will whenever the neutral universe fails to conform in some slight particular to the subtleties of the female vision. She was strong, she was agile, she could not have fallen merely to teach Hugh a lesson or merely to hasten the swimming party which, however, I knew full well she intended to enjoy before the last light of the day. But that faint cry, that soft cry tinged with the barest coloration of accusation, I had heard it and recognized it immediately as the clear cry Fiona never uttered unless she needed my help. So as unlikely as it seemed to me, perhaps she was hurt. Perhaps there would be no swimming after all.

Beyond the suddenly visible bulk of Catherine's shadow, I saw the white dress pulled up to the loins, the lifted knees, the slender face, the cavern floor, Hugh's crouching shape, the circle of dim light. We were below sea level and now we were crowding together in a small wet space hollowed out from stone and thick with echoes.

"What happened?" I asked. "Are you all right?"

"I slipped, baby. Me! I went down about twenty steps."

"Well," I said, laughing, fumbling with the rucksack, finding the sweater, "let's see if you can walk."

"I hope you're satisfied, Hugh," Catherine said. "Fiona might have broken her ankle."

"Climb into this sweater," I murmured quickly and calmly, "and then we'll check you out."

But was she indeed hurt? Catherine was kneeling beside Fiona, Hugh was crouching, in his one hand gripped the now dying torch. Fiona herself was still prostrate on the cold stone. For a moment I had the decided impression that Hugh had bolted into these ruins and dragged us into these wet depths of vaulted darkness for the sole purpose of discovering nothing more than Fiona herself lying flat on her back in the faint eye of the torch like the remains of some lady saint stretched head to toe on her tomb. The expression on Fiona's face seemed to bear me out, since her head was turned to the sound of my voice and since the slender construction of Fiona's face and the willful eyes and thin half-smiling lips were raised to me in something more than mere personal concern for the immediate situation of unlikely accident. What else could that expression mean if not that she understood what I was thinking and was momentarily aware of her own body and expressly erotic temperament as the very objects of Hugh's subterranean design? How else account for Fiona's expression of puzzlement and appeal if not by knowing suddenly that Hugh was quite capable of attempting to transform my faunlike wife into a lifeless and sainted fixture in his mental museum?

"Give me your hand, baby. Help me up."

But still no word from Hugh? No hint of his usually exaggerated concern for Fiona's interests, pleasure, well-being, safety? Not even taking advantage of the darkness to thrust himself against Fiona who was now holding my hand and scrambling to her feet and was nothing if not responsive to Hugh's slightest touch? But it was true, all too true. He must have known that today there would be no hugging and kissing, as Fiona had put it, long before Fiona had voiced that sad little conviction of hers, long before he had had his dream, long before he had banged his head on the rotted shutter.

There was nothing to do, I thought, except to hold wide the neck of the sweater and help Fiona, however clumsily, to pop her head through the opening and feel her way into the sleeves so absurdly long and tangling. And then, quite simply, I would demand the torch from Hugh and lead us calmly back up to the limitless pastel light of the burned court.

"As long as we're here," Fiona said then, "let's look around."

"OK," I said, once more changing my mind, shifting my stance. "There's nothing to see. But we'll take a quick look anyway."

I realized immediately that there was more to come, that Hugh had not yet shot his bolt of poison and that Fiona was not going to comply with my helpfulness and had already refused the possibility of wearing the sweater. But at least I managed to drape Hugh's sweater across her shoulders and loop the long sleeves around her throat. In due time Hugh, not I, would lead us back up to the courtyard. Agreed.

"There's no way out," Hugh said. "We're at the bottom."

"Buried, you mean. Buried alive."

To hear Catherine's determined voice, to hear Hugh's silence in response to it, to know that Fiona was once again looking for Hugh in the wet darkness, to be aware of this cold timeless space hollowed from the very roots of the sea—suddenly I wished again that Hugh's poor torch would discover a real effigy with a stone cowl, stone feet, stone hands pressed together and pointed in prayer. Or would discover a real row of iron-headed pikes along one of the vaulted walls. Or a steel glove, the blade of an ax, a gold cup, anything to justify all this shadowy suspension of our lives of love. Surely this empty place should offer up some little crusty memento to justify my separation from sun and sea and grass, to justify the unspeakable content of Hugh's dream. But then the memento, as it were, did in fact appear.

"Now, boy—how do you like it?"

"If I were you," I said softly, slowly, "I'd leave that thing here where you found it. That's my advice."

"Leave it," Catherine said quickly. "I don't want to know what it is. I don't want to see it."

"Old Cyril knows what it is. Don't you, boy?"

"Yes," I murmured, "of course I do."

"Tell us, baby. Tell us!"

"No, Fiona, it's up to Hugh."

"Damn right it is!"

And I who had never exposed Fiona to discomfort of any kind, I who had taken the exact same care of Catherine, I whose handsome and bespectacled face had always stood for sensuous rationality among the bright leaves, I the singer who spent my life quietly deciphering the crucial signs of sex, I who only moments before had decided that Hugh would discover nothing, nothing at all—now it was I, I alone, who shared with Hugh clear knowledge of the precise nature of what Hugh was dangling from the neck of the torch, as if I myself had sought it and found it and inflicted it on all four of us, silly and pathetic and yet monstrous memento of Hugh's true attitude toward all of our well-intended loves.

"It's a bad omen, Hugh," I said. "Leave it behind."

"My God, boy. Where's your sense of humor?"

The voices echoed in the waxen blackness. Three figures squatted around Hugh's pit, and Hugh himself stood waist-deep in this very pit which had emerged from beneath the beam of his torch only moments before. The cavern was empty, its wet walls and floor were empty, as I had thought. But the pit was not. Suddenly Hugh had found this small rectangular hole in the cavern floor and had leapt up to his knees in the refuse of coagulated fishing nets, broken clay pots and charred ribs of wood. In the midst of this pulpy refuse, he had poked with the torch itself until we heard the dull yet tinny sound of metal on metal, had thrust down the head of the torch and hooked what he was looking for and slowly, in rigid triumph, had raised the unmistakable object of his lonely search.

"I knew it was here. It had to be."

"OK," I murmured, "you found it. Now put it back."

"Not a chance, boy, not a chance . . ."

Then we were climbing, and in unchanged order (from top to bottom, from first to last), Hugh was perspiring in the lead, Fiona had obviously forgotten the effects of her fall and was pacing Hugh with renewed agility and fresh anticipation, Catherine was treading on Fiona's heels, while I went chugging upward with my concentration divided between the gloom of the coming moment, as I envisioned it, and the pleasure of the daylight burning somewhere above our heads. Yes, I thought, Hugh's exhibition in the courtyard was unavoidable. But after, after the silence, the disbelief, the dismay, perhaps then we would move on to long naked strokes in the bright sea or to a rendezvous of sorts with the small earthen-colored nightingale whose secret song I had recently heard not far from the villas. Or would the strains of this day dog us into the future, disrupt our embraces, diminish the peaceful intensity of all those simple idyls I still had in mind?

We stopped, we slipped, we climbed on.

"Thank God, baby. We're safe!"

Fiona with the empty sweater clinging to her back like the cast-off skin of some long-forgotten lover, Catherine with her eyes tight shut and hair awry and broad cheeks brightly skimmed with tears, I shading my face and easing off the uncomfortable and partially opened rucksack, Hugh holding aloft his prize and leaping through the weeds to a fallen pediment, Hugh turning and facing us with the little copper rivets dancing on his penitential denims and his mouth torn open comically, painfully, as if by an invisible hand—suddenly the four of us were there, separated, disheveled, blinking, and yet reunited in this overgrown and empty quadrangle that now was filled with hard light and the sweet and salty scent of endless day. I dropped the rucksack, squinted, fished for a fat cigarette. Fiona caught hold of the sleeves of the sweater at the wrists and pulled the long empty sleeves wide and high in a gesture meant only for the far-off sun. Catherine sat on a small white chunk of stone and held her head in her hands, Hugh tipped his prize onto the altar of the fallen pediment and flung aside the torch, reared back, and waited.

"But is that all, baby? It doesn't look like much."

"Take a better look," I said quietly. "You'll change your mind."

I filled my mouth and lungs with the acrid smoke, I squinted at Hugh, at Fiona, at Catherine. We ached with darkness, our eyes were burning with the familiar yet unfamiliar return to light, as lovers we were exhausted but not exhilarated. Hugh lifted his right leg and cocked his foot on the fallen pediment and rested his right forearm on the upraised thigh.

Catherine sighed and climbed to her feet. Fiona approached the cracked and fluted pediment, slowly Catherine and I moved into position so that all four of us were grouped around Hugh's improvised altar upon which lay what appeared to be only a thin circlet of pitted iron—frail, ancient, oval in shape, menacing. I looked at Fiona, she looked at me, all four of us stared down at the pliant and yet indestructible thin loop of iron that was large enough to encircle a human waist and was dissected by a second and shorter loop or half circle of iron wrought into a deliberate and dimly functional design.

"No," Fiona whispered, "no . . ."

On the opposite side of the pediment from Hugh, I also raised one heavy leg, placed one mountain-climbing boot on the gray stone, rested my forearm across the breadth of my heavy thigh, allowed myself to lean down for a closer look. Our four heads were together, in our different ways we were scrutinizing the single tissue-thin contraption that had already revealed its purpose to Fiona and now, I suspected, was slowly suggesting itself to Catherine as something to wear.

"It looks like a belt," I heard her saying. "But what are all those little teeth . . ."

I felt Fiona's lips against my cheek, my upraised hand was wreathed in smoke, the delicate and time-pocked iron girdle was lying on the gray stone and, I saw in this hard light, was the brown and orange color of dried blood and the blue-green color of corrosion. I concentrated, we were all concentrating. Thinking of the blue sky and mustard-colored walls and brittle weeds and this bare stone, I studied Hugh's destructive exhibition, studied the small and rusted hinge, the thumb-sized rusted lock, the rather large tear-shaped pucker of metal and smaller and perfectly round pucker of metal that had been hammered, shaped, wrought into the second loop and that were rimmed, as Catherine had just noted, with miniature pin-sharp teeth of iron—kept my eyes on this artful relic of fear and jealousy and puffed my cigarette, listened to Catherine's heavy breathing, wondered which strapped and naked female body Hugh now had in mind.

"Anyway," Catherine said, "it's too small for me . . ."

"No," I murmured, "it's adjustable."

"Don't be afraid," Hugh said. "Pick it up. Show us how it works."

"Baby. Let's go, baby. Please."

"The only trouble is that we've only got one of these things instead of two."

"Shut up, Hugh," Catherine said, "for God's sake."

"But maybe one's enough. What do you think?"

And relenting, changing her mind, Fiona reached out one bare energetic arm and suddenly cupped Hugh's frozen jaw in her deliberate hand.

"Do you want me to try it on for you, baby," she said. "Is that what you want?"

Later that day, much later, I knew that Hugh was by no means appeased. The hot coal of desolation was still lodged in his eye. For the first time he stripped to the waist, discarding his denim jacket on the beach not a hundred paces from the villas where the three children shrieked, for the first time he exposed to us the pink and pointed nakedness of his partial arm. But nonetheless he refused to strip off his denim pants and accompany our nude trio into the black-and-white undulations of that deep sea. And every time I came up for air, curving thick arms like the horns of a bull and sucking in broad belly muscles and shaking spray, looking around now for Fiona, now for Catherine, inevitably I saw Hugh stretched out on the black pebbles with one knee raised and his good hand beneath his head, the little black iron trinket clearly visible on his white chest.

"You haven't seen the last of it," he called out once, "believe me."

But then Catherine came rolling toward me through the waves, over my shoulder I caught a glimpse of the dark and distant fortress, I felt a splash, and suddenly, Fiona's wet face was next to mine.

"Baby, baby, baby, what can we do?"

The Flute Player

from DEATH, SLEEP & THE TRAVELER (1974)

After *The Blood Oranges*, travel and foreign countries were for
me inseparable from writing. I loved teaching, but depended
increasingly on already frequent leaves from Brown; I thought
endlessly of the next exotic place in which to work. Late in the
spring of 1970, at a party, a British novelist suggested Lesbos.
I saw it, this Greek island, and thought of sylvan groves, fallen
temples, goats, and shepherd girls with pipes. But Lesbos was a
long way off, the British novelist was known for his wit, and so
we hesitated, Sophie and I, and then decided to attempt a brief trip
to Lesbos before committing ourselves for any length of time
to an island that lay only five miles off the coast of Turkey.

We managed the trip, and took along our youngest child, then
eight. We flew to Amsterdam, then to Athens; then continued on
to Lesbos in a small plane with a badly tuned engine and a stewardess
who frowned at our interest in Sappho's island and told us that
Simi was a more interesting place and had the best beaches in
Greece. There were forty drab miles between the little landing
field at Mytilene and the village where we hoped to find a house
suitable for a longer stay. When we climbed down at last from the
dusty bus, tired and disoriented, we knew that we had made a
mistake. The heat was leaden, the sea flat and gray, at the end of a
short quay made of cracked concrete were hung dead and drying
infant octopi from a sort of clothes line. The Turkish coast was
a flat and ominous smudge on the horizon; there was a ruined
fortress atop a bleak hill, a few tortured olive trees, a beach of
pebbles and shards of rusty iron. Still, in the next few days an old
man from the village tried to help us. He took us to some concrete
rooms beside the beach, empty and with barred windows, and
showed us a gutted wooden house that could not possibly be made

habitable without months of work. Finally he proposed a villa, and up the hill we went to an immense house with smashed walls, broken windows, wires dangling from useless fixtures. It had once been used as the Nazi headquarters, the old man told us proudly, and in the corner of one of its desolate rooms Sophie discovered on a littered table an envelope scrawled with the name of the British novelist, who must have been more courageous than ourselves or was a bigger jokester than he was reputed to be. At any rate, his scrawled name was a sign, a laugh in the dark, and that night our little boy came down with a pain that the local doctor diagnosed as appendicitis.

Back we went to Athens, where we were relieved to learn that the village doctor had been wrong. But we felt that we had barely escaped from the underworld, and, longing for home, left Athens on the next flight. Over the mid-Atlantic, Sophie, for some reason, was reminded of a newspaper account she had read about a ship's officer, a Dutchman, who had been tried for the murder of a passenger with whom he had had an affair during a long cruise. The obviously guilty officer was acquitted because of the testimony of his wife, who later left him. It was then that I thought back to a young Dutch couple who had spent their days playing ping-pong at the hotel where we had spent our abortive days on Lesbos, and to a Dutch journalist and his beautiful wife and daughter we had known briefly in San Francisco. When I opened an airline brochure to a full-page advertisement for Metaxos brandy that showed a young woman dressed only in a halter of hammered gold and a golden bikini in the shape of a goat's skull with the horns encircling the slender hips, I knew that I had found my Muse and also the materials for a short novel.

In the next few months, I wrote *Death, Sleep & the Traveler* in a loft I rented from an artist friend in Providence. The book's narrator, Allert, is a fat, middle-aged Dutchman who tells the story of two love triangles: one involving himself, his wife Ursula, and her psychiatrist lover who is Allert's best friend; a second that occurs on shipboard and involves himself, a wireless officer, and a young woman, Ariane, who is an habitué of pleasure cruises and generally the lover of ship's officers and men alike. The psychiatrist dies in a sauna; Ariane disappears over the side of the ship and is thought to have been murdered by Allert. Ursula testifies successfully on Allert's behalf at his trial and then leaves him; Allert survives with the guilt he cannot admit into consciousness, and the memories of the only pure love he had known in his life, that given him by Ariane.

"The Flute Player" dramatizes the mythical world of the cruise ship, the start of Allert's affair with Ariane, and a visit they pay to a nudist island in the course of their ocean journey.

The Flute Player

There were gongs, there were whistles, there were blasts from high-pitched pipes, screams of compressed air. Even from where Ursula and I stood together on the crowded deck near the gangway I could see that the ship was high and sharp and clear, a paint-smelling flowered mirage of imminent departure over the lip of the earth.

"You see," said Ursula into my ear and laughing, nodding in the direction of the young woman leaning happily at the ship's rail, "you will not be alone, Allert. Not for long."

I turned, I looked again at the young woman who was leaning on the rail and smiling at the crowd on the pier, at the loading shed, at the other ships in the harbor, at the smoke rising more swiftly and blackly now from the pale blue smokestacks above our heads. The girl was standing with no one, she waved but not to anyone in particular down on the pier. And when I turned back to Ursula our own ship's whistle blew, its vibration filling deck, sea, sky, bones, breasts, and tearing us all loose from the familiar shore.

"She'll take care of you," Ursula shouted into my waiting ear, "you'll see."

"Mr. Vanderveenan," she called as I reached the top of the ladder and rose head and shoulders into the wind and glare of the uppermost deck, "won't you join me for a game of net ball? I can find no one at all to play with me."

She was wearing a blue halter, tight blue denim trousers, black dancing slippers, and her hair tied back in a knotted strip of orange velveteen. She was standing in the wind beside the high net and balancing in one hand a black leather ball six or eight inches in diameter. Her waist between the lower edge of the halter and the upper edge of the leather-belted blue pants was bare. I recognized that her costume was the standard one generally intended to cause the viewer to imagine the belt unbuckled and the pants unzippered and hanging loose and partly open from the hips, and yet the naked waist was as smooth and childlike as the expression on her guileless face.

"I would like very much to play your net ball," I said into the invisible wind. "But tell me, how did you know my name?"

We were close together and partially concealed by the two pale blue smokestacks that were oval in cross section and leaning back at a wind-swept rakish angle in the thrust of our journey. The ball in her hand was a tight ripe sectioned fruit of black leather.

"The purser, of course. Didn't you know that he's one of the officers at our table? He knows the names and faces of all the passengers on the cruise."

"I see. The purser. Apparently I have not been aware of him."

We were closer together and I was quite familiar with the implications of the belted pants, the lure of the naked midriff. It was a commonplace attire. So far she promised nothing that was not in fact commonplace, except that her nearest shoulder blade was bare and poignant and that the miniature features of her face were grouped together in distinctive harmony. Even if she was an adult instead of a child and was a person who had actually lived beyond her majority, as I assumed she had, still she could never have come even close to half my age, a notion that engaged my attention occasionally from this moment on.

"You don't know the purser? Really? He's the one with the handlebar mustache. He's a favorite of mine."

"And who is the young officer who has assigned himself the seat next to mine at our table?"

"Oh, that's the wireless operator. He's another favorite of mine."

"You have many favorites."

She was smiling, I was closer than arm's length to her naked shoulder, I told myself that she could not possibly wish me to kiss her lips or even to touch her small bare shoulder so soon despite the inviting way she balanced the black ball, and despite her smile, her steady eyes, her upturned face. And yet I could in fact imagine this young person readily unbuckling her tight pants here in the space for games and athletics between smokestacks fore and aft and two white lifeboats on either side. And yet the poles of sex and friendship, I told myself, did not always imply the bright spark leaping between the two, at least not immediately.

"If you don't know the purser," she said, glancing down at the black leather ball, "then you don't know that my name is Ariane."

I reached for the ball, I felt the heat from the nearest smokestack mingling with the chill of the invisible wind and the bright light of the sun. Far below us a steward was moving along the hidden deck playing the three impersonal notes of his luncheon gong. The young woman's breathing was reflected in her bare navel as well as in the natural rhythm of the breasts supported only by the triangulation of the blue halter. Between her shoulder blades the halter was tied, I saw, in a crisp knot.

"So," I said, giving the ball a small toss, "so you are Ariane. It's a lovely name."

My tie was struggling in its clip, my hair was blowing, the dead white net was high above my head, I thought of the young woman's name and saw the brothers, the sisters, the anonymous girl in the luncheonette, the shabby baptism of the first-born and female child receiving the elevated name she would so often discover in cheap magazines in the offices of social welfare.

"Whatever you're thinking right now," she said, slipping her hand inside my jacket and her arm part way around my waist, "is unworthy of you. You shouldn't think such things, Mr. Vanderveenan."

"But your name is indeed lovely. You must remember that I mean what I say—always."

Her arm was around my waist, the slightness of her entire body was brushing against all the bulk of mine, I could feel her small ringless hand playing with the folds of my damp shirt in the area of the small of my back. Had anyone discovered us standing there together between the smokestacks, he would not have been able to detect her arm and hand concealed inside the formal drapery of my unbuttoned jacket. But I could feel the slight pressure on my waist, the faint tugging and stroking motions of the fingers of her left hand, by leaning down was able even to catch a smell of her breath which was fleeting and natural in the context of the ocean wind. Her gesture was a surprise of course, and for an instant caused me to experience another one of those rare pangs of anxiety and anticipation in the face of the first hint of sudden attraction. I thought she was being friendly, I thought that her physical gesture expressed warmth and playfulness without intention. And yet we were indeed leaning together on the uppermost deck and one of her fingers had become somehow lodged between my belted trousers and my damp shirt. Already her entire manner should have told me plainly enough about her firmness of mind and her directness.

"Well," she said, raising her face toward mine and smiling, "you can't play net ball in your jacket."

"Just so," I said and drew my body away from hers, gave her the ball, removed my jacket, turned and walked into playing position on the other side of the net. The steadiness of the ship, the syllables murmuring in the wires overhead, the honed whiteness of the wooden deck, the symmetrical web of the high net, the sound of a ventilating machine, the wind at my back and the sun directly overhead so that time and direction were obliterated, these circumstances could not have been more concrete, more neutral, more devoid of meaning, more appropriate to the surprise and simplicity of the occasion at hand, when an unknown young woman was offering me something beyond innocence, companionship, flirtation. She was watching me as closely as I was watching her, and in both hands had raised the ball to chest level.

"You're traveling alone," she called, while I waited, raised my own hands in anticipation of her girlish throw.

"And you," I called back, squinting and waiting for the game to commence, "you too are traveling alone."

"But I'm different. I'm not married."

"Well," I called, laughing and wondering what had become of the desperate gulls, "I am married and I am nonetheless alone on this cruise. There's no more to say."

She raised the ball above her head. I took a step backward, I cupped my hands in the shape of the suspended ball. The ship was carrying us not toward any place but away.

"Often I go on these cruises," she called. "Often."

"Excellent," I called back. "Are you going to throw?"

She waited, this small anonymous female figure in an athletic pose. And then staring at me through the remarkable vibrations of the taut white net, slowly she lowered her arms until the ball, still gripped in her two hands, came to rest in the upper triangulation of her thighs, which were slightly spread. Her halter and tight pants appeared untouched by the wind, while on my back and shoulders and heavy legs my shirt and trousers were flattening like sails.

"I don't think so," she called without moving. "I think not."

I understood. Suddenly I began to understand the absolute presence of the girl who was waiting on the other side of the net and whose name was periodically carried on the passenger lists of ships such as ours. So I nodded and ducked under the net; she dropped the ball which, moving in accordance with the wind and slope of the deck, drifted under one of the lifeboats and disappeared over the starboard side of the ship.

We embraced. The skin of her naked back and shoulders was as smooth and glossy as the skin that has replaced burned skin on a human body. Her kissing was wet and confident, prolonged and wordless, and included even my nose, which she sucked into her small entirely serious mouth.

"You must never pity me," she said when we were ready once more to descend the ladder. "That's what I ask."

I heard the tapping on the door. I heard excited voices and the sound of feet moving quickly across the deck outside. I heard the sound of her voice calling softly through the louvers of my cabin door.

"Allert? Are you there? We are passing the island. Won't you come and look?"

I waited, stretched flat on the coverlet, and quite distinctly I felt some alteration in the position of our tonnage as it shifted in the deep sea, and could not prevent myself from hearing the hivelike excitement of those passengers who were gathering on the starboard rail. I could hear the wind in the straw hats, I could hear the bodies crowding each other at the mahogany rail.

"Allert? Will you answer? I know you're there."

I was of course thoroughly certain that she could not possibly know that I was lying tensely inside my cabin since I had taken care to draw the green curtain across my porthole. And yet the very ordinary sound of her voice as well as her faith in my whereabouts, prompted me to reply.

"It is only an island, after all," I said evenly. "It is not Atlantis."

"It's important, Allert. Open the door."

"Very well," I said then. "In a moment."

"If you don't hurry we shall be past it and then there will be nothing to see."

I swung myself up from the bed and buttoned my shirt, drew on my trousers, opened the door. The intense light of midday, the ungainly binoculars on a strap around her neck, the now louder sounds of the expectant passengers, it was all exactly as I knew it would be, concreteness rotating toward illusion. And in my doorway, or nearly in my doorway, she was smiling and resting one small gentle hand on the binoculars.

"And Allert," she said in the voice that only I could hear, "have you been sleeping?"

"No," I said, closing and locking the door behind me and taking hold of one of her frail but well-proportioned arms, "no, I have not been sleeping. I have been meditating. As a matter of fact, Ariane, I have been wondering exactly who you are."

"But, Allert, you know who I am."

"More important, perhaps, I have been wondering exactly who I am."

"But I know who you are, Allert. And that's enough."

"Perhaps you do," I said, gazing to sea and thinking that her declaration was somehow more than an assertion of innocence, "perhaps you do indeed know after all. But where did you get that man-sized pair of binoculars?"

"From one of my friends, of course. We'll use them for looking at the island."

"Of course. From one of your friends. But tell me," I said then, diverting us back to one of the subjects I had been considering in my cabin. "What is your age?"

"Twenty-six, Allert. And yours?"

"Oh, I am much too old to say," I replied in a thicker, more milky voice. "Much too old to say."

"As you will, Allert. I really don't care about your age."

"But then it's probably true that in matters of shipboard romance, at least, the greater the disparity between the ages the better."

"You're in a very difficult mood today. I wish you'd stop."

"In a moment," I said then, and squeezing the thin arm, "in another moment I'll growl at you in Dutch."

She laughed, we were walking in step together, she caused her little hip to fall against my big pillowed flank, she laughed again. And yet it seemed to me that even so she was still not completely reassured.

At this moment we rounded the great glass front of the observation lounge and strode hand in hand into the windy open space of the forward deck where, precisely as I had envisioned the scene, the group of passengers was gathered birdlike at the starboard rail. I was interested to see that they were more bizarre and yet not so numerous as I had thought. In particular I noticed one man whose body was not unusually masculine but who was naked except for a pair of khaki-colored shorts and an enormous rouge-colored conical straw hat that went down to his shoulders. A woman, heavy set and bold, was holding a small wicker basket filled with fruit, as if preparing to drop it quickly over the side.

"Allert," Ariane whispered as we squeezed to the rail, "they're all looking at you. They're all jealous because your companion is so young and so attractive."

"Yes," I whispered back, "they cannot imagine what we do together, but they have ideas."

"Oh, Allert," she said then, suddenly putting her hand on top of mine, "surely the captain is going to crash into the island!"

For a moment it seemed even to me that what Ariane had said was true. Because the island, a dry, treeless and apparently heart-shaped knoll, was rising out of the sea directly off our starboard bow. Considering the various angles of vision between masts, cables, diminishing horizon, approaching island, and considering the vast expanse of totally open sea in which the ship and island were the only two concrete points—one fixed, one free—and that the space between the two was disappearing as quickly as breath, given all these circumstances it did indeed appear true that the captain was subjecting us all to unnecessary risk by changing course and by aiming the prow of the ship directly toward the arid heart of volcanic land anchored so permanently in the deep sea. Then I recovered myself and realized that for the first time during the voyage I was out of sympathy with Ariane, who, after all, was quite as capable as I was of common sense.

"Look," I said brusquely, "anyone can see there will be no collision."

"But we are very close to the island, Allert. Very close."

"Close," I said then in a gentler tone, "but safe."

We veered to within perhaps a hundred meters or so of the island. The man in the rouge-colored hat cried out and in an instant trained on the burning island the telescope of his terrible motion-picture camera, a camera I had failed to see, cradled as it was against his eye inside the cone of his hat. Ariane and I stood quietly touching each other and sharing the black binoculars, in the process of which she allowed her fingers to slide unconsciously over my buttocks while I, in turn, wet the vulnerable spot behind her ear with the tip of my tongue.

"It's so barren," she whispered, "so beautifully barren."

"Yes. And notice how the goats apparently manage none-theless to survive on an island without food."

"It's because they're unreal, Allert. That's why."

But the goats were real enough for me, and though there did not appear to be a blade of grass or the slightest sign of fresh water on the island, still the community of goats stood ruffled and silhouetted atop the nearest hummock and stared at what to them must have been the specter of a white ship bearing down on their final garden. Through the binoculars I could see the spray crowning the tightly spiraled horns, could see how old and young alike crowded together haunch to haunch, horns among horns, posing in the certainty of survival in the midst of pure desolation. The animals were as still as rocks, though their horns were flashing and their coats of long hair were blowing and ruffling in the emptiness of the ocean wind.

"The goats are real enough," I said. "But they are a strange sight. Even a haunting sight, perhaps."

"Allert," she said then, as if she had failed to hear my observation, "let's not allow them to disappear so easily. Come, let's watch until there's nothing more of them to see."

But it was only too clear that she neither doubted nor required my acquiescence, since she had taken back the binoculars and was already making her way out of the crowd and toward the stern of the ship which appeared now to be coasting past the island at an ever-diminishing nautical speed. Ariane walked swiftly, then ran, then walked swiftly again until finally she stood at the last extremity of the slowly moving ship, motionless with the binoculars dwarfing her face and her hard shoulder braced against the slick white glistening surface of the ship's flagpole.

We were crossing the pointed tip of the island, the goats

were fading. I was standing directly behind Ariane who was pressed against the rail and against the flagpole, her small bare shoulders hunched in the intensity of her gaze.

I squinted at the disappearing island. I respected Ariane's concentration and did not press the front of my body to the back of hers, but waited as she sighted across our wake toward the island blazing less and less brightly in the dark sea. The hair was blowing at the nape of her neck, the ends of her halter knot were blowing between the shoulder blades which my own two hands could have so easily cupped, concealed, shielded. However, it seemed to me that Ariane was elated but also desperate as she attempted to hold in view the brown earth and the remote and mournful goats, so that I did not press the front of my pants into the seat of hers, no matter how gently, or put my finger where the wind was stirring the fine hairs on her neck. At the stern where we were standing together but separated, it was impossible to hear the engines or any other sounds of the ship, because that was the area most engulfed by the crosscurrents of the wind, the singing of the dead wake, the thrashing of the great blades just below us and just beneath the frothing chaos of the surface.

"Well," I said at last, "I'm glad you roused me for this event. It was an interesting sight. The abandoned goats, an island as bare as that one."

Slowly, as if once more she had failed to hear me, or as if she could not admit that now there was nothing to see except the empty sky, the unbearable sunlight, the gunmetal gray reaches of the ocean that was both flat and tossing, slowly she turned around and revealed her face from behind the disfigurement of the black binoculars, and leaned back against the rail, looked up at me, smiled, spread her legs somewhat apart. Her expression was open, clear, inviting. I noted how dark her skin had become since the start of the journey.

"But Allert," she said then, and her eyes were large, her teeth white, "the island we just passed belongs to me. Didn't you know?"

"Do you wish to explain yourself?"

"I do. Yes, I do. But another time."

Together we leaned on the rail and side by side stared at what we were leaving in our wake, which was nothing. But had I understood her meaning at that moment I would have bruised her in the agony of my desperate embrace.

"Mr. Vanderveenan," she said, "will you come to my cabin for a moment? I have something to show you."

At the edge of the pool and in utter privacy she straddled the upper diving board like a child at play while I lounged upright and draped in my towel against the ladder. She had mounted to the upper diving board and now sat straddling the board backward so that I, holding the aluminum rail and she, hunching and leaning down with her hands braced forward between her spread wet thighs, were able to look at each other and to speak to each other as we wished. How long we had posed together in this tableau I could not have said, though at the sound of her invitation I felt on the one hand that we had never existed except together and in our tableau of mutual anticipation, but on the other that we had only moments before arrived at the pool's edge and that she had still to dive and I had still to help her dripping and laughing from the pool.

"By all means," I said, squinting up through the cocoa-colored lenses of my dark glasses, "let's go to your cabin."

She descended. I lifted her from the ladder. Hastily we used our towels, silently we collected our straw slippers, our books, our towels, our lotions, our straw hats for the sun. Her skin was brushed with lightlike pollen, I decided that the two flesh-colored latex garments in which she swam had come from a cheap and crowded department store. The energy of her preparations, doffing the rubber cap and so forth, caused me to hurry.

"Not now, Mr. Larzar," she called to a broad-shouldered man dressed like the rest of the ship's officers in the somehow disreputable white uniform, and waving, "I have an engagement with Mr. Vanderveenan." And then, to me: "He wants his trousers pressed."

"But you are joking," I said as we descended to the dark corridor, "only joking."

"Whenever I am on a cruise I press the trousers of the ship's officers. I am not joking at all."

"I see," I answered. "But at least I would not want you to press my trousers."

"But of course you are not one of the ship's officers," she said in the darkness of the corridor below and laughed, shifted the things in her arms, unhooked the brass hook, stood aside so as to allow me to enter first, then closed the door.

Blue jeans flung on the bed in the attitude of some invisible female wearer suffering rape, underclothes ravaged from an invisible clothesline and flung about the room, a second two-piece bathing costume exactly like the first but hanging from one of the ringbolts loose and protruding from the porthole, and cosmetics and pieces of crumpled tissue and a single stocking that might have fit the small shape of her naked leg, and magazines and sheets of writing paper and mismatched pieces of clothing—in a glance I saw that the context in which her personal trimness nested, so to speak, was extreme girlish chaos of which she herself was apparently unaware.

"You may sit on the bed," she said, noting the antique typewriter in the upholstered chair, and without hesitation dropping towel and robe and slippers and so forth into the plump impersonal chair with the old machine. "Just clear a place for yourself. It doesn't matter if you're a little wet. Do you like my cabin? Is it as nice as yours?"

"Tell me," I said then, deliberately and gently, "why are we here?"

"I'll show you," she said, kneeling on the unmade bed where I was propped, "but I like this cabin because the porthole opens directly in the side of the ship. Whenever I wish to, I simply kneel on my bed and lean in my open porthole and smell the night or watch the sunlight in the waves. Do you see?"

While talking she had knelt on a pillow and pushed wide open the porthole and now was leaning out head and shoulders with sunlight falling on her narrow back and tension concentrated in her nearly naked buttocks made firm by the bending of her legs.

"That's a very agreeable demonstration," I said, "but for me it produces a certain anxiety."

"Why is that?" she asked, drawing in her head from the wind, the spray, "are you afraid I'll fall?"

"You are not very large, whereas in comparison to you the porthole is big and round. So I do not like you to lean out of it. My feelings are simple."

She knelt beside me, she studied my eyes, with both hands she better situated one of her small breasts in the little flesh-colored latex halter, the sun was a bright ball of light on the opposite wall.

"Mr. Vanderveenan," she said, "you are an old maid. I would not have believed it."

"I am not a man generally teased by women," I said slowly, filling the sentence with the white cadences of my native speech, and extending my hand which for a moment she lightly held, "and I do not enjoy the prospect of open portholes."

She was sitting on her heels, her knees were spread, I could

see the outline of a label sewn inside her bikini pants as well as
a little pubic darkness protruding like natural lace at the edges
of the crotch. The sensation of her two hands on my extended hand was light and natural.

"Very well," she said, "I don't wish to cause you anxiety."

She smiled, I noted just below her navel a small scar in the
nasty shape of a fishhook, for a moment she raised my hand
and touched it with her two dry lips. And then she drew back
from me, got off the bed, rummaged about in an open drawer
from which whole fistfuls of cheap underthings had already
been half pulled, as if by some aggressive fetishist, until she
found what she wanted and rose from where she had squatted,
displaying to best advantage the roundness and symmetry of
her little backside, and returned to me with the battered
oblong case clutched to her chest. I rolled up from my slouching position. I sat on the edge of the bed. She sat beside me
with the case on her knees and her shining skin smelling of
talcum powder.

"So," I said as she opened the case, "so you play the flute."

She nodded, she smiled into the case at the sections of the
silver instrument tarnished, I saw, with the myriad sentimental stains of a poor childhood focused at least in part on
music. Then slowly and expertly she began to fit together the
sections of the aged instrument which already reminded me of
a silver snake suffering paralysis. It could not have been more
clear to me that the poverty of her childhood had been forced
to make way, finally, for the flute, as if the musical instrument, like a fancy name, would prove to be one of the
avenues away from broken fences and a poor home. It was
typical, it seemed to me, and the assembled anomalous instrument was proportionately much longer than I had thought.

"But this is a surprise," I said. "I did not know you were
musical. Did you learn as a child?"

She nodded, she tapped the metallic keys, she arranged her
arms and elbows in the contorted position all flutists assume

when they commence to play. She tested the broad silver lip of the flute against her own small lip that was smooth and dry.

"I learned as a girl," she said, without lowering the old and battered flute from her childish mouth. "I was one of those fortunate schoolgirls to play in the local orchestra."

"And since that time," I said, and laughed, "you have continued to play your flute. It's a surprising accomplishment. It's quite wonderful."

"I think it is. And I want to play for you right now."

"By all means," I exclaimed, filling my words with white-wash and ducks and potato soup, "a little concert. Excellent, excellent."

"I know what you're thinking. But you'll see that my flute playing is not what you expect."

"Come, come, I'm listening," I said, laughing and attempting to strike the condescension from my heavy voice. "Let me hear what you can do with your flute."

"Very well," she answered then. "But it may not be as easy as you think. You see, I play in the nude."

And there in the little pathetic chaotic stateroom she did just that. With the door locked and the porthole wide to the menacing trident of the god of holidays, and standing within easy reach of my two clasped hands, slowly she removed her latex halter, stripped down the latex bikini bottom, seated herself cross-legged on the end of the bed, picked up the instrument, puckered her lips, stared directly at me with soft eyes, and began to play. The first several notes moved me and surprised me even more than her nudity, since the notes were deep prolonged contralto notes, sustained with a throaty power and intention that suggested some mournful Pan rather than a small and ordinary young woman on a pleasure cruise.

"Forgive my banter," I whispered, allowing myself to slouch back again on the unmade bed and listen and to stare into the eyes of the naked flutist. "Your talent is serious."

From lonely little girl among stupid old men lewdly picking their strings and blowing their dented horns, from school orchestra composed of indifferent unskilled children, from days of practicing in an empty room smelling of beer and damp plaster, from all that to nudity and self-confidence and the ability to set into motion sinuous low notes loud enough and plaintive enough to calm the waves. And I had expected none of it, none of it. So I lay there propped on a heavy elbow. I was sexually aroused in the depths of my damp swimming trunks as I had not been since long before the disappearance of the ship's home port, and yet at the same time I was thoroughly absorbed in the shocking contralto sounds and the body bared as if for the music itself. I listened, I heard the reedy undulations, I noted the hair like a dense furry tongue in the fork of her canted thighs, I saw the flickering of the pallid scar and realized that she was taking no breaths, that the sound of the flute was continuous.

"Please," I said in a low voice, and momentarily allowing my free hand to cup the mound of my sex, "please do not stop."

Her mouth was wet, her eyes were on mine constantly, except when occasionally she glanced out of the porthole or at the heavy helpless grip of my hand that was now the fulcrum on which I was minutely rocking, though still on my side. And throughout this improbable experience, simultaneously gift and ordeal, she was apparently unaware of the incongruity of all she was giving me behind the locked and louvered door.

And then in mid-phrase she stopped. She removed the flute several inches from her small chafed reddened mouth. Wet armpits, steady eyes, no smile, small breasts never exactly motionless, old flute held calmly in a horizontal silver line, the song quite gone, thus she abruptly stopped her performance and spoke to me as if nothing at all had happened.

"I'd like to relieve you now quickly," she said. "And will you spend the night here in my cabin?"

Then she moved, and in the silence of the disheveled cabin I could hear that all the low notes of the silver flute were still making their serpentine way beyond the porthole and in the transitory wastes of sea and sky.

But how could I have remained unawakened by our descending anchors? How could I have allowed myself to sleep through the actuality of my own worst dream? After all, Ariane had forewarned me that we would be reaching the shores of the island in the darkest part of the night and would be dropping anchor. And it was indeed so because now the sun was rising in the lowest quadrant of my porthole like blood in a bottle, and I was wide-awake and nursing my premonitions. The ship was at anchor.

I climbed to my knees on the wet bed and opened the porthole. I saw that the sun was flooding the horizon but that the island was nowhere in sight. And kneeling with my head in the porthole and the sun in my eyes, I recalled how the night before I had refused Ariane's invitation to go ashore on the island of nudists. And squinting into the ominous and bloody sun, once more I determined to prevent our exposure to the boredom and distaste of bodies bared merely for the sake of health or naturalness.

And yet with unaccustomed haste I dressed, seized my straw hat and went out on deck in search of my young friend. The ship was silent, the gulls were gone, the hot deck might have been embedded in concrete. I tapped insistently on the door to her cabin, I assured myself that no one was enjoying the use of the pool, I understood that it would be several hours at least before juice and coffee and rolls were served in the dining saloon. The locked cabins, the empty bridge, the damp blankets heaped up in the peeling deck chairs, the silence—this, the death of the ship, was what I had always feared.

I crossed from the starboard side to the port and there against the rail were a half dozen passengers and, in the dreamlike distance beyond them, the low brown sandy island that so appealed to Ariane. I joined the passengers who did not intend to visit the island, I gathered, but who nonetheless were determined to look at those who did and, further, were hoping for a glimpse of the distant nudists. With them I stared across at the hazy island and down at the white motorboat now moored to the foot of the gangway lowered against the ship's white side.

Except for Ariane and the wireless operator seated hip to hip in the forward portion of the white launch, and except for the young crewman slouching in the stern with a rope in his hand, the long white motor launch was empty, occupied as it was by only three persons instead of sixty. I decided to become the fourth.

I descended the gangway at precisely the moment the crewman was preparing to cast off. I took my seat behind my young friend as the motor began its muffled bubbling. I glanced up at the remaining passengers propped like wax figures against the rail and under the hot sun. There was no waving, in a half circle we moved away from the high side of the anchored ship.

"Allert," she said, smiling, reaching out for my hand, "you've changed your mind."

"Yes," I said, "I too will visit your nudists."

"Without you it would not be the same."

"Well," I said, accepting and squeezing her proffered hand, "Allert also can be a good sport, as my wife would say."

We picked up speed, there was a dawn wind blowing, Ariane smiled and tilted back her head as if to take deep breaths of the burning sun. The wireless officer and I exchanged no greeting. Behind us lay the white ship, diminishing but stationary, while ahead of us lay the scorched island that was expanding minute by minute for our watchful eyes.

"I did not sleep well last night," I said. "I had intolerable dreams."

"Poor Allert. You will be able to sleep on the beach."

The sea, on which there was not the smallest wave, was now changing from opaque blackness to a turquoise transparency. Twenty or thirty feet below us shelves of white sand were reflecting the light of the sun back up through the soundless medium of the clear sea. I was relieved to notice, over my shoulder, that no smoke was visible from the blue smokestacks of the anchored ship. Ariane's hair was blowing in the wind, the long black sideburns of the wireless officer contradicted in some disturbing way the rakish angle of his white black-visored cap. My young friend in her blue jeans and a halter of orange silk, through which the shape of her small breasts was entirely visible, was an antidote to the wireless officer's unusual mood of sullen reserve.

"Your island appears to be uninhabited," I said, clutching the brim of my straw hat against the wind, "since there is not even one nudist to greet the eye."

"Allert," she said, "don't be skeptical. Please. There is a village on the other side of the island. The beach is momentarily concealed from our view inside its protective cove. The village and beach are connected by a dirt road which is excellent for bicycling. You must remember, Allert, that I have been here before."

I touched her cool arm and again I saw over my shoulder that our diminishing white ship lay unchanged, unmoving. I disliked the way the wireless operator sat with one foot on the gunwhale and his tunic thrown open to display the unwashed undershirt, the cross on a chain. Also I disliked his sideburns, his bad complexion, the angle of his white cap, the hand he was hiding in the pocket of the white tunic.

"My wife persuaded me, against my better judgment, to take this cruise," I said, smiling into the girl's dark eyes, "and I am not sorry. Now you have persuaded me, also against my better judgment, to journey off in a mere motorboat. And though I distrust open motorboats even more than I distrust large ships, perhaps I will not be sorry. But I am not skeptical, Ariane. I am never skeptical. I know you will take us directly to the beach of the nudists and then return us safely to our waiting ship."

But even while my heavily accented voice hung on the air, causing Ariane to laugh and the wireless operator to scowl behind an unclean hand, our motorboat veered slowly around a finger of dark sand and headed directly into a small cove that was clearly the entrance to the hidden beach of Ariane's description. The strip of pure white sand, water of the palest blue, the row of weather-beaten bathhouses like upended coffins—it was all exactly as I had pictured it from my young friend's words. The sky was an infinitude of burning phosphorus, the sand was as soft as facial powder, surely the empty bathhouses would smell of urine. The vision of the cove was familiar yet unfamiliar, I was drawn toward the listing bathhouses and yet repelled by them.

"Hurry," Ariane called the moment after our prow had touched the sand and she, in childish haste, had leapt ashore, "we really must not lose a moment of this joyous place!"

The wireless operator, in open tunic and rakish cap, was the next to jump to the dry sand where, quite unavoidable, he turned and faced me. His greasy sideburns appeared to be pasted down the sides of his jawbone. He was not smiling.

"What have you done with my photograph?" he said, with his feet spread wide apart and his hands in his tunic pockets and his hat pushed in slovenly aggressive fashion to the back of his head. Obviously he was the kind of young officer who would get drunk with ordinary sailors, abandon a ship in distress, commit strange psychopathic acts of violence.

"I do not know what you are talking about," I said. "But I do not like the tone of your voice."

"After all, you are not the only one who needs the stimulation of an illicit photograph."

"I refuse to listen!"

"Return it tonight," he said and stuffed his hands deeper into the tunic pockets, and lunged off through the sand like a crazed survivor of a wreck at sea.

"And you, Allert," my young unsuspecting friend called from the bathhouses, "won't you hurry?"

I wiped my hot face on my sleeve, I began to walk slowly up the beach toward the row of narrow listing wooden structures where I, like my companions, was to divest myself of all clothing. But physical nudity was one thing, I thought, whereas psychological nudity was quite another, especially when the self was being stripped to psychological nudity by a man as ruthless and devious as the young man on whom the entire ship depended. My need was for self-control against the brutal clawing of that young man's repellent hands.

"But no, Allert, no!" she cried when I emerged from the bathhouse, "you may not wear your straw hat on the beach of the nudists!"

She laughed, standing quite naked in the hot sand. The wireless operator also laughed, though now his concentration was suddenly and unwillingly fixed on the gentle nudity of Ariane.

"What," I said, "not even an old straw hat?"

"Nothing, Allert, nothing. Not even a hat."

"Very well. But sunstroke is a serious problem, Ariane."

"But you must trust me, Allert. You said you would."

The sunlight was as intense and diffuse as any I had ever seen, the kind of sunlight that would bake alive infant tortoises buried though they might be in their thick shells deep in the sand. In the midst of this directionless glare Ariane's nude body was of the size and weight of a young child's yet it was not childlike. She was plump but at the same time thin, curvaceous but at the same time compact, and in the glare of the sunlight, which decomposed all colors to white and hence made of the island landscape a brilliant unreality, Ariane was shrouded, softened, protected in her own emanations of mauve-colored light. In the midst of our frightening white scene she alone was desirable and real. She had allowed her black hair to fall down her narrow back, her eyes were large, her small calves were shapely, there was a curious dignity in the plumpness of the small naked belly exposed without embarrassment to the wireless operator's watching eyes and mine. Her little familiar scar was hooked into the bottom of the belly like a gleaming barb, the small modest breasts and sex made me think of some overdressed Flemish child preserved on dark canvas.

Though the wireless operator was lean and muscular, while I was large and poorly shaped, still the chemical horror of the gleaming sun reduced us equally to the dead white quality of the beach itself, exposed quite equally our blemishes, our black hair curling from white skin, our genitals which in this light appeared to have been molded from cold butter. I was not pleased to find myself as unattractive as the wireless operator.

"Ariane," I said, when the three of us emerged from the path between the dunes and onto the beach, "I hope you do not find my weight entirely offensive."

"Allert," she said, and her throat was as thin and tender as a child's, "you are a handsome man."

"But tell me," I said, raising my voice and filling it with the disarming resonance of the kindly Hollander, "if a man is not used to nudism, if he is not used to being among members of the opposite sex without his clothes, in such a situation might he not display quite suddenly all the awkward aspects of sexual desire? If so, would not this lack of control be embarrassing?"

The sand was hot, my eyes felt sewn together with invisible sutures, the beach ahead of us was a glaring crescent. Behind us the wireless operator was shielding himself with Ariane's purple satchel and grunting in discomfort and disapproval.

"Allert," she said, interrupting our walk across the sand to touch my hip, to stare up openly into my wet face, "what you describe is entirely possible. But it is also natural. To me it would not be at all embarrassing. In fact," she said, more slowly and gently but also more clearly, "if such a thing occurred in my presence, I should be flattered. I should be warmly pleased."

"Thank you," I said, glancing over my shoulder at the stricken eyes, the body bent sharply forward at the waist. "Your sympathy for that situation is most beautiful. But were I in your place, for instance, and in the presence of a man who could not control himself, I would be far less charitable. In fact, toward such a man, I would show no charity at all."

"But, Allert," she said, smiling and pressing her fingers against my wet forearm, "you are a good-hearted person, Allert. I know you are."

I saw the blue of her eyes against the white of the sand, the white of the sun. And despite the fire flickering already to and fro on the tops of my shoulders, for another moment I endured with pleasure the uninhibited inspection of Ariane's soft eyes which, when they met mine, were bluer, moister for what they had seen.

"Every man is an island," I said. "I am like the rest."

"But Allert," she whispered, "you are a very special person. You are the talk of the ship."

But before I could object and point out the obvious untruth of this curious remark, Ariane reached up and covered my mouth with the smallness of her cool hand, then embraced me by flinging her arms around the enfolded fat of my naked waist and resting her head on my chest. Then she turned and with unexpected swiftness walked to the water's edge where, ankle deep in the clear undulating sea, she proceeded brightly up the white crescent of beach followed, as she knew full well, by her two naked companions, one of whom was already the color of sickening red.

"You ought to see yourself," came the voice at my back, "if you could see yourself you'd leave Ariane and me alone. A man like you shouldn't go around without his clothes. She just doesn't want to hurt your feelings. Couldn't you tell?"

I did not reply. Instead I concentrated on the sensation of the pale water against my skin and on the sight of the young woman who had thick black hair to the small of her back and who now was standing beneath the leaves of a tropical tree and waving. The island, or what I could see of it, was empty except for the eager girl beneath the tree and a far-off cluster of golden figures who, in their various sizes, suggested one of those stable families who respect the old and cherish the young and divest themselves of clothes for moral purposes. Even from this distance I noted the sweep of a patriarchal beard, the flash of a cherubic body. I looked away, I realized again that the sand of the beach was like white ash. But it was the naked wireless operator, not I, who was turning red.

"Come," called Ariane, "the shade is lovely."

Even here in the shade of the lone tree, only Ariane among the three of us looked real. Only her skin retained its natural color, only her black hair remained alive in the breeze. On either side of Ariane, where she sat upright and smiling against the tree, the wireless operator and I were merely white, except for the florid sunburn spreading like some poisoned solution across the young officer's shoulders, chest, and listless arm. The wireless operator's sallow face was wet with sweat, his head was hanging.

I held out my hand for one of the peaches which Ariane had extracted from the satchel. My hands were wet with the juice of the peach, the warm sweetness was dripping down my chin. In the distance a golden old man was tossing a golden infant into the air. And I noted in a casual glance that the wireless operator was drooping, dehydrating faster than ever, burning. If Ariane was aware of the seriousness of his condition, she gave no sign.

"Allert," she said, biting into the wet yellow fruit and unconsciously touching her left nipple as if to induce new sensation or confirm its size, "isn't that naked family beautiful? They have no shame."

I licked my fingers, I nodded. Her eyes were bright, her armpit was slick with perspiration, on her other side the wireless operator was staring at me speechless and with dead white eyes. Portions of his slumped naked body were assuming the complexion of a fatal plum.

Suddenly I heard a thin distant voice crying, "Papa! Papa!" and at the same time heard a single fragment of the far-off mother's laughter, and at this moment Ariane and I, in perfect accord, rose to our feet and, holding hands, walked slowly to the water's edge. I knew that behind us the wireless operator was helpless and that his lips were cracked, his shoulders blistering.

The light was the color of merciless pearl, the sand was a sheet of white flame, together we rolled in clear shallow water.

"Allert," she said, stretching her little flat body beneath the water and raising her face, extending her arms and clasping both my stolid ankles, "you are so good a lover, Allert. Maybe because your mouth is so large and says so many sweet things to me."

We rose, we walked outward from the shore of the island that was as dry and livid as a glimpse of paradise preserved in a hostile photograph, walked outward until I stood waist deep in the placid water and Ariane stood facing me sunk up to her shining breasts. The air was white, the sea was pale, all around us the air now smelled of invisible dead ash.

"We do not want the ship to sail without us," I said in a whisper.

Later, after we had performed, as I thought of it, like two unshelled creatures risen together from the white sandy floor of the sea, and after we had immersed ourselves totally in the calming waters, and after we had quit the nudist island and regained the ship, it was then that we faced the condition of the wireless operator. We eased him into Ariane's cabin and stripped him bare, discovered that the entire burned surface of his body was patterned with the clearly visible shapes of tropical leaves. Thus the wireless operator became the sick occupant of Ariane's narrow bed, and thus Ariane became his eager conscience-stricken nurse. For days the wireless operator filled her cabin with the smells of his chills and fever. For days the smell of a strong unguent filled that cabin in which there was no place for me.

"Allert," she said quietly and behind my back, "it is not necessary to wash my underpants. You are always kind to me. But you shouldn't bother to rinse my panties."

"Oh, but it is nothing," I said, and felt the life of the ship in the soles of my naked feet. "It is an unfamiliar chore for me and one I like. But surely if you can press the clothing of the ship's crew it is somehow appropriate that I rinse your panties."

Sitting as she was on the far end of her rumpled berth, small, indifferent to the hour of the day, Ariane was not within range of the small mirror fastened above the porcelain sink. I could see the familiar disorder of the little stateroom whenever I glanced from the frothy sink to the mirror, and even had a splendid reflected view of the opened porthole above the berth, but I could not see Ariane and could only assume that she had already removed her bathing suit as I had mine. At the sink I stood with a towel knotted around my waist but assumed that Ariane would not care to wrap herself in towels.

"Well, you are doing a very thorough job, Allert," she said behind my back. "But don't you want to hurry a little?"

"Two more pairs to go," I said into the empty mirror that was quivering slightly with the pulse of the ship. "Only two pairs. And do you see? They look as if they belong to a child."

"But, Allert, I think you have become a fetishist!"

"Oh yes," I said heavily and raised my face to the glass. "Yes, I am a deliberate fetishist."

I nodded to myself, I submerged my hands to the wrists and scrubbed the little shrunken garment that felt as slippery as satin on a perspiring thigh. I was enjoying myself, half naked before the sink and rinsing Ariane's six pairs of off-white panties. They were not new, those panties, and the crotch of each pair bore an unremovable and, to me, endearing stain.

"There. You see? I am done. Now we shall hang them to dry."

But that day Ariane's wet undergarments on which I had worked with such prolonged and gentle satisfaction, remained in a damp heap in the porcelain sink. In a single instant I forgot all about Ariane's damp panties (reminding me of the clothing shop windows into which I used to peer as a youth in Breda), because in that instant I turned from the sink to find that she had not resorted to a warm towel, as I was convinced she would not, but also that there on the other end of the rumpled bed, with the wind in her hair and her legs drawn up and crossed at the ankles, she was far from that complete state of nudity in which I had thought, even hoped, to find her. But I was not disappointed.

I did not know how to respond, I felt a certain disbelief and breathless respect. But I was not disappointed. Because Ariane sat before me girdled only in what appeared to be the split skull and horns of a smallish and long-dead goat. It was as if some ancient artisan had taken an axe and neatly cleaved off the topmost portion of the skull of a small goat, that portion including the sloping forehead, the eye sockets, a part of the nose, and of even the curling horns, and on a distant and legendary beach had dried the skull and horns in the sun, in herbs, in a nest of thorns, on a white rock, preparing and polishing this trophy for the day it would become the mythical and only garment of a young girl. What was left of the forehead and nose, which was triangular and polished and ended in a few slivers of white bone, lay tightly wedged in my small friend's bare loins. The goat's skull was a shield that could not have afforded her greater sexual protection, while at the same time the length of bone that once comprised the goat's nose and hence part of its mouth gave silent urgent voice to the living orifice it now concealed. The horns were curled around her hips. On her right hip and held in place between the curve of the slender horn and curve of her body Ariane was wearing a dark red rose. I recognized it as one she must have taken from the cut-glass vase of roses that had adorned our table for the noon meal.

"Allert," she said at last and into my puzzled and admiring silence, "how do you like my costume for the ship's ball?"

Slowly I shook my head. The bikini made of bone and horn was the ultimate contrast to the hidden and vulnerable sex of my young friend. I now felt that the towel around my waist was a vain and undeniable irritant.

"Yes," I said gently, "you are Schubert's child. Who but my Ariane would fuse her own delicacy with the skull of the animal Eros? And the rose, the rose. It is a beautiful costume. Beautiful. But it is not for the ship's ball."

"But I promised the purser, Allert. What can I do?"

"You may cease your teasing right away."

"Very well, my poor dear Allert. I have been teasing. I will attend the ball dressed as a ship's officer. Are you satisfied?"

"Completely," I said then, dropping my towel. "Completely."

I sat beside her on the berth. I removed the rose. I seized the two horns and smelled the dark and living hair and the tangled sheets and the sea breeze. Gently I tugged on the horns until they came away from her with the faintest possible sound of suction. I could not believe what the goat's cranial cavity now revealed. The goat's partial skull fell to the floor but did not break. I smothered my small friend in my flesh, a huge old lover grateful for girl, generosity, desire, and the ax that long ago had split the skull.

To be wanted in such a way, what was there more?

Dead Passion

from TRAVESTY (1976)

For part of still another summer, in 1974, we lived on the edge of a village on the Brittany coast. There were miles of nearby beaches frequented by French tourists. Our farmhouse was filled with black flies and stood beside a field where cows grazed among silent menhirs, those strange upright stones from the time of the Celts. And once again, place and coincidence conspired, now touching off the most ironic narrative I had hit upon so far. First, one afternoon I found in that farmhouse an English edition of Camus' short novel, *The Fall*, picked it up, and flicked through it. I remembered that when *The Fall* had first appeared, twenty years before, I had looked at it and, noting that it was a monologue, and thinking monologues singularly tedious, decided not to read it. Now I changed my mind and had the pleasure of savoring at last the superbly ironic voice of Camus' anonymous lawyer.

A few days later there was a catastrophic automobile accident on the narrow country road leading to the beaches, the sort of accident that only French drivers could contrive. The cars must have been traveling at their usual fierce speeds and the drivers had not given an inch and had collided head on. We were told that not one member of those two families survived. Beach toys and picnic gear and unrecognizable parts of the tinny cars were scattered everywhere; deposits of pulverized glass lay on the road and in shallow pockets in the bordering dunes.

That evening I remembered reading about Camus' death in a car crash. In my faulty memory I saw him behind the wheel of a handsome sports car speeding through a dark and rainy night outside Paris. I thought too of Camus' insistence on the importance of the question: why not suicide? I had never much liked that question and had my own abhorrence of suicide, since our friend who had shot himself was never far from mind. I disliked intensely what I took to be Camus' philosophical alternatives: reasons to live or suicide. It was then that I decided to ask the opposite of Camus' question and to attempt to discover fictionally, not reasons to live, but what might possibly justify the act of suicide.

We went back to Vence at the end of the summer and I spent the rest of that year working on *Travesty*, which is a monologue exactly the length of *The Fall*. My monologuist, who is known only as the "privileged man," is accompanied on a suicidal night drive over a dangerous stretch of road in the south of France by Chantal, his nineteen-year-old daughter, who crouches terrified in the back seat, and by his best friend, a poet named Henri. The privileged man is driving at the highest possible speed and intends to crash his elegant sports car into the three-foot-thick wall of an abandoned farmhouse, thus committing suicide and murdering both friend and daughter. The privileged man's monologue, "impossibly" spoken in the last minutes before the crash, is a discussion of Henri's love affairs with Chantal and also with Honorine, the privileged man's wife, and is an argument stating that no effort of the imagination could be greater than trying to imagine one's own death— which is what the privileged man is attempting to help Henri and even Chantal to do. It is this effort, the ultimate exercising of the imagination, that reveals the privileged man as more of a poet than Henri, and that justifies, to him at least, the horror he causes.

In *Travesty* I hoped to write a comic novel about the fatal importance of the imagination. But when I had finished writing it and allowed myself to read the published accounts of Camus' death, I learned the details of that calamity for literature, and was faced with a final and disturbing irony I could not have anticipated: Camus was in fact a passenger in the car in which he died and not its driver. At least there is our close friend, a German scholar and critic, who insists that *Travesty* is not at all a travesty of Camus' work but an homage to Camus himself.

"Dead Passion" is an account of the privileged man's own brief excursion into adultery.

Dead Passion

Our villages carved out of old bone, our forests shimmering with leaves the color of dried tobacco, our village walls over which the dead vines are draped like fishing nets, the weight of the stones that occupy the slopes of our barren hills like sculpted sheep, the smell of wood smoke, the ruby color of wine held to the natural light, the white pigeon drawn to the spit even as he becomes aroused on the rim of the fountain —surely there is no eroticism to match the landscape of spent passion. There is nothing like an empty grave to betray the presence of a dead king in all his lechery. The blasted tree contains its heart of amber, you can smell the wild roses in the sterile crevices of ancient cliffs, suddenly you find the whitened limb of a tree sleeved in green. Yes, ours is a landscape of indifferent hunters and vanished lovers, *cher ami*, so that but to exist on such a terrain, aware of blood and manure, of the little paper sacks of poison placed side by side with bowls of flowers on the window ledges of each village street, or aware of the unshaven faces of our local pharmacists or of the untended pubescence of the girls who work in our markets and confess their fantasies in our darkened churches—yes, simply to exist in such a world is to be filled with a pessimism indistinguishable from the most obvious state of sexual excitation. I am a city person and not without my own form of pragmatism. And yet whenever I have seen from the window of this very car a glimpse of a distant woodland, I have thought of the royal hunting party mounted and in pursuit of a fevered stag, and thought of the sound of the horns, the lovers in that boisterous army, pretty and plumed, flushed and separated on their tossing horses but riding only in wait for the day of the chase to give way to the night of the tryst, when the mouth that took the brazen hunting horn by day will take the elegant and ready flesh by night. Yes, we who are the gourmets and amateur excavators of our cultural heritage know in our cars, our railway trains, our pretentious establishments of business, that we have only to pause an instant in order to unearth the plump bird seasoning on the end of its slender cord tied to a rafter, or a fat white regal chamber pot glazed with the pastel images of decorous lovers, or a cracked and dusty leather boot into which some young lewd and brawny peasant once vomited.

Yes, dead passion is the most satisfying, *cher ami.* You have hinted as much in your verses. But no wonder I have always thought of Honorine as mistress of a small chateau and nude beneath a severe black hunting costume for riding sidesaddle, though she has never been on a horse in her life. And you can imagine my pleasure when Honorine did in fact inherit from her mother, that noble woman, the small chateau which I myself named Tara and which you and I have filled with the deadest of all possible passion. You don't agree? You disclaim anything but vitality and tenderness in your relations with Chantal and Honorine? Then perhaps it is only my own passion that is so very dead, *cher ami.*

But the owl is watching us. And look there. Rain. Just as I expected. Soon the invisible camera will be trained on us through the wet and distorting lens of our windshield.

But I too once had a mistress. You did not know? Well, I hope that despite all you have been told about the power of your sullen allure you do not consider yourself the only person to have received the gift of love as seen through the prism, as I may call it, of another woman, though it is true that my own experience was confined to a single mistress and not to a pair. Never in my lifetime would I have contemplated a pair of mistresses. I am one of those lesser and hence more limited men, as you well know.

But little Monique was quite enough for me at the time. At the beginning of our friendship she was only a few weeks into her twentieth year, which, come to think of it, was exactly Chantal's age when you, in all your mysterious naturalness and unconcern, determined to extend to her the love of the poet, if you will indulge the expression. Then too, Monique was a shade smaller even than Chantal, a fact I take to mean not that I was trying to duplicate my daughter in my mistress but simply that I was lucky enough to win Monique with a single glance and that she was the smallest person with whom I ever shared what she used to call the dialogue of the skin. Her size was important to me not because it mimed specifically the small size of Chantal and Chantal's lovely grandmother, but only because it bore out so perfectly an idea that has obsessed me since earliest manhood: that the smaller the woman one regards the greater one's amazement at the vastness, fierceness, of the human will.

So Monique was remarkable, then, for her startling size, the utter harmony of her physical proportions, the immensity and even dangerous quality of her will. Her self-assertiveness was staggering. Of course she never failed to obey me, and yet even when she conformed to my simplest suggestion (about what to eat, what not to eat, some article of clothing, and so forth) she did so with beautiful vehemence, as if she were acting on her own prideful volition instead of mine. But never fear, she gave as good as she received.

If I loved Monique for her size, I loved her equally for the nature of her skin and its complexion. Tight, painfully and wonderfully tight over the entirety of her little face and limbs and torso, so thin and tight that actually I used to fear the consequences of a slip of the threaded needle. And of course her skin was white, almost glazed, in fact, and whiter even than Honorine's fair skin. And you know that my predilection for whiteness is just as intense as my appreciation of the Mediterranean hues.

Short skirts, short hair, bright blue lacquered shoes, occasionally a blouse tastefully crocheted, and the inevitable silk stockings as if always to confirm her threatened womanhood —I can still see her, one of the most inventive girls and strongest human beings I have ever known. I used to meet her twice a month on a schedule so strict that it did not vary more than several minutes from one occasion to the next. We were equally intolerant of lateness, though the flowers I carried and the luxury of the car I drove always gave me the advantage in these matters of time and demonstrations of anger. But we enjoyed each other's anger, and vied with each other in the creation of embarrassing public displays of bad temper. It was as if we shared between us an unspoken agreement to parody the lovers' quarrel, the domestic disagreement, whenever possible. Yes, even now it gives me oddly pleasurable satisfaction to recall how often I submitted to the insults she shouted at me on the most crowded of street corners (in the sun, in the rain, in the darkness after a splendid meal), and how she in her turn bore with quivering fury the disciplinary blows I so often inflicted with the edge of my heavy fork on her fragile wrist, usually under the eager eyes of an old waiter in the most elegant of restaurants. But as I say, it is a familiar and convenient pattern, this happy ritual of disruption and reconciliation. We relied on it totally, Monique and I.

At any rate Monique was proud, opinionated, hostile, inventive. It never failed to delight me that she could be so cruel of tongue, so vicious, or that a chest as small as hers was capable of such heavy breathing, or that she could become so quickly subdued and smaller than ever once seated in the rich interior of my powerful and highly polished car. But let me tell you that this Monique, whose youth and personality were so impressive, nonetheless and of her own free choice was the living example of all the uninhibited nudes I courted in the pornographic magazines of my own late and isolated boyhood. Not only was she a natural actress in the theater of sex, not only did she become in her mind and body the very flesh and activity of all those distant uncountable images of mine, but on top of everything else she collected in her small overfurnished rooms every conceivable kind of pornographic or erotic book, magazine, photograph that she was able to discover in our museums, kiosks, bookstalls, establishments devoted to the equipment and stimulation of the sexual drive. She lived her very life in unwitting competition with that rare photographic study which I prepared over the years of Honorine's own erotic womanhood. But Monique's performances were cruder, much cruder, than my study of Honorine. And at times they suddenly revealed my young friend's sense of humor, whereas there was no place for humor in my nude or partially nude views of Honorine.

Quick to take offense, quick to become aroused, quick to laugh at herself and at such exaggerated sexual animation in one so small—there we have our tireless Monique, who thrived on her pornography old and new and liked nothing better than to adorn her own little nude figure in the outlandish black lingerie of those ladies of the boas who in another era so incensed our forefathers. Yes, she collected and wore all those belts and harnesses and spangled black stockings as avidly as she immersed herself in her books and magazines. And do you know, *cher ami*, she had a palate that demanded only the finest of white wines. Only the finest.

But then there came at last that warm spring night when, suddenly inspired, I spanked Monique. It was not entirely my fault, and it was the only time in my life when I fell so close to being the sadistic villain lurking everywhere in the stories, photographs and fantasies of my little mistress. You will agree that no one wants to find himself becoming nothing more than a familiar type created by a hasty and untalented pornographer. We do not like to think of ourselves as imaginary, salacious and merely one of the ciphers in the bestial horde, to put it somewhat strongly, *cher ami*. But it was not totally my fault, as I must repeat, since the night was rainy and since the hour was late and since there was provocation, a provocation I did not even think to resist.

Well, you have the picture: spring rain, the city sleeping in its tile and stones, a wash of faint light from a bulb in a rose-colored shade, the warm little room smelling of the new season and of the oil of peach seeds with which Monique had scented her hot douche, and of course the two of us lying nude among the bolsters (except for Monique, who was wearing one of her scanty black harnesses known in the parlance of our grand temptresses as a garter belt). There you have it: the small, young, nearly naked girl on her stomach, the stockings which she had already removed adrift on the floor, the two of us slowly passing between us a set of large new photographs as rich and stimulating as ripened cheese. It was a scene that might have come directly from the writing desk or cold and shabby studio on one of our poor, dull, unshaven pornographers.

But as I have been saying, I had not the slightest thought of causing Monique even a moment of pain that night; I was not unusually aware of her childish, upturned buttocks twitching occasionally in the rose-colored suffusion from the lamp in the corner; I felt no need to exert any special mastery over Monique amidst the muffling softness of so many tasteless (but appropriate) oriental bolsters. And yet when all at once the moment of provocation was upon me, and in fact it was nothing more than a pouting underlip and some sort of pert, injurious remark quite lost now to passing time, it was then that I knew without any hesitation that I wanted to spank

Monique—and to spank her in the conventional position, with my bare hand, with conscious determination and as hard and as long as possible. Mind you, until that instant I was absolutely uninitiated into that commonplace practice of familial punishment. And yet I did not hesitate, it did not occur to me to spare Monique one trace of humiliation or one grain of pain: I was not interested in justice or the possible sexual consequences of that event. To the contrary, thought and action were as one and I seized Monique abruptly, joyously, and like a vindictive father of long experience pulled my little startled mistress across my naked lap where I held that sprawled and squirming body in a grip that made escape impossible. The pleasure of the first long, deliberate blow was immense. Simply immense.

Well, the palm of my hand was a cruel and relentless paddle. Monique cried out, I gave not a thought to the sleeping neighbors, I spanked Monique with a lack of restraint astonishing even to myself. It was as if I could not bring the flat of my hand into hurtful contact with the soft, private world of her buttocks often enough or hard enough, so that I increased my efforts and gave myself total consciousness of touch and sound and enjoyed to the fullest the agitation of her helplessness. And then breathless, delighted, feeling the heat in my hand and a sparkling sensation throughout my own nakedness, finally I stopped. Only then did she cease resisting. Only then did she go limp, roll slowly away from me, and smother her angry sobs in one of the bolsters. Her weeping was a shameless exploitation of her childlike appearance, but it was an agreeable addition to the pleasure I was then savoring in my exhaustion.

So I myself fell back among the bolsters, surprised at what had happened but smiling, hearing the rain, feeling my own body filled, as it were, with crystals of vigor. Partially on my side and in a condition of curious alertness, peacefully I contemplated the body lying in rare quiescence and with its back to me. Yes, the buttocks were still pink, and pinker yet because of the lampshade. Every now and again a tremor passed down the spine or through one slender leg as if, released from my grip, she was striving now to relieve the discomfort of her small *derrière* by settling her body more deeply into the rolling, Oriental softness. The spare, black, lacy harness was low and loose on her little hips, one of her hands crept back and of its own accord began to rub and soothe the afflicted area. I watched her, I smiled. I did not for a moment think I had done any genuine harm. It even occurred to me, and with reason, that Monique in her sobbing was actually just as expectant as I was in my smiling. Of course by now my great bird, if you will allow the poetic license, was soaring in flight, so that it was only natural that while I watched Monique's small hand moving to pacify the hurt in her buttocks, my own firm hand—the very one with which I had performed what she later called the abomination—became a skilled and willing communicant with my distended sex.

How long we were held together in that wordless state of sexual torpor I do not know. Only the movements of our hands, fingers, suggested that even we two nude luxuriating figures lay under the spell of time. But then Monique herself effected the transition to what would lead, or so I quite wrongly thought, to our embrace. She turned her head and looked at me. One moment I was merely the comfortable *voyeur* who in actuality sees very little, the next I was looking directly into the small, handsome face of my Monique and growing suddenly expansive at the sight of the tears on the cheeks, the wet nose, the familiar, hard, dark scrutiny which I seemed to detect in the filmy eyes. Yes, I felt that now I was performing, so to speak, not merely for myself but for Monique's own attentive contemplation. She was watching me, she was waiting, I thought that in a moment she would creep to my arms.

But how wrong I was. Because even now and betraying not the slightest sign of her intention, Monique was already preparing herself to become like nothing so much as a cat in a sack. She smiled, I felt forgiven. In a spasm of her former childish energy she was on all fours, I rose on an expectant elbow. She leapt to her feet on the floor and struck and held a suggestive pose, I responded with more explicit and vigorous manipulation. She stripped off the little black threatening belt, in eager anticipation I sat up and held out one beckoning arm to her. She raised the belt above her head (rather than tossing it away as I thought she would), and even then I merely exposed myself still further to what I thought was going to be some new form of erotic stimulation. Would you believe it?

Even when I beheld and felt the first lash across my thighs, I thought she meant only to whip me lightly to ejaculation, a process, which, at that moment, I imagined as a fulsome and brilliant novelty. But when I received the second lash, this time across the eyes so that instinctively I covered my face with both my arms, and then received full in the lap the pain of the little metal grips affixed to the tips of those four silken straps, of course I realized that she meant quite the opposite.

Yes, with terrible precision and on an ascending scale of strength and tempo, my little mistress thrashed me on face and lap, chest and lap, until I thought the very possibility of sexual discharge was no longer mine. I groaned, I tasted blood, I cowered. My great bird was dead. And yet throughout the ordeal, while attempting hopelessly to protect myself, still I was somehow admiringly aware of the legs apart, the dark flashing eyes, the vindictive, animated dance of that small, nude girl, the black straps that flew from her fist like the snakes from the head of some tiny and gloriously tormented Medusa. She flayed me. She did so with joy. And even that was not the end of it.

Because when at last she stopped, not from fatigue but from an unbearable excess of exhilaration, she flung the now useless garter belt into the very lap she had but a moment before so fiercely beaten. It was a gesture of superb contempt. But as if that gesture of contempt were not enough, for an instant she looked around the room helplessly, trapped in the passion of her distraction and clear purpose, and then in wickedness and exasperation flung herself down beside me among the bolsters and with the furious fingers of both hands brought herself to an orgasm that would have satisfied even a cat in a sack. At least it satisfied Monique. In my defeat and discomfort I too felt a certain relief, a certain happiness for Monique, and if in the midst of helplessness and pain I had nonetheless been able to photograph her benign expression, surely I would have set up the tripod, triggered the blinding light. As it was I merely gave myself to the sound of the rain and finally, on all fours, made my way to my clothes.

Well, it was an instructive night, as you can see. An hour, two hours, and as from nothing a new bond of accord was suddenly drawn between Monique and myself. I learned that I too had a sadistic capacity and that the commiseration of Honorine was even vaster and sweeter than I had thought. But what is still most important about that particular and now long-lost night is that it reveals that I too have suffered and that I am not always in total mastery of the life I create, as I have been accused of being. Furthermore it illustrates that I am indeed a specialist on the subject of dead passion. At any rate, and for better or worse, I abandoned Monique when you entered our household. Somehow your presence made Monique's unnecessary. But of course there are moments, such as this one, when she still dances inside my head with a vividness quite comparable to that of the life enclosed within our own small world which is moving—need I say it?—with the speed and elasticity of the panther in full chase.

I am always moving. I am forever transporting myself somewhere else. I am never exactly where I am. Tonight, for instance, we are traveling one road but also many, as if we cannot take a single step without discovering five of our own footprints already ahead of us. According to Honorine this is my other greatest failing or most dangerous quality, this propensity of mine toward total coherence, which leads me to see in one face the configurations of yet another, or to enter rose-scented rooms three at a time, or to live so closely to the edge of likenesses as to be eating the fruit, so to speak, while growing it. In this sense there is nowhere I have not been, nothing I have not already done, no person I have not known before. But then of course we have the corollary, so that everything known to me remains unknown, so that my own footfalls sound like those of a stranger, while the corridor to the lavatory off my bedroom suddenly becomes the labyrinthine way to a dungeon. For me the familiar and unfamiliar lie everywhere together, like two enormous faces back to back. I am always seeing the man in the child, the child in the grown man. Winter is my time of flowers, I am a resigned but spirited voyager. Of course the whole thing is only a kind of psychic slippage, an interesting trick of *déjà vu*, although Honorine insists that it is a form of mystical insight. She is inclined to idealize me in her own reasonable and admirable fashion. But then I must add that at certain times she has found my mental disappearances, as she calls them, not merely disconcerting but fearful. And yet I have never given Honorine literal cause for anxiety, I can promise you that. She will be the last to propose any ready answers when she learns what has become of us tonight.

But no doubt I have been meaning to say that every more or less privileged person contains within himself the seed of the poet, so that the wife of each such individual wants nothing more than to be a poet's mistress. In this respect Honorine has been especially fortunate.

The Martyr of La Violaine

from THE PASSION ARTIST (1979)

My mid-life crisis, as they call it, has been no mere single convulsion for a while paralyzing the spirit around the age of forty or fifty (when the ax falls, according to a friend), but has been a continuing presence, a mildly menacing condition that has lasted for the thirty or so years since my early manhood, or so it seems. And yet I did experience, just once, the full flowering of depression. We were again in Vence for a year free for the writing of fiction. Our French friends feasted us on Provençal rabbit; the hills were yellow with genêt, the heady blossom that Henry Plantagenet always wore on his hat. But I was in the grip of a dark surging, for no reason that I knew of, and saw the clear light of the Côte d'Azur as dulled through the waves of my own misery. I could not eat the rabbit, took no walks, could not bear to listen to the soft sounds coming from the dovecote.

Whenever I entered our house I thought that I saw my father's coffin propped in front of the cold hearth on one of those sinister contraptions that are usually found standing incongruously upright in the dark corners of small churches everywhere in Europe. I had this vision even though both my parents had died by then and were buried in a lovely little town in Maine. Each morning I sat benumbed and mindless at a small table of polished cherry wood. Each morning Sophie left a fresh rose on my table, but even these talismans of love and encouragement did no good. All was hopeless, writing was out of the question.

Then there came an invitation for lunch in town and Sophie insisted that we accept it. Our hostess, a vivacious Frenchwoman, tried to cheer me up with a lively bit of gossip about a middle-aged man who went one day to pick up his young daughter at a school in Nice, only to discover accidentally from one of the child's

· 233 ·

classmates that his daughter was an energetically active prostitute already gone, that day, from the playground to a sexual assignation. I listened to that story, drank a glass of wine, and saw myself walking jauntily toward a lone girl and some empty swings. Our friend's anecdote about the disillusioned father prompted two more essential associations. I remembered one of my own father's stories of how, as a young member of the Connecticut National Guard, he had volunteered to help quell a riot in a woman's prison, and I thought that in this story I had the plot of a novel. Then I recalled a Marxist critic whom I had encountered at a conference on the novel at a small college in the Middle West. When this critic scorned works of the imagination as degenerate, I commented that he really belonged at some other conference, perhaps one on problems in social science. Thereupon an irate and self-righteous young faculty member leapt to his feet from the audience and demanded that I apologize to the Marxist critic. I, who could not bear rejection of any kind and had for a lifetime depended on approval bestowed on me by Sophie and two or three close friends, was forced to apologize there and then in a packed auditorium to a white-faced devil who hated fiction. In Vence, at my table overlooking our grape arbor, the memory of my humiliation smoked and fumed around me until suddenly I knew that if I could invent my most loathesome male character to date, I would have my protagonist. So the shattering of my fragile vanity on the campus of that small mid-western college gave me, finally, Konrad Vost, who is just as appalling as I wanted him to be.

The Passion Artist is set in an imaginary central European city whose life revolves around its prison for women called La Violaine. The prison lends its name to the café across the street where the relatives of inmates gather to be close to wives, daughters, sweethearts, mothers. One of the frequenters of La Violaine the café is Konrad Vost, who grieves for his dead wife, Claire, and maintains a sterile home for his schoolgirl daughter Mirabelle. He awaits the release of his aged mother who has been incarcerated in La Violaine the prison since Konrad Vost's childhood, when she murdered his ineffectual father. Konrad Vost learns that Mirabelle is a prostitute, has sex with one of her young friends, then denounces his daughter to the police. When a riot breaks out in La Violaine, he becomes one of the force of volunteer policemen, which also includes one Spapa, attempting to subdue the women inmates. However, the valiant women drive out the police, take over the prison, and eventually capture Konrad Vost in a swampy marsh beyond the city. When Konrad Vost is returned as a hostage to La Violaine, he meets his mother at last, and before his death is introduced to the beauties of sexual love by her closest friend.

The "martyr" of La Violaine is a young woman whom Konrad Vost has brutally beaten in the prison yard. In the following pages, Vost comes across her bathing in a millpool in the swamp, spies on her, and causes her death.

The Martyr of La Violaine

A bright red dragonfly on a half-sunken post, the claw of the small yellow earth remover clutching the air, the rusted treads of the abandoned machine resting partially on the torn soil and partially in a pool of clear sun-filled water, his thin black shoes appropriate only to city streets but already bespattered with the mud of the marsh: thus he paused in that area of contested desolation where both marsh and city met, faltered, struggled, flowed and ebbed in the rhythm of natural infestation. For all his walking, he had never before stood exactly here, though the yellow machine was a familiar monster and the dragonfly, its transparency gleaming with the color of blood, was catching the light and quivering as if adorning not the rotted edge of the tilted post but the black surface of the back of his gloved hand. Never had he stood beneath such a distant sun; in the brightness of the ferns at his feet he saw only the strangeness of vegetation that grows in the wake of a holocaust, while in the shell of the small upturned automobile that lay nearby in a bed of silt he recognized the remains of the vehicle Claire had spent her life desiring. Everything was here and nothing. A wire dangling from the iron claw contained the power of electrocution; an empty concrete conduit emerging from a lip of clay had been meant for sewage; a black shoe cupped in a clump of marsh grass might have been his own. With every breath he smelled the salty fetid smell of air that is always fresh, never confined, always stagnant, forever drifting in random currents between layers of water, layers of light. He stared at the marsh that receded in all directions like an immense pebbled sheet of purple glass. He could see nothing of hut, barn, haystack, cluster of young naked trees, yet these too were embedded in the distant glass. Konrad Vost was alone and unable to move in a landscape without shape or meaning, belonging to neither city nor countryside: it was worse than bearing his disfigurement through the dawn streets and indifferent crowds. For him there was only sun, emptiness, the smell of salt and putrefaction.

But then the air around him, vagrant, powerful, cut adrift from tides, earth, light, shifted its fetid currents and brushed aside the grass, rolled aside the still marsh water, and exposed momentarily what otherwise he could not have seen: the curling iron rails of some anomalous narrow-gauge railway track long ago destroyed and long unused, long buried in the flat and shifting marsh. Through the parted grass and water shone the deep orange light of the bent and splintered rails that now consisted of nothing except the splendor of rust which even while he watched was flaking, burning, as the iron itself continued its slow process of disintegration in the light of the sun. But a severed train track across an empty marsh? Rails and bonelike ties rising into sight from beneath blankets of sand, sludge, drifting water? He shaded his eyes and smiled. The sight before his eyes was unaccountable, but suddenly he remembered Claire and understood what previously he had merely feared: the unaccountable is the only key to inner life, past life, future life. From the silence of the purple distance came the rattle of couplings, the sound of gunfire, the chugging of a locomotive that did not exist. Air, rust, water, grass: had he not once ridden a train on these very tracks? And hidden himself in village streets now buried beneath the city streets at his back? He listened. Here, now, alone at the edge of a marsh, suddenly he knew that he had once been a child in flight. The sounds of the locomotive were coming no closer. But he was comforted.

He nodded to himself, compressed his lips, and without

hesitation stepped into the water that lay between the shelf of mud where he stood and the section of railway track, once again hidden beneath the water, behind the grass. The tracks were gone but he had seen them; they were there, for his own use if not for the use of any actual train.

The water rose to midcalf and, as he could not have expected, was as cold as a blade. It dragged at his trousers, he felt the mask of his face reflecting the shock in his legs. The water eddied away from him as he pushed on toward the brackish spot where he had seen the tracks. Silt, water, algae clogged his shoes, his socks, his trouser bottoms, his nakedness. He would never again be dry or free of the dead smell of the marsh. But what did it matter? The inner landscape had become externalized. He would cross it with the ruthlessness of a police patrol following leashed dogs.

At precisely the moment when the smell of natural decay and artificial decay was strongest, and when behind him the dragonfly quit the safety of the rotten post and disappeared, leaving in its place only a droplet of shimmering water, then simultaneously he found his footing and climbed aching and dripping onto the all but concealed bed of ancient tracks. Again he shaded his eyes, waited, felt the water descending his calves inside the trousers now heavy and shapeless from his wading. The horizon was empty. He knew that he was becoming more gaunt than ever; he knew that behind the steel shutter of La Violaine, the shutter that was still down and would remain so until calm was again restored to the prison across the street, the silent figures of those men loyal to the rebelling women were gathered already for morning coffee or beer. He knew also that there was no longer a chair for Konrad Vost in the closeness and darkness of the café. So much the better, he told himself, and started off down the tracks that led, apparently, to the deepest easterly recesses of the marsh.

The tracks had been constructed on a roadbed nearly level with the deceptive surface of the marsh, so that occasionally he found himself again walking through sheets of water. Now he was totally exposed to the sun and was, he knew, an all too visible target to anyone lying prone and watching him from no matter how great a distance out there in the purple or deep green spaces; now he was well hidden behind walls of yellow and undulating grasses that rose higher than his head and whispered like thin blades sharpening each other. As he progressed, stumbling and adjusting his stride to the ties, it became increasingly apparent that the marsh was not merely flat. Shallow ponds concealed the wide mouths of wells that dropped downward for immeasurable distances; stands of pale trees suddenly sprang up from the mud; he could see the vestiges of an immense canal undulating through ribs of sand; off to his right lay a geometric arrangement of wet stones where primitive buildings, long since dissolved, had sheltered both men and animals. More fence posts, the rotten ribs and backbone of a small boat, brightly colored marsh plants festering in sockets of ice, the fragments of a shattered aqueduct gray and dripping where moments before there had been only flatness and emptiness, abrupt discolorations that revealed quicksand or underground rivers: it was all an agglomeration of flashing mirrors, the strong cold salty air was impossibly heavy with the smell of human excrement and of human bodies armed and booted and decomposing under the ferns, behind piles of rocks, in the depths of the wells. Had it once been a landscape of nighttime skirmishing? Was it then the terrain of at least some kind of history? At any moment an iron ship might loom before him, or the vast trench of a communal grave.

He stopped, wiped his face, looked back in the direction from which he had come: the city was now only the faintest line of little concrete teeth littering the horizon. Soon when he turned again to look there would be nothing. He felt as if he were walking on the crushed or broken bones of the world's dead. His shoes, socks, lower trousers were still damp and dripping; his upper body was growing warm in the sun. When he again paused and looked backward down the length of track at the distance he had already come, the city was gone.

Not a bird. Not a scurrying animal. Not a fish to leave bubbles or ripples on the clear or purple glass of the water. No insects. Nothing but the light, the swollen breath of life in decay, the muddy plains and fissures of the deceptive topography.

Toward midmorning he heard the unmistakable sounds of men's voices. Later, before he had time even to conceal himself within the shelter of a growth of high yellow grasses rising suddenly on his left side, he watched as three men, who were wearing the familiar kepis and dark blue uniforms and carrying weapons hung from straps on their shoulders, passed in single file across the line of his vision far down the tracks. In another moment they were gone, these representatives of the Prefecture of Police, disappearing abruptly as if into a tilted mirror. But he had seen them. He was not alone in searching the marsh. Again circumstance had borne him out, again he had been proven correct: where else to hunt down the fugitives of La Violaine except in the marsh? Still later, from a different direction, came the faint snarling of brutal dogs baring their teeth and straining on their leashes of black leather. Then again there was silence, with only the sounds of his own breathing and walking to scratch in his ears.

How long it had taken for the sun to climb directly overhead he did not know. But the hour of cessation had arrived; the light of the marsh was stronger, more evenly diffused than ever, as if it could not possibly intensify or fade; and in this hour of midpoint he felt suddenly safe, disarmed, stiff and fatigued from his walking, curiously freed from the purpose that at dawn had impelled him to enter the muddy, crystalline, uncertain reaches of the marsh. He rested, sitting on the edge of the track with one knee drawn up and the black hand lying inert at his side. He was on top of a low embankment from which he could see on an island of black soil a stone hut oddly intact, a threadlike road that might have been made with the tip of a finger, a long glassy stretch as of the sea. He clasped his raised knee with his active hand; he was conscious of the breath of decay that was in his clothing and the pores of his skin; he was at peace with the incongruity between himself and all this low wilderness. In face, neck, arms, chest, his muscles and tendons were slackening, coming to rest. The smell in his nostrils was like that of a naked human shoulder green with mold. He felt himself in a waking sleep, suspended between clear sight and silence: this was the landscape that had swallowed legions; everything and nothing lay at his feet. It was then that he heard the one sound that even he, in all this wet or spongy vastness, could not have anticipated: laughter, the shrill tones of what could only be an old woman in the grip of laughter. He listened, he held his breath. For the first time since leaving the hospital he was on his guard. The pleasures of the high sun had evaporated. In this place what could be more alarming than the sound of an old woman's laughter?

Carefully, propping himself on his left hand, disengaging his right from a circlet of thorns that had sprung up beside the rails, slowly and quietly he descended the embankment and entrusted himself to the shadows and sudden light of a thicket he had failed to notice from his vantage point above. The earth was silent beneath the wet soles of his shoes. He moved between the slender white trees with all the stealth he could summon, and despite fear and urgency he was entirely conscious of how the tall young trees dispersed and focused the light so that now, all at once, the thicket was warm and filled with star-shaped patterns of bright flashing light. Again came the sound of the laughter, high-pitched, close, trembling with the broken music of an old woman long confined among other old and laughing women. He knew without thinking that it was a sound to fear, that loud sounds of unreasonable pleasure were not to be enjoyed vicariously but to be feared. But he could not have imagined that within this thicket of flowering warmth and whitened light he himself could be so violent.

Her back was to him in the narrow clearing, and yet he recognized her at once. Despite the deceptive clothing, the black gown and, on the head, the black shawl holding the hair, still he recognized at once the same old woman who, from her barred window, had stared down happily at the chaos of men and women in the yard below. Now she was laughing to herself, without reason, here in the gentleness of shadows and light, as if she were not one of those condemned long ago to La Violaine.

He reached the small black figure in a single stride; she turned; the astonished face was staring up at his own. Now they were so close together, he and the old woman, that they could have clutched each other's clothing with angry hands, and though she was bent and though her face was far below his shoulder, still it was shockingly upturned toward his own in one of the brightest rays of light to pierce the leaves overhead, so that every feature was thrust upon his consciousness and sealed there in heat and light. He and the old woman were stock still, he tall and at the mercy of his fury, she bent and twisted in her attitude of vanished laughter. The two of them might have been about to embrace or to grapple together in unequal contest there in the new growth of trees. Within easy reach the ancient face was turned up to his own and brought alive, though unmoving, by the focused light. He

stared down at the warmly tinted expression of fear and
surprise, and there could be no question of identity: it was
she, the old woman who had savored the chaos of La
Violaine as a private spectacle. The open mouth with its three
amber-colored teeth and the breath of a great age, the small
twisted ears that appeared to have been sewn to the sides of
the skull with coarse thread, the skin that was shriveled
tightly to the bone beneath and cured in sun and salt until the
wrinkles were deep and permanent, the soft facial hair that
flowered around the lips and on the cheeks like a parody of a
bristling beard, and above all the yellow eyes, which alone
reflected the ageless crafty spirit in a face that otherwise was
only a small torn mask of leather: these were the elements that
made his recognition a matter of certainty, and that inspired
in him a rage which, even to him, bubbled and frothed in
excess of what the emotion, the time, the place or the old
woman herself might have justified. But the very texture of
her age affronted him, as did the cleverness that burned so
youthfully in the yellow eyes of someone who should have
been confined to an iron bed or rickety chair in a prison for
women. He was appalled by her disguise, her freedom; he
was infuriated that someone so old was still a woman. But in
this instant, when warmth and speckled light cushioned the
proximity of gaunt bony man and shrunken woman, suddenly
he understood that the old creature's eyes were telling him
that she knew full well that in her he despised the pretty bud
that has turned to worms.

When he raised his arm he had no intention of letting it fall.
He had not even meant to lift his arm, but when he felt his
right arm moving upward and backward until it was higher
than his head, he did so in the knowledge that he intended
only to frighten the old woman, nothing more. Yet he too
was shocked at the length and breadth of the gesture that
carried the arm that had been inert at his side to the top of its

arc so that the black hand was poised at its summit, prepared with greatest strength to strike its blow or fling a great weight to the ground. In the extremity of his vision he had seen the upward passage of the black hand, and when it was no longer in sight, raised at arm's length above and behind his head, still he saw the uplifted hand as did the old woman: black, clawlike, murderous, some interminably heavy and destructive weapon that would travel at a great speed down the terrible distance from its place in the air to her own small weightless self, at which the blow was aimed. But he intended none of it. He did not in fact swing down his arm.

For the old woman, however, it was otherwise. Before he could move and while the black hand was quivering high in the air, at that very moment she must have felt that the black hand would fall and must have felt the inevitable rush of air and the breathless pitiless impact of the blow itself. In that instant his own body was as unwieldy as an awkwardly drawn bow; his black hand was still in the air; he stared down and in disbelief as the old woman's eyes squeezed shut and the face gradually changed its expression from fear to girlish supplication to the pinched and luminous grimace she had saved for her doom. Death lit up the old woman's face as from within. She dropped at his feet.

Slowly he lowered the black offending hand to its place at his side. He heard a voice shouting and noticed, a short distance beyond where the dead woman lay, a great pile of fagots tied with a rope. He could not move, his scalp was bristling, he felt as drained of blood as was the small deflated body in its heap of rags. Obviously the old woman had been carrying the fagots on the little saddle of her bent back; obviously in this sunny spot she had decided for no reason to throw down her burden meant for the hearth. It was for this that she had been laughing to herself in the speckled light. Now the querulous voice was calling; now he felt as if he had been seized from behind by powerful bare arms locked around his waist. He thought of himself as that Konrad Vost who had again been wrong. He turned and fled.

For Konrad Vost, he told himself, the world was now in a constant state of metamorphosis, duplication, multiplication; figures deserving existence only within the limits of the dream now sprang alive; the object of least significance was inspired with its secret animation; no longer was there such a thing as personal safety; in every direction there rose the bars of the cage. What could be worse?

He gained the tracks and immediately, without wiping his face or glancing backward and downward toward the tranquil stand of trees where he himself had committed an act that had erupted only from his own contemptible imagination, and without waiting for a glimpse of the old man who was now discovering the sack of rags in the clearing, he broke into a clumsy run which defied his characteristic bearing and which he was able to sustain until his pained chest brought him again to a walk. He forced himself along, despite shortness of breath, the swinging arm, the clamminess of his legs and feet. As he hurried down the lengthening tracks, not in flight from evildoing, as he reminded himself, but only in pursuit of legitimate or even heroic ends, still he formulated what he had learned in the grove of laughter: that whatever his own previous misconceptions, nonetheless age never obliterates entirely the streaks and smears of masculine or feminine definition. Never.

He longed for water. Slowing his pace but walking on, he found it ironic that he who was making his lonely and treacherous way across a marsh, which was nothing if not the residence of a retiring sea, that in such a place a man as determined as himself should suddenly be compulsively concerned with drinking cold cups of water, immersing himself in water, when there was none. The hut where the old woman had lived with the querulous man would have had its well, its ladle, its ancient bucket on a length of dripping chain; even here, now, the light through which he moved was like a bright clear fluid which he could almost cup in his hands and drink. But it was light, not water, and for some reason the vista now surrounding him was dry, murky, muddy, barren, without any trace of water that might cleanse him, quench his thirst.

Now the light was changing, the mirrors were tilting, the tracks were lying exactly at sea level, and now the light that had so filled his eyes was spread in a miragelike sheet of water across the entire landscape, which, before, had consisted merely of parched grass or mud. The level of the roadbed so perfectly matched the level of the surrounding water that now the way of his journey appeared to be carrying him through the water itself.

Again it was a sound that brought him to a dead standstill in the midst of the emptiness. Suddenly his perspiration disappeared in a cool breath; the brightness of the light diminished to normal intensity; the air became clear; the mirrors of the marsh were again adjusted so as to be conducive to the ordinary sight of his eyes: still water, islets of crab grass and, to the left, a frieze of tall thin pale green trees aligned exactly parallel to the rusted tracks which lay now like broken lines of fire across the water. Behind the trees something was wetly gleaming. But also, and more important, the sound he was still listening to was coming from behind the trees.

Small but unmistakable, it was the sound of splashing. It reached him faintly, musically, yet without rhythm, like a bell deliberately tinkled to destroy rhythm and prevent anticipation. Again it came to him, the sound of water disturbed, water tossed into the air, water set randomly and sweetly in motion behind the trees. But dare he risk again leaving the solidity of the tracks? There was no way of knowing, for instance, the depth of the water between himself and the tall green trees that were spaced evenly and closely together like the stakes of a fragment of a gigantic fence. Yet here, after all, was the substance of what he himself had been desiring: the calmness of green trees, the freshness of water.

Abruptly and with a few awkward movements he hid his right hand from view in his suit coat pocket, attempted to judge the distance between himself and the trees, and then decisively and silently entrusted himself to the flat water. He felt as if he were gliding toward the screen of trees; underfoot there was firmness, the water rose only to his midshins. The splashing sounds drew closer, the structure behind the trees was brightly shimmering. The trees appeared to be clothed in pale green skin and, as he approached them in haste and silence, revealed the webbing of white vines that, never climbing more than a meter from the water's surface, laced the trees together trunk to trunk. His thirst was intolerable, he was surprised at his eagerness to see beyond the trees which, he knew full well, were watery replicas of those other trees, which had proven to be a grove of death.

He stooped, held his breath, with his left hand seized the green thinness of the nearest tree, and then bracing the side of his head against the tree, and crouching like a phantom in the still water, he stared at the spectacle that some master stroke had surely fashioned only to feed the needs of his own psychological function in this instant of suspended time. The crumbling remains of the old mill, for such was the structure that had gleamed through the trees, consisted of a high partial wall of jagged and blackened stones and a great iron wheel rusted into the antithesis of motion, and stood before him at a small distance like a dripping theatrical backdrop before which a single young naked woman was enjoying the water. The enormous wheel could not turn, could no longer bear water to the top of its arc, and the air itself was a dry transparency, and yet both wheel and wall were, on all their surfaces, totally and freshly wet as if from some invisible but constantly replenished deluge of clear water.

But the small young naked woman? This childlike creature quite unaware of the dripping ruin which, behind her back, could only exaggerate her nakedness, her small size, her dripping skin? But even in the first glimpse he knew conclusively that she who was now splashing herself in the pleasure of natural privacy was the selfsame person whom he and Spapa had beaten into unconsciousness in La Violaine. He could not be mistaken: the very bruises that blurred his own elation in a flash of shame gave absolute identity to the young woman who had in fact survived the combat in the prison only to experience now the privilege of being herself in her skin. The black and blue welts were all too visible, the eye puffed shut gave him a stab of pain, in particular he recoiled from a star-shaped bruise on the little haunch. She was disfigured, more so than he, and on her body bore the livid signs of his own righteousness. But her beauty remained: the freely hanging dark hair, the sun-darkened tan and pink complexion of the wet skin, the shocking symmetry of a body so small that in its childlike proportions it exceeded the beauty of the life-sized woman it was intended to represent: in all this his powers of recognition were even more confirmed than in the physical evidence of her injuries, the sight of which so offended, suddenly, his proud and sentimental eye.

She was facing him, she was close enough so that he could study as if in the magnification of a large and rapturous lens the eye that was open, the scarred stomach he could have contained in his hand now clinging to the tree, the naked breasts which had somehow escaped the damage inflicted by Spapa's brutal stick and his own. Facing him, in the water that reached above her knees, and in silence, without either song or laughter, merely reaching down and splashing her hands against the water or scooping it up and allowing it to trickle on the shining hair, the oval face, the waist where the skin was tightening in the exertions of her self-absorption, on the wet thighs that, together, preserved her modesty. As for himself, surely he who had beaten her on head and body could now be allowed to spy on her innocent nudity; after the first violation, peering at her through green trees was nothing. So he watched as the hands fluttered, as a knee rose, as one thigh crossed the other, as the shoulders dipped, as the muscles played beneath the skin about the navel, as the water flew from the fingertips and the mouth smiled. Alone, turning toward him her diminutive naked profile with its curves freshly dipped in light, it was she who imparted to the sinister ruins behind her back a lifelike pastoral completion. The wheel might have been steadily revolving, the water might have been coursing in its productive fall, the grain might have been gathering in its stone bowl, while on the other side of the building the old men might have been lounging among their waiting donkeys, unaware of her who, naked in the millpond, was causing the wheel to turn, the grain to flow.

Not once did he blink. Standing fully clothed in the same water in which her nakedness was flowering, now he was suddenly aware that the object of his spying had turned her back to him and was bending down to stir the waters. The sight of her body bent down from the waist in precocious but unconscious self-display destroyed in the instant his tranquillity so that loathing the repetition of the sensations that had been aroused in his trousers only days before, and determined to preserve in his mind the vision of the bather, he loosened his hold on the tree, turned away reluctantly from his secret view of the pond, and crouching, silent, stealthy, waded back across the water to the dry tracks.

He paused once to hear again the splashing. He noted that

his thirst was quenched. He told himself that he could not have harmed her person for a second time or dared to interrupt her bright bare immersion in air and water. Abruptly he set forth again and the sounds of splashing faded, his own unwanted sensations faded, while only the vision of honey, light, water and dark hair remained. He could not have been more soiled in his dress, or in his blood, his bones, his tissues, and yet he carried with him the clear indestructible sight and, despite discomfort and weariness, was now increasingly animated by self-satisfaction: he had looked at her, but he had not harmed her.

If he had known the identity of the little martyr of La Violaine, as he soon came to think of her, he would have suddenly understood his own death the day it arrived; and if he had not allowed himself to be consumed by the vision of the bather he had spied on through the green trees, he in turn might have prevented her martyrdom.

As it was, he walked with a fierce exhausted pleasure, he walked while bearing the entire millpond inside his head, he had eyes only for the nudity of her whom he had spared, he towered and staggered along bemused and unaware of the dangerous tracks and making no effort to recall his dream: he who knew better and should have concentrated on the path of his journey. But it was of course too late.

The snarling of the black dog destroyed the vision as swiftly as the fangs of the beast would have seized his thigh were it not for the leash. The terrible lean creature lunged at him from no place of hiding that he could see, while the loudness of the weapon being prepared for firing came to him exactly as if the dog had not been snarling but had instead been frothing and straining at the leash in silence. They came from nowhere, the vicious dog and the armed unkempt man wearing the familiar blue uniform and, on his head, the kepi cocked at an arrogant angle. From nowhere, man and dog, yet suddenly his way was obstructed; the muzzle of the gun was aimed at his chest. The beast was straining so fiercely on its leash that its front feet were free of the ground and its snarling jaws were not a hand's length from the center of his own body where lay the living entrails the animal clearly wished to rip and masticate while still steaming in the heat of his blood. As for himself, he fell back from the murderous pair, he raised his left hand in self-defense, in supplication, and managed to restrain himself from flight. He could hear the dog's breath and the guttural wet tones of its lust and hatred; he could hear the creaking of all the wrinkles in the thick uniform of the man who was leaning his weight backward against the pull of the leash wrapped several times about his left wrist and leveling with his right hand the weapon suspended from his shoulder by a leather strap. The stub of a yellow cigarette was caught between the lips, the careless stubble of beard on the coarse face glistened with the exertions of his search through the hot marsh. Even while noting these details he, Vost, was thinking that in a moment or two he would be shot by the man and eaten by the dog.

In shocked and cowering haste he heard the sound of his voice in his rancid mouth: "But I have discovered one of them, there, in the pond behind those trees where she is in the nude. She's alone. She's yours for the taking. . . ."

The silent yellow eyes of the thick man cloaked in his barbarous officialdom stared into his own wide eyes as steadily and ruthlessly as the eyes of the dog. The man said nothing, holding both gun and dog, while the animal continued to choke and gnash its teeth. Perhaps the escapee naked in the millpond was not enough enticement for this man who bore on his body the smell of his dog; perhaps he would take the woman captive and, even so, fire his weapon into the tremulous breast of himself, Konrad Vost. But the image of the naked bather seemed to form at last inside the thickness of the broad cranium; the man in his suspicious but slowly growing interest lowered his gun; he jerked once on the leash and gave the quivering animal an incomprehensible command. Darkly this cruel pair circled around him, where he stood crushed in his shame, and set off toward the screen of trees.

But what had he done? Was it possible? Had he sacrificed the purity of his vision and the freedom of his former victim merely for the sake of his own well-being? Or merely because he had been so taken by surprise by the brute maleness of the man and dog that he had simply collapsed in the stench of their intimidation? But there was no excuse. With a word he had snatched the bather from her clear pond and imprisoned her once more, in some makeshift cell in the city. And who could say to what further mistreatment she, who had already suffered enough, might be subjected by her wordless captor once he had tied the leash to a tree?

It was then that he heard the burst of shots. Not a single shot but several. A sound like the dog snarling. But they were shots from a gun. He heard them, they hung in the air, they faded, he swung wildly around and then, in the stillness of the echo, seeing nothing of trees or man or dog wherever he turned, then in the silence and failing light he stood alone to bear as long as he could his incomprehension, his complete understanding. He did not know what had contrived the terrible correctness of his knowledge. But it was true: he himself had killed the little martyr of La Violaine.

His shoulders sagged, his head was bowed, his grief was centered in the pain of the face he dared not expose to the darkening air. When at last he took his hand from his face, he found that the formerly brilliant light of the marsh had given way not merely to dusk but to fog. Gauzelike, thick, tinted here and there with a wet pinkness, it lay in strips or massive handfuls on the tracks, on the nearby water, between blasted stumps and hummocks of cold grass, covering the entirety of his now subterranean world wherever he looked. Two thoughts came to him at once: that he could not determine which direction led back to the city, or which away from it; and that now the fog was smothering the small naked figure as it drifted, face downward, in the pond. But she too was gone, the millpond was gone, while for himself there was only the sightlessness that resulted from the paradox of the increasing whiteness of the fog and the growing darkness of the approaching night.

An Amorous Bestiary

from VIRGINIE, HER TWO LIVES (1982)

Sophie and I heard about Venasque, which is thirty miles from Avignon, from a writer friend who spoke about that perched village with all the vividness that fills her fiction. We had never lived in a place as small as Venasque, with its population of four hundred, but we had in fact read Laurence Wylie's *Village in the Vaucluse*, an evocative study of the complexities of life in a small French provincial community, and were already predisposed to that part of France. Our friend told us of a house in Venasque that we could rent; we learned that Venasque is only twenty minutes by car from Wylie's village.

As it turned out, Venasque is close to La Coste, where stand the ruins of a chateau made infamous, to those of his time, by the Marquis de Sade; nearby is the ominous and still very much intact chateau of Maussan, to which de Sade, as an unruly child, had been exiled to the care of an uncle. In another direction is La Fontaine de Vaucluse, where Petrarch lived and wrote, faithful to his pure love for Laura. And in still another direction lies Lourmarin where Camus is buried. Further, this is the Provence of the troubadors, lovingly evoked by Ford Madox Ford in his book *Provence*.

When we arrived in Venasque in the fall of 1980, we knew we had come to the end of the line in a long search for vineyards, rude beams, red tiles, Picasso's dancing goats, literary voluptuousness. That year Sophie studied medieval French at a table in an eighteenth-century tiled kitchen and I worked in a little room overlooking the Ventoux (windy mountain) and a valley of scattered villages once walled against the Plague.

Three years earlier, when writing *The Passion Artist*, I had read Michel Leiris's extraordinary work *Manhood: A Journey from Childhood into the Fierce Order of Virility*, as well as a violently erotic short novel by Georges Bataille, *The Story of the Eye*. Also, I had re-read de Sade's *Justine* and had become obsessed with the idea of writing a novel based on the life of de Sade. I thought of his self-sought and undeserved persecution; I was awed by his fixation on the terrible theme of innocence (it is mine too) which is the subject of *Justine* and so much of de Sade's work. But despite the several times I interrupted *The Passion Artist*, I could find no way to make use of de Sade's life and writings in a narrative of my own. However, one afternoon we were walking on the road cut into the cliff that inevitably aroused my vertigo, with all its sensations of thrill and terror, and suddenly I thought of Pygmalion and imagined a seventeenth-century aristocrat who would be known only as Seigneur and who would spend his life transforming women into worthy objects of passion. Seigneur would be an "artist" of love: he would teach a variety of women the art of love. Next I remembered a beautiful little girl who appears in *Travesty* and knew that this child must become Seigneur's Cinderella, his confidante and companion throughout a long series of sadistic, poetic lessons in eroticism. Her innocence, as incorruptible as Justine's, would lie at the center of the story; in Seigneur I would satirize the artist at work. Again, as in *Second Skin*, *The Blood Oranges*, *Travesty*, and *The Passion Artist*, I would attempt to write seriously about the imagination.

So when the time came, Venasque, and not Vence, was the place in which I would hear the voice of my eleven-year-old narrator Virginie. She has two lives, this eager innocent, the first in 1740 (the year of de Sade's birth) and the second in an imaginary Paris, in 1945, where her brother turns their drab apartment into a brothel. It was thanks to "Le Sexe Shoppe," which Sophie and I discovered one afternoon in Avignon, and to the book I impulsively bought there—*Long Live the Bride*, a splendid pornographic story "told" in a series of magnificent color photographs—that I decided that there was indeed a similarity between the pornographer and the lyric poet. Also thanks to *Long Live the Bride*, I thought of the irony of giving little Virginie her second life in Paris. By the end of her story, Virginie dies two deaths: once when she joins Seigneur, who is burned at the stake by a band of his women bent finally on revenge, and a second time in her brother's incestuous embrace in a fire that consumes his brothel.

In "An Amorous Bestiary," one of Seigneur's more willing victims undergoes two initiatory lessons.

An Amorous Bestiary

As the bird cares for its nest so I cared for my hearth. I banked the coals, I swept its vast warm floor with a broom of twigs as long as I was tall, and I shoveled out the ashes with an iron shovel I considered to be my own, stooping and pushing and scraping my shovel like someone tending the hot lair of an unappeasable beast. As for the iron pots great and small that hung from hooks and chains like ranks of bells in a tower, these I removed one by one, systematically, with considerable effort, and scoured inside and out at the stone trough in Adèle's kitchen, and then one by one replaced where each belonged, so that my hearth was always filled with scrubbed iron vessels that I knew by touch as well as sight. My hearth was so large that I could move about within it freely, at will, avoiding the hanging pots and applying to both chains and pots the slightest caress of my fingertips. But mine was not a life confined to the hearth; no one exiled me to sleep in the place where the fire roared and the flames died. I was not a captive relegated to the blackened pit, the lowliest and ugliest and most frightening chamber of the château, since I myself chose to inhabit that enormous hearth. Precisely for the sake of paradox I became the keeper of the vault of fire. The very paradox of child and hearth, small girl and revolving spit, thin creature and arch of stone, was exactly what provided my sense of self and gave me pleasure. Chosen freely, the hot dungeon became for me the cell of my contented solitude, and I wished for no other. Around the hearth I worked for my own amusement; inside the hearth I slept in the warmth and comfort of the forest turned to ashes, the tree to smoke, the ringing ax, the sledge loaded with wet logs, the music of the invisible bird or hidden spring, the charred beef brought to table. Well I knew that all my associations of the hearth signaled, for me, the presence of Seigneur. It was he I tended in sleep or in my waking hours. It was he who was my secret reason for loving the hearth.

Though womanhood was not for me, sometimes I thought that everything Seigneur imparted to Magie and to Finesse, Volupté and Colere and Bel Esprit, he was imparting, actually, to me. Sometimes I thought that I, the child without past or future, was actually the object of his most severe and ardent interest. No wonder I was the constant shadow on his black or roaring hearth. Not a single person could know what I was thinking, not even he. But inevitably my thoughts gave rise to but one word: fidelity. No woman who passed through our château could claim that word. Fidelity.

I awoke quickly, vividly, silently, of my own accord. I shivered as I usually did upon arising, for the dead hearth in the morning never failed to provide me with the brief thrill of all that was gone, and then I crept forth and shook myself, performed my ablutions, and seated on a high stool ate my buttered bread and drank my spring water from the stone crock. The air was cool, the day barely begun, the entire château lay around me like a labyrinth that only I might explore. Straight-backed on my stool, drinking and eating, I experienced a moment of that curious pride when she who is assumed to have no consciousness knows, for one instant, that she herself is the vessel brimming with all the world for whom, this instant, she does not exist. Hence I saw them all in the mirror that was myself: Adèle in her nightcap, Finesse and Colère and Volupté and little Bel Esprit and dear Magie all sleeping unclothed but under heavy sheets in their separate cells that were more austere and more sensuous than I can say, and Père La Tour who would soon be polishing his saddles, and Dédou alone and whimpering in the hay, and of course Seigneur, the first to rise, the last to sleep, now wearing only his ivory-colored breeches so that had the vision been actual and reflected in a real glass, I would not have looked.

I drank, I took a bite of my bread, with my other hand I touched the thick and bloodstained wooden surface, chopped and scarred, of the table that stretched away to my left and right so far that it might have provided fifty horsemen places at which to eat. But I sat alone and in the center of the single ray of light that came down thick and broad, like the blade of a weapon, through the high and vaulted window. Rivers were running within me, I tasted milk and grass. I allowed myself another thought of Seigneur tying the black bows at his knees, and donning his strange collarless and tight-fitting shirt. I saw the dovecote inhabited by cooing birds all of which were white except for a single male, dark purple and preening. I saw the soft nose of Cupidon poking and sniffing above the edge of the door to his stall. There I saw the sundial in the shape of the sun's face on a high sand-colored wall, and there the iron cock of the weathervane pointing in the soft breeze and the real cock strutting in regal loneliness in the cloister. Poplars and cool fields stretched away from us in all directions and it was dawn, I was awake, Seigneur was fully clothed at last. The doves made their sounds of burbling water and wood twisting in wood. I sat in the light and around me lay a labyrinth of light. What was it all if not the very domain of my purity?

But then the still morning erupted into all the fragments of its actuality, and I said good morning to Adèle, noting as usual the sleep in her eyes and the persistence of the little nutlike mole at the edge of her mouth, and carried to Seigneur his black coffee in its large white china cup that was molded inside a second skin of silver, and to each of our five new women I carried dates and bread and coffee and a single flower lying wet and freshly cut on each tray. As I went down the cool corridors of our labyrinth, and tapped on the narrow wooden doors that bore in bas-relief a sheep or sweeping hawk or head of a goat, and bid good morning to Finesse, Colère, Magie, Volupté, or little Bel Esprit, admiring anew each woman now unadorned and barefooted and wearing only the single ankle-length gown of her own color (violet, black, orange, red, and finally white, respectively), as I the morning's envoy went thus from room to room and brought to all of them this beginning of the new day, even then I had in the back of my mind two questions, as I always did: Who shall she be? What shall she be made to do?

I use the word "labyrinth" deliberately. It was Seigneur who taught me long ago the meaning of that word.

So inside the labyrinth I greeted Finesse and Colère and dear Magie and the rest, and carried my trays and collected them, and experienced once again the clarity of my morning perceptions, so that the very veins in the leaves of all the greenery in the enormous stone pots lining the corridors reached my eye as if in magnification, all those tiny veins as hard and sparse as the shining legs of little birds. I saw the sad expression on the face of a porcelain woman in a stone niche; I was aware of the occasional high-backed and empty chair that I came upon around a corner; I smelled the sunlight within our confines of warm stone. Yet even inside the labyrinth, seeing only what was before my hand or hanging on slender chains from the high ceiling above me, still I also saw our château as if from without and afar: the gates bearing their incomplete designs of ivy, the walls the color of dark sand, in one corner the single low tower that was plump to my eye and roofed in its gently sloping cone of black slate which, from near or far, looked always wet as in some cool clear shower of rain just past. Who but I could know what occurred both within and without? And all the while I carried in the back of my mind those small morsels of the morning that were mine alone: Who shall she be? What shall she be made to do?

Then through the noise of morning, a clacking of dishes and sighing of looms and neighing of horses and the laughter of a woman who might have been Magie, through all this I heard distinctly the cold tinkle of the bell in our chapel that was situated beyond the stables and which at this moment would be entirely empty, I knew, except for Seigneur. And so it was, when I arrived, although my anticipation had been too pure, too strong, investing in that scene an excessive emptiness, since when I arrived at the call of his bell, I found Seigneur not entirely alone but accompanied by the two whippets quivering on his either side in all their whiteness and uncertainty. But for the man and the two tall dogs there was nothing else in this white chapel which, before my time if not Seigneur's, might well have been furnished with prie-dieux for kneeling penitents, and golden icons, and an altar decorated with a single vast bouquet of dripping gladioli gathered by some humble retainer from our seas of those stately flowers. Now there was nothing except man, dogs, and on the air a trace of resin as if from some distant cere-monial of grief or joy.

"Good morning, Virginie," said Seigneur without moving, without smiling. "I would like to see Magie in Le petit jardin."

How strange, I thought as I always did, looking up at Seigneur's impassive face and showing none of my own feelings except in my eyes, how strange it was that most of our days began in a chapel stripped of every relic, every appropriate sign, and containing only Seigneur who always stood where once the altar had stood. How strange that from such a place, all the more devotional for having been rendered meaningless, should come the conception that so determined the pain or pleasure of our days. How strange to see the man flanked by his dogs in an otherwise empty chapel. But I had my answer, at least for the moment, and was relieved or at least partially relieved since I loved Magie already and, of all the possible places for our rendezvous, I much preferred Le petit jardin, in which no form of violence could occur.

Mere moments later the man and his two white dogs and the young woman in her orange gown and I the messenger and confidante, despite my mere ten years, were all locked together in that little enclosure of Le petit jardin, where we might have existed together for all time and all time to come. When the gate closed I could not help but feel that sensation of mystery induced as nowhere else by the man, the beasts, the seated woman, and most of all by the nature of Le petit jardin itself.

On four sides rose gray walls higher than Seigneur was tall; the gate was narrow and composed of straight and close-spaced iron bars; over two of the four opposing walls came the massive watery foliage of two weeping willow trees planted outside the garden instead of within, so that those of us inside Le petit jardin were sequestered among the heavy tendrils of trees we could not see. Along these same walls were cultivated rosebushes carefully pruned and blooming, no matter the season; in the center of Le petit jardin was a small carpet of the greenest lawn, upon which sat Magie in her high-backed chair that had a red cushioned seat and was carved with representations of climbing vines and the heads of animals never found in any field or forest. And then, as if flowers, green plot, intruding willows and anomalous chair and seated woman were not enough, the back wall, opposite the narrow gate, consisted of a family sepulcher of twelve ancient crypts. As always I marveled at the soft pure atmosphere of this little place. How wise of Seigneur, I thought, to bring us here. What better place in which to forge the first bonds between man, child, and seated woman?

"Magie," Seigneur said at last, "I want you to study the eyes of this child. . . ."

Smiling woman with her hands in her lap, and standing man flanked by his dogs, and the sun almost directly overhead and not a single bird or insect to remind us of all that lay beyond Le petit jardin: this was the context in which I once again stepped forward and raised my chin at Seigneur's bidding, and I thought that my narrow face was falsely modest, since I too had studied my eyes in pool and glass and knew them to be quite worthy of what Seigneur was about to say of them. But Seigneur positioned himself beside Magie; I faced them both; the two dogs stood so closely together that their bodies touched. Seigneur held out his hand as if to cup my raised chin—yet it was only an airy gesture since Seigneur had never touched me in any way, no matter how slightly. There I stood as always and looked not at Seigneur but at Magie whose pinkish curls were loose and who returned my gaze. I thought that Magie already saw in me what Seigneur saw.

"Magie," he said, "note the largeness of this child's eyes. Note the roundness. Note the deep shades of brown with which they shine, a color of the darkest brown that nonetheless in the proper light, this light, appears also to reflect the yellow of invisible daffodils growing not in a garden but in the mind. You can see these eyes as well as I can, Magie. You are already capable of noting how they dominate the face and hold the attention of the viewer like no other two eyes you or I have ever seen."

He paused, as always. He nodded, as he always did. He allowed himself the briefest smile while I waited, arms hanging and head raised, trying to keep my body still while

Seigneur talked about my eyes as if they belonged not to me but to some other child who now stood in my place.

"Magie," he said, while I waited before the standing man and seated woman in all my outward shyness and inner pride, "the question is not merely one of beauty. Not at all. For now you must lean forward, without blinking, and see in this child's eyes what I myself have come to call the seven precious expressions in the eyes of innocence. Look closely, Magie, and concentrate. Know now that you are looking directly at the seven precious expressions which are, in the eyes of innocence, as follows: Joy. Attention. Calm. Surprise. Grief. Incomprehension. And finally the veiled painful accusation of her whom one must wound—inevitably. Do you see them? Do you understand the power of this child's eyes? But I want you to achieve in your own eyes these same expressions and to learn what you could not until this moment know: namely, that these same precious expressions which seem so rare to us in the eyes of the child are to be found, no matter your incredulity, in the eyes of a dog. . . ."

The crypts of the nameless dead were a somber gray, the willows were like thick falls of water, and the grass was serene, the clear light diffused, the pure air sweet with the "breath of Virginie." In all the suspension of this gentle place we waited, holding Seigneur's last softly spoken words still in our ears. Magie was smiling. Seigneur was not. As for me, I was by no means dismayed at his comparison since I too had knelt and hugged the two white dogs about their necks and used my eyes and hence already knew that Seigneur's comparison was exact and true.

"Yes, Magie," Seigneur continued, "I want you to court these rare creatures until you have seen for yourself that the innocence of Virginie shines forth, in fact, from the eyes of dogs. And now," he said after another pause, "now you must lift your skirt into your lap and woo my dogs. The degree of your success shall be determined by the dogs themselves. You see, they are private creatures and not easily aroused."

Had I been seated as Magie was seated in her high-backed wooden chair in what I thought of as this sacred place, I would have complied immediately with Seigneur's request so that my child's skirt would have been already lifted and my legs already exposed, if that was what he wanted. But Magie's eyes were still on mine; her receptive smiling face was unclouded by the slightest doubt; she sat without movement as if she were as much a fixture of Le petit jardin as crypt or weeping willow.

"Incredulity, Seigneur?" she said at last. "But you know I am not easily taken by incredulity. You know as well as I that this is one lesson I need not be taught, one trial I need not be subjected to. But no matter. I am happy to demonstrate what you have in mind."

Then with the simplest and easiest gesture Magie gathered the forward folds of her orange skirt into her lap. She no longer smiled. She sat with her legs exposed from lap to toe against the backdrop of that underportion of the orange skirt that came down behind her legs from the hidden edge of the chair to touch, in a simple silken curl, the grass where chair and naked feet were placed. Her legs and lap were bare; her hands were posed in the simple gesture in which she still held the bottom edge of the skirt; her milky thighs were swept, I saw, with a faint dusting of golden hair like pollen wafted from one white flower to the next. I knew that in this unhurried gesture of compliance she had quite forgotten Seigneur, where he stood to one side boldly, expectantly, with his hands clasped behind his back, and also had quite forgotten me, though mine was the very innocence, after all, that was both the object and the substance of this morning hour.

"Look at the dogs, Magie," he said in his lowest and most quiet voice. "Concentrate. Concentrate. The larger with the black collar is the male, the smaller with the yellow collar is the female. You must appeal to them both. You must win them over."

She did nothing, said nothing, and the dogs did not move. Yet the two dogs now pressed themselves against each other all the harder, and by their eyes revealed that they well understood that the atmosphere in Le petit jardin had changed and that now they had fallen suddenly under a scrutiny they could not ignore. How could I help but marvel at the whiteness and thinness of these dogs with their fragile bones and underbodies tightly shrunken to the purposes of speed? How not marvel at their uneasy eyes and gathering self-consciousness? Oh, but from where I stood at the edge of the green I marveled as much at the dogs' self-consciousness as at Magie in all her naturalness.

She leaned forward. Without knowing it, she had twisted her gathered skirt into a long roll which she now drew tightly backwards against her lower stomach and rounded hips. Without knowing it, she was looking steadily and even quizzically into the moist brown eyes of the dog in the black collar. How I waited! How I watched the shifting paw, the flickering of nerves beneath the white coat, the hardly perceptible movements of the long thin head to the left, to the right, and watched the dog's poor efforts to escape the steady scrutiny of dear Magie!

"Come, Le noir!" she might have said with her eyes alone, since giving a little lurch the poor beast pulled himself away from his mate and with tall broken steps complied exactly with Magie's wishes and crossed the patch of green between them. He stood beside her, looking desperately to the left, the right, then finally laid his thin head across her upper thigh in the peaceful, obedient, trusting gesture of the suppliant dog.

And: "Come, La jaune!" she might have said, again with her eyes, since after a moment's hesitation the dog in the yellow collar slowly followed the example of her mate until her own long head was resting across Magie's other thigh. Nose toward nose the two dogs pointed their still heads across the downy thighs of Magie, whose face appeared to me to be both pleased and pained.

"Well done," said Seigneur under his breath, "well done." But it was clear, at least to me, that Magie had not the slightest need of his encouragement.

So far these morning circumstances had affected my own consciousness, or lack of it, in exactly the way Magie's had been affected, since without knowing it I had clasped my hands and assumed a kneeling position on the edge of the grass, though I came to myself and realized the extent of my happy submersion in this morning hour as soon as Magie let go of her skirt, as she now did, and lightly rested her open hands on the heads of the dogs. Well could I understand the warmth she was feeling from each of the dogs' heads against her thighs; well could I imagine the sensation in her palms and fingers of the frail elongated bony skulls lying just beneath the living skin and coverings of white hair. For the moment she did not stroke the dogs watching each other across her lap, but merely rested her loving hands on their warm heads. It was a sight so stationary and paradoxical that suddenly it caused this question to come to my mind: mightn't the Tapestry of Love consist of some such scene, so that now I was viewing in life precisely what I had never been allowed to see in art? Perhaps, I thought, perhaps, since never yet had I seen whippets and woman so warmly and symmetrically arranged. There had been past times, in fact, when the dogs had cowered in the corners of Le petit jardin, or kept apart, or huddled against the legs of Seigneur, or approached the partially naked initiate only one at a time. Now animals and woman too were making order of this vulnerability. Now I myself had become their supplicant.

"Speak to them, Magie," urged Seigneur in a whisper. "Use your voice as well as your eyes."

But she did not, and yet she caused the dogs to lift their heads, turn their heads in search of her eyes, and then, simultaneously, to rise up and balance themselves on hind legs as brittle as dried bones, and simultaneously to position their front legs across the thighs where their heads had rested, so that now the two white bodies were stretching upwards, and the two white muzzles were very nearly in the same plane with Magie's face. Merely by lifting her gentle hands and holding them above the heads of the dogs in a gesture of benediction exactly the same, I noted, as that which Seigneur himself offered at times to the lowly animals, she had indeed caused the whippets to rest their front legs on her thighs and to elevate themselves so as to approximate in standing the way she sat. Their tails were tucked in nervously between their hind legs; they formed a white heraldic triangle over the naked lap; beneath her hands, now covering the shoulders of each beast, they stood as if paralyzed in comfort and made not a move except now and again, timidly, and in unison, to point their dry noses toward the fair face.

Unmoving dogs, seated woman, standing man, kneeling child: thus we remained immobile in Le petit jardin until Magie, who alone was mistress of all that happened, of all we saw, and who alone was the first to move, quite simply and slowly raised both her hands and in them clasped Le noir's warm and pensive head and with her own brown eyes stared seemingly forever into the eyes of the dog. I watched her face, the frowning of the forehead and the dimpling around the mouth. I watched as Le noir submitted his head to her hands and his eyes to her loving eyes. I watched as the smaller dog awaited without moving the attention that she too would receive, and did receive, from Magie, who was now lifting Le noir's ears, and breathing into them, and stroking the thin muzzle, and touching the tip of it with the tip of her nose, and above all else was peering again and again into the brown eyes of the whimpering animal. I saw what Magie saw: my own brown eyes and the seven coppery circles in the depths of them, and currents of air the color of an orange sun invisibly setting, and vast expanses of space the color of cut wheat. The longer she looked the more the dog whimpered. The more she smiled the greater was the agitation she caused in his breast. The greater her pleasure the wider the poor creature's unresisting eyes until, at last, she freed Le noir and with the briefest laugh, which was the only sound she made, turned to La jaune and with eyes and fingers lavished on La jaune the affection she had all but spent on Le noir.

The elk in snow, the swan on the pond, the blood-colored flower on a country road: all these and more she must have read in the eyes of the smaller dog, which, seemingly forever, she held in exactly that same thralldom in which she had held the larger. Then, quite suddenly, she ceased her stroking, her nuzzling, her kissing, and, allowing her hands to fall to her sides, shut tight her eyes and relaxed her naked legs and laughed her brief laugh, as if she could have known in advance that these were precisely the gestures with which to liberate the whippets from their constraint and to signal to the larger dog and smaller her receptivity to that eagerness which, until this moment, they had held in check. As if by a voiced command they fell to licking the fair smiling face of dear Magie and to nudging her willing head in her aroused affection, and all the while moving their hind legs, suddenly, in the tight and lively circles of an impossible dance. With wet and frantic noses they probed now the dancing curls, now the loose and unconcealed lap, La jaune kissing a partially hidden ear just as Le noir gave himself free rein to explore the open and inviting lap, the two creatures then reversing themselves from leg to cheek and cheek to lap despite the significance of the yellow collar and the black.

She allowed it all. She encouraged it. She smiled and kept tight shut those very eyes which the two dogs simultaneously or in sequence licked again and again with their purpling and excited tongues. How generously she received their ravishment, I thought. How blindly she accepted that close scrutiny which, only moments before, had been her own. At last, and when she knew by all her senses, excepting sight, that the dogs had finally forsaken her for each other, still she waited, blindly enjoying what Seigneur and I were the first to see: that bestial pantomime which might have been embossed on a silver coin or represented in a field of white mosaic.

"Open your eyes, Magie," said Seigneur in his most gentle and admiring voice. "Open your eyes and see what you have accomplished. In fact," he said, as if musing only to himself, "the sight of what you have accomplished tempts me to spare you the sight of what the end of this long day will bring. And yet," he said, in his suddenly quite distant voice, "I shall not spare you that sight or any other. In fact, I shall spare you nothing. Ever."

It was then that Magie opened wide her eyes while for me the sight of the white dogs gave way to the horror I foresaw at the end of the day.

Was I not the busy child? I who climbed the tower stairs to scan the terrain of sensuality that surrounded us? I who swept and swept again my hearth? I who wove another rose into the unfinished tapestry on the loom that was mine? And with my own hoe worked another furrow into my small portion of the east garden that I loved? And carried grain to the doves and wood to my hearth and paused periodically to watch the declining sun pass time on the sun's own face? Yes, I was the busy child shining pots of iron and pans of copper and goblets of glass that gleamed, and hurrying down one empty corridor only to return by another, my hands and body occupied by space and keys, flagons and baskets, while my thoughts went from task to task as though my hurried efforts might somehow surprise me with time safely past and the fated end of that day avoided. It was all impossible, I knew, and yet I kept to myself, and only occasionally stopped abruptly when the approaching fate of the day fell across my path like the shadow of a great wing brushing the earth, and then, and only then, I asked myself why it was that Seigneur did not relent, or told myself that perhaps this very moment he was in fact relenting, though I knew he was not. In all my experience of Seigneur's creativity, nothing, I thought to myself with the black wing stopping my way, nothing was quite so difficult to bear as what I had hoped he might dispense with or at least postpone this day. But even as the thought occurred to me, while gathering eggs that were still warm or turning the pages of my book of hours, still I knew that Seigneur was a man of principle and that I had only to prepare myself as best I could for what I could hardly admit to consciousness or allow to memory, though it was there, in my memory, like a barbed hook piercing a heart that throbbed.

The doves grew quiet. The looms fell silent. Inside their hive the very bees were stilled. High on its wall the sculpted face of the sun was now partially concealed by a shadow that no longer moved. As for me, I could not help but notice that we had reached that ending of the day when the light is clearest and the executioner is brave enough, at last, to don his hood and seize his ax and climb his scaffold where the waiting victim is already all but headless in the final and purest light of day. Then, reluctantly, I took myself to the courtyard, where the gates were closed, and all, I saw in a glance, was ready.

The high-backed chair so recently positioned on the green grass in Le petit jardin now stood alone, and how oddly, ominously, in the center of the courtyard, from which, I knew, there was no escape. Tranquillity had given way to barrenness, and there sat Magie with hands folded as before and the curls as resilient as before, in the morning, and on her face the same expression of smiling and ordinary confidence which conveyed all too clearly, I thought, that she had heeded no warning, had seen no ravens clouding her clear skies, had passed the intervening hours as if for her there could be nothing more arduous to face than a pair of white whippets in a secluded bower. For once the woman was more innocent than the pure child. Joining her and standing beside her as was my simple role in this grim scheme, I recognized in a breath her innocence, and my heart fell. Could she not feel the emptiness that filled the courtyard? Or note Seigneur's unsmiling countenance and his silence and the way he stood at a distance with his feet wide apart and that strange mechanical staff gripped in a firm hand, its butt in the sand and its small iron beak towering above his head on the end of the staff? Wouldn't this sight be quite enough to instill in most grown women the faintest shade of fear or the first unpleasant taste of apprehension? But it was not so, and there was nothing I could do but remain as best I could at Magie's side in the clear light, even as I understood that the moment had come, and that the day was at its fullest, and that the day was dead. Only in the prolongation of its death did this day exist. At times the clearest light, I knew, was indistinguishable from the darkest night.

"Magie," Seigneur called across the space between us, "at this day's beginning you enjoyed the pleasure of what I shall call the generosity of vision. Now, at its end, you must know what it means to see with the eyes of pride. No lesson is more essential, no sight more necessary to the womanhood you shall at last achieve. The generous eye is desirable, but without the eyes of pride the person who aspires to womanhood is blind. It is one thing to impart your natural generosity to a pair of dogs and thus, by the expenditure of natural innocence, to recognize in turn that the timidity of the united dogs is noble.

But it is quite another to be the passive recipient and, further, recipient of the gift unwanted, and thus to discover that it is harder by far to accept the gift than to give it. She who is able to receive the gift, no matter the nature of that gift, is proud; the more unwanted the gift the greater the woman's pride in accepting it. And a woman's pride is the glory of the womanhood that is hers alone. It is pride that makes a woman loved, or makes her desired, and the greater a woman's pride the more she is loved. The heart of womanhood, Magie, is pride. . . .

"So now I am going to forge your pride: you shall not be touched, you have nothing to fear, nothing to do. Yet you must know that this day's final event is for you and you alone. You are the cause of this event, and its inspiration, and its center; what is to happen would not happen were it not for you, though you do nothing and say nothing and merely sit in your chair until this charade is over and the light fails. The amount of pain implicit in the gift is the only measure of a woman's pride. The greater the pain the more valuable the gift and the fiercer her pride. And the extent of her pride is the only measure of a woman's worth. So the gesture I am about to perform is an indication, at least, of the vastness of the value you represent to me. Accept what I am about to give, Magie! Be proud! It is all for you!"

This speech, so like a period of drums and horns, I thought, increased the distance between Seigneur and ourselves, and revealed the potential of the man's own pride, and with the last of its exclamation, died in our surrounding silence like the thump of the ax, the fall of the severed head. What, I asked myself, could be more ominous than the death of this rhetoric? My brief and somber sidelong look at Magie revealed that she too, at last, was beginning to appreciate the seriousness of this occasion. Gone was her smile, gone her faint flush, and visibly fading were all the happier aspects of the innocence that informed her life, no matter the adult she was or the fact of her motherhood. The silence that roared in our ears at the conclusion of Seigneur's speech was just as dark, I thought, or just as fraught with menacing cadences as the sound of the long-dead wave in the broken shell or the very shape and color which lone man, lone woman, lone child exacted from the space around us. In such clear light and heavy silence I was tempted to reach for Magie's hand and hold it, though I did not.

What terrible noise was this? For even as I heard the random blows of the hooves and heard the loud snorting of the beast that smells danger on the air, and as I saw the four attendants with their peculiar tools and saw Père La Tour leading into our midst the desperate horse that was taller and blacker than Le Baron's horse or any other such horse I had seen before, even as all the elements of Seigneur's cruelest drama filled the emptiness of our sad stage, even then as I remembered fleeting sights and cries from past performances and knew without question what was yet to come, still I cringed inside myself and in my mind attempted to deny, impossibly, what I saw and heard and what I would see and hear despite myself.

Seigneur made not a move, still facing us, as if he cared nothing for the horse and men behind his back, or as though they were not there, loud and struggling and tumultuous in the bright uncanny light of our dead day. Men and horse could not have more disturbed the emptiness of the courtyard, nor more destroyed the silence into which Seigneur's distant speech had fallen like a loud voice shouted down the deepest well.

"Don't move, Magie!" he called across the space between us. "But don't be afraid. You shall come to no harm."

Once again, as I had done before, I attempted to calm myself and brace myself by cataloguing on the very pages of my inward agitation all the particulars of this gathering scene. Père La Tour, for instance, was controlling the frantic horse by means of a short thick stick containing at one end a small loop of rope into which the horse's nose was caught and held by the simple expediency of twisting the stick and hence the loop, which tightened around the tender nose, quite naturally, with every turn of the stick worn smooth with use. Whenever the horse attempted to rear, or attempted to lunge away from Père La Tour, or attempted to toss its head and thus dislodge the painful sensation in its poor twisted nose, Père La Tour had only to give his stick another turn to heighten the madness in the horse's eyes but also to subdue quite easily the urgencies that inhabited all the great weight of the struggling beast. It was a clever device, I thought, yet sickening.

As for the attendants, those four disheveled men whom I somehow recognized but could not remember, men who wore tight and faded shirts and knee breeches and old lumpy shoes long used to plodding in manure and raising dust, of these four frightened and bare-armed fellows there were two who were equipped with long and blunted poles of iron which, each to a side, they thrust against the heavy haunches in order to prevent as much as possible the lateral movements of the black horse, while their two comrades carried between them a great cagelike iron mechanism which in itself might well account for the bloodied flecks of terror in the animal's poor rolling eyes.

Still Seigneur made not a move. Still he faced us, as if the breathless and fearsome activity behind his back were no concern of his. The light held, like mercury in a column or rain in a cloud, while all around us lay the listening château and its silent occupants, each one arrested in whatever her act of butchering, weaving, reading, singing, daydreaming at open casement, or producing sweet tones from an ivory flute—all quiet and waiting for the screams which, except for

Adèle, they could not possibly know would issue suddenly from this near-empty courtyard from which, for the time being, they were excluded.

"Magie," called he who was master of this scene, "don't worry about our handsome but uncooperative animal. Once he complies with what I have in mind, and gives up his gift, which is actually mine as well as his, he shall spend the rest of his days among heavy and compliant mares in rolling fields filled with shadows and sunlight, green grass and yellow, and long meandering streams of clear water. Fear not for yourself, Magie, and fear not for the horse."

But what effect could such words have if not to increase our apprehension? Yet I knew that this was not Seigneur's intention, and also knew that never did he say what he did not mean. So I nodded to myself and wished the horse away to his fields and Magie to her peaceful bed and me to my hearth, at the same time finding my attention more firmly fixed than ever on the commotion barely contained behind Seigneur's back.

The two men with the iron prods were moving them, I saw, and were muttering under their breaths in their now greater efforts to prevent the horse from thundering in a terrified half circle to the left, to the right, to the left, and from striking down his sweating tormentors with his glistening hooves. At the head of the poor beast the other two attendants were lifting high the great cagelike mechanism, which was actually a halter of sorts, but made of iron strips instead of leather, and, while Père La Tour turned ever tighter his rude but effective stick, were shoving and pushing and manipulating the iron halter so as to encase within it, finally, the horse's head. The black ears lay back, the eyes were white and bloodied in their sockets, the pink nose was so constrained and distorted in the loop of rope that the enormous creature was able to breathe only through the open mouth which, in turn, was partially obstructed by the wet tongue engorged with pain and also by the as yet muffled sounds the poor beast could not help but generate between his open jaws. Then they were done, the two thickset men, who were among the lowest underlings in our handsome stables, and Père La Tour (who loosed his rope) leapt back and flung aside his stick.

Now the true purpose of the iron halter could no longer remain a puzzle or be denied, even by me or, more importantly, by dear Magie, whose very self, I thought, deserved to be swept away this instant by some saving wind that would obliterate horse, men, seated woman, everything in fact except Seigneur and me. But there was not the slightest breath of wind to destroy or in any way obscure the now only-too-evident purpose of the iron halter imprisoning beyond a doubt the great handsome head of the poor horse. What was now inescapable, since I saw it and remembered it as well, was that the iron halter differed from an ordinary halter not merely because it was made of thick iron instead of supple leather, but mainly because it housed a ratcheted device which, something in the manner of the bit in a bridle, and something like a skeletal duplication of the beast's own jaws, sat inside the frothing mouth and compressed the tongue and held apart the mammoth jaws to any degree of openness desired. That was in fact the diabolical difference between this riveted and hinged device and the soft and comfortable halter which my own Cupidon and all our horses loosely wore throughout their peaceful days in our richly appareled stables. Now I could not help but see that the black horse's jaws were forced open to their fullest extent and perhaps beyond. The locked and gaping mouth, the chastened tongue, the large and yellowed teeth still wet to the watching eye: could there be any iron device more unnatural? any intrusion into the animal world more cruel? any spectacle more shameful to those compelled to see it? For a moment I thought to close my eyes, but I could not.

I watched, Magie was watching. In the silence in which
time itself was suspended, and the clear light too, we heard
the helpless unrhythmical pounding of the hooves, the un-
voiced oaths of the attendants, the loud and labored breathing
of men and horse alike. Père La Tour stood well out of the
way and wiped his brow. Those to the rear of the horse
poked and prodded the gleaming flanks. At the head of the
poor beast the other two attendants, with straw in their hair
and dung on their shoes, stood to either side of him fiercely
gripping at arms' length the two long iron rods that were
affixed in a swiveling manner to either side of the iron mask.
All was in motion, yet nothing moved. With backs bent and
feet shuffling, the four men fought the plunging and swaying
horse to a standstill. The horse expended his energy as if at a
gallop; the four men clung to their iron poles and kept him
captive, great mouth high and open in the still air.

"Magie!" called Seigneur across the space between us. "Be
brave! Be proud! In all your days to come, and without
thinking and as a matter of fact, you must expect to receive
from each and every lover, master, lord of your life, precisely
that kind of gift to compare favorably, in quality, with the
gift you shall now receive from me. Nothing is too good for
you, Magie! Nothing too abominable! Nothing too rare!"

With these words he quite suddenly turned his back to us
and, like a warrior brandishing his pike, grasped in both firm
hands the iron staff, that had about it an aspect curious indeed,
and frightening, and spread his feet, one slightly before the
other, and bent his knees, gathered his strength, hoisted high
the mysterious staff and faced the horse. But how could I
have failed to understand, as memory and actuality joined
again, and I saw that Seigneur was using both hands to
operate, rather than merely hold, that which was no mere
staff but was instead a long and slender pair of pincers all the
more malevolent for its simplicity, its thinness, its great
length, its sinister originality of design? Pincers, and I swayed

in dizziness beyond my years while noting, nonetheless, that Magie's understanding lagged but a hair behind my own, since now she was standing up in a movement of surprise and defiance which could only have been prompted by that same recognition that had come to me and now had found its second mark and was rending the unsuspecting nature that was herself.

"No!" she cried, as Père La Tour stepped forward, at Seigneur's curt nod, and reached up his hands and, in one deft gesture, clamped the little ugly beaklike head of Seigneur's pincers to one of the two square teeth lodged by nature so tightly in the front of the black horse's long upper jaw. "No!" she cried again, as Père La Tour jumped away to safety and Seigneur squeezed shut his slender instrument and held it ready. "Injure me if you must," she then cried in a final breath. "But spare the horse!"

I saw the flexing of bold muscles, the shifting of feet, the motions of Seigneur's grand head, so violent as to shake loose the black ribbon binding his thick hair at the base of the neck. The horse squealed once, squealed again, as if a suffering pig were lodged inside its belly, and these sounds were so inappropriate to the great size and noble stature of the horse that they made me gasp. Then Seigneur leaned back on the end of the pincers. He applied all the tension he could impart to the upper end of the pincers. Thus, in sudden silence, the mighty horse stared down at Seigneur with a liquid steadiness that imparted to both enormous eyes a wild concentration which, in itself, must have spurred on Seigneur to the extraction that was the final purpose of this day.

I felt the sudden protective sweep of Magie's left arm and found myself smothered face-to-stomach against her warm body. I heard the splintering of bone. I heard the breathy expulsion of the man's relief. I heard the high protracted screech that issued once from the mouth of the horse in tones that were human. Sightless, I still knew that the light had failed.

"Your prize, Madame," Seigneur cried above the pain of the beast, and wheeled upon us, and extended the pincers. "Come take your prize!"

That night I forsook my hearth and spent the darkness seated beside the woman who wept in her sleep yet lay upon her bed as straight and unmoving as a stone effigy lying with folded hands upon its tomb. Though I could not see it, I knew that on a small and polished table next to the head of the bed there rested a silver bowl of spring water containing in the form of an eternal gleam that which, on the morrow, the waking woman would dispassionately remove, and dry, and enclose in the waiting locket that would hang from its silver chain around her neck.

In my single dream that night I heard the distant voice of Seigneur calling out to a group of new arrivals as he always did: "Welcome to Dédale! Welcome! The women you shall become await you here. . . ."

In Taku Bay

from ADVENTURES IN THE ALASKAN SKIN TRADE
(in progress)

In Venasque, Sophie and I knew that when the next year off from teaching arrived, as it now has (it is January 1984), there would be nothing to do but stay at home in Rhode Island instead of going to France. This, then, is my first full year for writing in Providence, and in our attic, which provides as much seclusion as any shepherd's hut in Provence, I have tacked before me on the wall a postcard illustrated by one of Topor's great drawings. A small man with his face in shadow wears a fedora and a long brown overcoat, and stoops under the weight of two shabby suitcases. He is chained by an ankle to a tree in such a way that he can go nowhere except around the trunk of the tree whose branches bear not leaves but little barns, little houses, a little church with a spire, the tiny face of a woman. The drawing is entitled "The Adventurer," and every morning it proclaims its wry and vaguely dreadful message: off we go, yet here we remain.

Sophie brought me full circle by suggesting, in Venasque, that for my next novel (the one I'm working on now), I try relaxing into the pleasures of autobiographical fiction, and *Adventures in the Alaskan Skin Trade* is intended to be as autobiographical as I can make it, though its narrator is in fact a thirty-nine-year-old woman, twenty years my junior, who runs a whorehouse called "The Alaska-Yukon Gamelands" in Juneau, the town of my formative years. Sunny, as she has been nicknamed by her dead father, is also an airplane pilot, a wilderness guide, a woman whose bumper sticker says "SWORN TO FUN, LOYAL TO NONE." Sunny tells her story of growing up a tomboy only to become, at an early age, a tough-minded sensuous version of those women who, in the days of the Yukon gold rush, were never sisters, wives, mothers, or sweethearts, as the old prospectors said. Sunny also tells the story of her father, a charming, unwitting misogynist who went to Alaska to search unsuccessfully, but in all the flush of his idealism, for riches as well as for a totem pole rumored to carry at its top the figure of Abraham Lincoln. As Sunny says, her whorehouse is the gold mine her father never found.

In the following excerpt, Sunny and her father, who calls himself Uncle Jake, and her mother, nicknamed Sissy, are on their way north by steamship from Seattle, and are treated to a tourist's glimpse of a glacier as they draw close to Juneau.

In Taku Bay

It had a prow of iron, a salt-encrusted hull, our dark ship making its slow way out of the dawn, this *S.S. Alaska* bearing its small band of unwary travelers north to the night.

It was 6 A.M. on Monday, May 11, 1930, our fifth day at sea and last full day before docking at Juneau. (Population 2,800 plus 900 Siwash Indians.) Most of the travelers were on deck as bidden, since yesterday evening it had been announced that in ten hours the ship would detour somewhat from its course in order that those who had never seen a glacier might do so now. Tony, the skipper, as my father called him (Uncle Jake had a way of achieving instantaneous intimacy—another of his favorite words—with those in positions of authority, and was himself a nautical person, thanks to his naval duties in the Great War), had urged everyone to rise early and be on hand to see the sight, and most had obeyed.

At 6 A.M., the rainy darkness smelled of salt tides and the vast cold atmosphere that shrouds black reefs, uninhabited shores, wrecks at sea. The wooden starboard rail, where near the bows our small band waited, was wet to the touch, and the iron plates beneath our feet shook and trembled to the beat of the engines that were buried far below us and were straining, ever straining, to push us on through oceanic treachery, swift cross currents, sullen swells at a speed of approximately eight miles per hour. The ship was a monster making monumental efforts merely to crawl. Occasionally the wet and foggy dawn smelled of diesel fumes or of some hot breath of cooking loosed from vent or open hatchway; we were moving, not moving, there was nothing to see, shivering as we were at the starboard rail and waiting for the mouth of the world to yawn and display its marvel.

Everyone not appropriately dressed for the vigil went below and returned with coats, jackets, hats, ship's blankets which they draped about their shoulders or over their heads like survivors on a drifting hulk. Everyone, that is, except Uncle Jake, who was immune to the cold, generally indifferent to wind, snow, rain, and now stood tallest among those at the rail and wearing his gray double-breasted suit and white shirt, blue polka-dotted tie, crisp white handkerchief in the breast suitcoat pocket. No hat, no raincoat, no blanket for my father. He had made his toilet at 5 A.M. and his dark hair was parted in the middle and stiff and shining with brushing and the cream he applied each dawn. With a large hand cupping my shoulder, he held me to him protectively; on his other side, Sissy clung to his arm, though the ship was as steady as a barrel and there was no risk of being lost in that little crowd. Sissy and I were hatted, coated, she in green, and shivering, I in my sailor's hat and coat, warm dress, and under it my leather leggings with straps that fitted around the insteps of my patent leather shoes. My head came to Uncle Jake's mid-thigh; with my left arm I encircled his enormous leg, happily, rhythmically, to the laboring pulse of the old engines. Near me, a great white life preserver was affixed to the rail. It was slick with the fog and intermittent rain, in black paint it announced itself: *S.S. Alaska.*

"There," said Uncle Jake to the group at large, "Tony has changed course. Do you feel it? Twenty degrees to starboard. And he's reduced speed. We've entered Taku Bay. The light will come up in about five minutes and then Tony will give us the spectacle of our lives."

He spoke as if he were a ship's officer, as if he were a frequent traveler on this ship, as if he were old friends with the ship's skipper and had done all this and seen all this before—which I thought he had. Now he released my shoulder and rested his large warm hand atop the sailor hat on my head. I squeezed his leg. From the bridge far behind us came the faint brassy sound of a bell—distant, mechanical, impersonal. Sea water was smashing irregularly against the sides of the ship. I freed myself from Uncle Jake and stepped around him, took Sissy's hand in mine and leaned against her.

"Darling," she said, "are you warm enough?"

I was.

And was I not like my father? Size and gender aside, I was his replica. I had become the sit-in drummer of the three-piece ship's orchestra, had thrown great platters of candy-coated garbage to the angry gulls, with Uncle Jake had sat at Tony's table when the seas were high and thick and all the rest of them were below in their berths, with Uncle Jake had visited Tony on the bridge and steered the ship. Sailors in wet undershirts and blue threadbare pants were forever hoisting me onto their shoulders; I had smiled at the greasy men in the engine room; I was the wireless operator's friend and had worn his headset, tapped out messages in code; hand-in-hand had strolled on wet decks with the purser, and was the favorite of the cook, second officer, chief engineer. The ship was Uncle Jake's and mine as well. And I was first to fire drills, which frightened Sissy, and first to meals, where I, not Sissy, sat to Tony's right (on three thick books from the ship's library), and first to see the porpoises or anything else of interest that hove into sight. I was the girl mascot of the old *Alaska* and knew it well.

"Now," said Uncle Jake suddenly and still to the group at large, "here's the light. . . ."

At that moment the fog lifted, the day broke, like a white continent the fog rose up from where it had lain pressed to the sea and hovered above us, grew translucent, admitted to the panorama disclosed to us a dead but welcome light that was without heat, without brightness, as if there were no sun at all above the fog. But at least it was all spread visibly before us, and even this first daylight, receptive to nothing but impending rain, was preferable to the blackness in which that handful of passengers had been standing, waiting: the broad mouth of Taku Bay was already behind us; the rocky, untimbered reaches of land were in the distance to the left. To the right, off the starboard bow, rocking gently on the long swells and so close that we might have run it down had not the fog lifted and the ship slowed, the surprise of an Indian fishing boat with a man and woman side by side in the stern and holding mugs of coffee. And dead ahead, a half mile distant, the gray-white face of Taku Glacier.

"Now there," said a short, fat man standing close to us, "now there's a glacier!" And he put his hands on his hips and smiled as the others joined in to share his awe, his elation, and for the first time on the voyage began using their cameras though the light was poor.

"It's Taku Glacier," said my father. "In the old days they used to cross glaciers like that on horseback."

"And look at those people in that little boat," said the fat man. "We have an escort!"

"They're Siwash Indians," said Uncle Jake, "from Juneau. They're about two hundred miles from their usual fishing grounds. They're after cod."

The S.S. *Alaska* was aimed directly for the center of the icy wall and slowly, ponderously went forward, black iron drawn dangerously to sullied ice. Again the bell sounded, the engines slowed, the ship continued on toward the ice which loomed larger, revealed jagged vertical fissures in its face, small chunks and slabs bobbing where the wall of ice met the dark sea.

The Indian stared up at us, then tossed the remains of his coffee over the side, bent down, started his own dismal little gasoline engine, began to follow us in toward the ice. A gull that had been sitting on the roof of the pilot house rose and sailed off, swooping and crying through the flat dawn. The Indian woman stooped and went out of sight into the dark and smoky hovel of the cabin. From the tall, narrow, rusty smokestack that jutted above the pilot house came a thin trail of bright blue exhaust. The little boat listed, sat low in the water, was smothered in heaps of netting, coils of frayed rope, rusted chain, seaweed. The Indian, in faded blue shirt and pants and rolled-down hip boots, stood ankle-deep in fish heads, moldy canvas, buckets of slime. He steered with one hand and all the while looked not toward the approaching glacier but up at the passengers who were now leaning over the rail and waving down at him. He did not wave back. His gas engine made a muted, metrical popping sound in the wake of the small unpainted boat.

"I think we're wanted on the bridge," said Uncle Jake, now speaking softly and only to Sissy and me, instead of to the group at large. "Tony wants us up there. He has a treat for Sunny."

And so saying, he smiled at Sissy and me, disengaged himself from clinging wife and clinging child and, on long sea legs, walked aft in the direction of the iron stairway that led up to the bridge. We followed, Sissy holding me by the wrist, I tugging and straining after the promised treat.

Across the stairway, hanging from a wet chain, was a wooden sign that said *No Admittance*. Uncle Jake unhooked it, led the way above.

The bridge was open to spray and gales, sleet and rain, and it was here that stood the ship's skipper to supervise the intricacies of docking, say, or to direct his crew whenever the safety of the ship and all aboard her was jeopardized, or whenever the ship was involved in any maneuver that was not merely run-of-the-mill, such as now. And now we ascended to it, met Tony (who was wearing a slicker over his white uniform), surveyed the forward portion of the ship, the passengers down there in the bows, the vista of the wide bay, empty except for ourselves and the anomalous fishing boat, and the suddenly towering glacier.

"Oh, Jake," cried Sissy, clutching the chest-high iron skirt that enclosed the bridge on three sides, "oh, Jake, it's much too close! We'll crash!"

He smiled, shook hands with Tony, lifted me into his arms so that I could see.

"Sissy," he murmured, laughing, "there's no danger. And isn't it a splendid spectacle?"

Then Tony, the captain of the *S.S. Alaska*, put his hand on her shoulder. "Good morning, Sissy," he said quietly. "You know, we do this on every northbound trip. You needn't worry." Then, hand still on her shoulder, he turned toward the open door of the ship's pilot house, and in his soft voice spoke to one of the men inside. "Hard astern," he said, and the man rapidly worked some levers, rang the brass bell.

High in my father's arms, absently flattening his hard black shiny hair with both my hands, high above them all I stared at the immensity of the rising glacier. I glanced down at the panic on Sissy's heart-shaped face, I craned to see into the pilot house when Tony gave his order. When I looked again at the shaggy whiteness, I saw that it was higher than the masts of the *S.S. Alaska*, and that off to the port at the ocean's edge there was a dark cave as big as the *Alaska* herself, and that the cave was growing larger and more darkly blue even as I looked at it. All around us the black water was making whirlpools because the direction of our propellors had been reversed, and I saw that there was now a large claw-like bird skimming the peaks of gray ice, and felt Uncle Jake's pleasure through the hands and arms that held me so high. Sissy begged him to put me down, but he did not, and in joy I began working myself up and down in his arms and ruffling and smoothing the black hair that had the shiny texture of dried glue. In his arms I thought that Uncle Jake and I were alone in marveling at what we saw.

"Stop engines," Tony said over his shoulder, and the shuddering ceased, the churning in the water ceased; through the abrupt silence came the sounds of spoons and kettles in the galley and the popping of the fishing boat's gas engine, louder than ever. We were motionless before the glacier and had not even begun to drift. The little boat to starboard was still rocking and pitching in the echo of our thundering halt and the Indian was staring up at Tony. I smelled the smells of tar and thick white leaded paint, salt on the cold wet air, Uncle Jake's cologne, the stench from the fishing boat below us. Dead ahead, the bird was hovering over the great wall of ice.

"All right, Jake," said Tony, "time for the show. Sunny may do the honors."

"Oh, Jake," said Sissy, "please, can't you put her down?"

But Uncle Jake merely smiled—I felt his smile with my fingers—and still carrying me on high stepped over to the narrowly protruding roof of the pilot house.

"Sunny," he said, twisting so that he could turn up to me his blue eyes, his faintly colored face, his aquiline nose, his sensuous and smiling lips. "Sunny, do you see that lanyard hanging down there from the roof of the pilot house? Pull hard on it and don't let go until I give you two good squeezes."

I nodded, reached out, took hold of the red handle dangling at the end of the short length of rope, and then tugged down as hard as I could with both hands and clung to it, held the red handle down with my weight.

It was the ship's whistle of course, and that blast of sound cried out for help, shrieked danger, sent its long imperious bellow of dissonance resounding for miles. Stays, guywires, deck plates, the entirety of the *S.S. Alaska* was vibrating to the powerful off-key note it was sounding. We were inside the sound, inside some terrible gathering of lighthouses with fog horns chorusing all together in the midst of a storm. Ships might have been colliding all around us; catastrophe was booming. The basso blast consumed the very atmosphere. On it went, unvarying, stretching my arms, tearing the shocked smile loose from my small face, knocking my sailor hat to the deck. In the instant Sissy was all but toppled, and only Tony's strong arm saved her. Below us, the passengers were crouching, wrists to ears, and the little Indian boat was foundering in the weight of the noise. But we hung on, Uncle Jake and I, and I knew that I alone was the cause of the electric whistle's withering, ungainly noise, and that soundlessly Uncle Jake was laughing. Together we reveled, he and I, inside the vast paralysis of that deep dreadful voice which is heard only at sea and which I alone pulled down upon us.

Then he squeezed me twice and I let go of the rope.

It stopped. It left behind a silence more majestic, more painful, more deafening than the sound it had made only moments before. And in that silence, suddenly, we heard an answering crack, a lofty splintering, a deep sound of breakage so abrupt, so loud, that it might have been caused by the largest of electric bolts driving straight down through the layers of gray mist above us, but was in answer, of course, to the terrible tremors of the ship's whistle. All eyes were open. Everyone was watching. And there to the accompaniment of that loud crack, there before us and for all to see, one great icy crag of the glacier trembled, split away from that high white barrier, fell forward, dropped, and slowly plunged into the black and waiting sea. The spray rose, the tip of that immense, torn tooth reappeared from the cold depths to which it had sunk; the long low cave off to port was suddenly no more to be seen, filled as it was with the black waters displaced by the girth and length of the sharply pointed tooth of ice extracted there, before our eyes, from the assaulted face of the glacier.

Below us, and forward, in the bows, the passengers began to clap.

"It was a big one, Tony," said my father. "Wasn't it beautiful, Sissy? Sunny was surely the author of grand havoc."

"Well, it pleases the tourists," said Tony.

"But this was out of the ordinary," said my father. "This was a spectacle for Sunny."

Then in the silence and desolation of Taku Bay, there came a small and angry piping: below us, to starboard, the Indian was holding his boat's horn to his mouth and blowing on the tinny, reedy horn repeatedly, while shaking his free fist at Tony. The Indian had let go of the wheel, the fishing boat was swinging in aimless circles, and atop its pilot house sat the angular black bird that had been skimming the glacier.

"Quarter speed ahead," said Tony, tightening his hold on Sissy and glancing down at the Indian who, standing amidst rusty hooks and tangled netting and fish heads slick with blood and slime, was still blowing his horn and shaking his fist.

"Hard to port," said Tony in his soft and mild voice, and again we were rumbling, turning, gathering the momentum that would put us back on course. Behind us Taku Bay was already filled once more with the densest fog, and there was nothing to see.

In the middle of that night, the last night of our voyage, since we were among the six passengers disembarking at Juneau and the ship was due at Juneau at 6 A.M. on the morning of May 12th, I dreamt that the wind rose, that the darkness was filled with stars, that the seas became willful, more willful, causing the ship to climb, fall, climb again through crackling and tumbling fields of floating ice. And I dreamt that side by side in the very prow of the ship, Uncle Jake and I stood barefooted in pyjamas and hallooing through our cupped hands at a ghostly mountain of ice lying dead in our path. We were dancing up and down and hugging each other with every shard of ice we sent rushing and shattering into the sea with the force of our voices. I heard the ice crumbling, saw the stars descending, clapped as Uncle Jake pulled loose the enormous life preserver and, in all his grand benevolence, tossed it down to the Indians trapped on a listing block of ice in the tumult. My sea legs were as good as Uncle Jake's; the perilous night itself imparted to our clear cries a tone so strong and lyrical that it might have been shaped by the brass of the ancient Deauville hunting horns. He picked me up, he dangled me over the side so that I could wave to the Indians. Behind us there was not a light to be seen anywhere on the dark and tossing ship—no riding lights to locate us for other ships, no lights in the lounge or cabin windows, and yet faint bursts of sparks and phosphorescence were skimming through the wires and around the tops of the smokestacks like crowns of fire and across all of the black wet surface of our ship in the night. My little skull was a lighthouse. I was deafened by the noise I myself was making, and now Uncle Jake was singing to the glacier, destroying it before we crashed into it head on, as two wet figures hauled themselves over the rail and slid aboard.

Then I awoke. We were in fact still rising, falling, wallowing, and even as I slipped to my knees in my top bunk and pressed my face and chest to the porthole, a wave crested, unfurled, and flung itself against the glass. I shivered happily, safe behind the thick glass and in the blue light that lit the cabin. Again we wallowed, the porthole was again submerged, and happily I breathed in the smells of heavy linen, fresh paint, warm blankets, brine. I pressed myself to the porthole like a starfish, lost my balance, fell back, rolled to my side, and looked over the perilous edge of my high bunk. There on the other side of the narrow cabin sat my father, fully dressed, on the edge of the bottom bunk where Sissy lay sleeping. She had not awakened, could not know how rough it was, yet there sat Uncle Jake beside her, drawing the bedclothes about her shoulders, stroking her hair, tucking her in as he might have tucked me in.

We rolled, we burrowed into the bed of the deep sea, I hung on and watched my father until I heard someone tapping on the cabin door. Uncle Jake stood up, braced himself, opened the door onto the red and yellow light of the corridor, and from Jim, our steward—for it was he—received a plate covered by a heavily starched white napkin. They whispered a few words, lurched suddenly—I heard Jim laugh—and then my father gave him a coin and closed the door.

Beneath our bunks, the life jackets were stored like chunks of gray wood. Most of our luggage was already packed and strapped and, out in the corridor where it was piled ready for our debarkation, slid and toppled to the rhythm of the willful seas—as I had heard and seen before the door was closed. Sissy's green robe swayed from the hook where it hung. Down we rolled, up we came, there was a sudden impact, we stopped dead in a trough, then came the painful recovery in slow motion and again, safely, we began to make headway against the storm.

In three easy strides, Uncle Jake was across the cabin and standing beside my bunk, plate in hand, his head just level with mine where I leaned over the low protective rail of the bunk and reached out to him. In the blue light, which shone for the sake of emergency and thus keyed me up for the gravest danger and yet persuaded me all the more of our safety, my father's hair was groomed, his shoulders square, his features more relaxed and comforting than ever, as if in the deadly cast of the blue light it was his life that shone forth.

He gave me the plate, smiled, covered my head once with a warm hand that was so large that it held me as if my head had been a mere softball in his gentle grip, then returned to Sissy's bunk and sat beside her, drew up the blanket, wedged a pillow between her slender figure and the bulkhead.

It was a sandwich. A chicken sandwich. He must have arranged much earlier with Jim to bring me a chicken salad sandwich at the height of the gale, knowing how I would fill my little mouth with soft white bread, golden crusts, cold lettuce, mayonnaise that could not have been creamier, the firm wet cubes of chicken flavored with all the succulence of a secret childhood meal at the height of a gale. And there I lay, propped on an elbow, bracing myself with naked foot, knee, elbow, and savoring, as he knew I would, my plump white sandwich while the cabin reeled and the porthole ran with water and the wind howled. The storm drove my face into the sandwich, smeared soft butter and softer mayonnaise on my lips, my nose, my eyebrows, my cheeks, which I wiped with the back of my hand, which I then licked. Chewing turned into rumination and slow bliss. I was my father's replica, my father's child, I carried the taste of the treasured sandwich back to the bottom, down to the dreamless sleep of my peace and pleasure.

Then: "Rise and shine, Sunny!" I heard him say and woke again, awoke at once, in an instant transformed myself from the child curled in the deepest sleep to the child upright and kneeling amidst the tossed-off covers and quick and bright with the event which I knew was nearly upon us—arrival at last.

"Down you come!" he said. "We'll dock in about half an hour."

"Good morning, darling," Sissy said. "We're almost there!"

The plain white narrow cabin was filled with sunlight and there was no wind, the seas were calm. For the first time since we had started north by ship the fog and rain, lowering mists and sudden squalls had given way at dawn, at the dawning of this day, to the sun, which we had forgotten. Now in the warmth and brightness Uncle Jake was at his most composed and yet as eager as I was, obviously, for the event we three had awaited from the start of our shipboard journey. A new home, a landscape unlike any we had ever seen, the prospects of the last frontier, as he called it—it was all contained in the press of his fawn-colored suit, the tightly-knotted red and white polka-dotted tie, the camel's-hair coat which Sissy was holding ready in her arms along with my sailor coat and her own light green wrap with the silver buttons. In the sunlight Sissy was as content and eager as Uncle Jake and me and wore her dark green Scottish highlander's hat (with the dark ribbons down her neck) at a trim and jaunty angle.

For a final time I pressed myself to the salt-encrusted porthole, looked out upon the unexpected light, the unexpected flatness of the sea on which we were moving at what appeared to be a speed we had never attained until now in our final hours. Then I leapt into my father's arms and he swung me down. Sissy, still holding the coats, and cheerier than at any time since the rainy midnight when we had left the *S.S. Alaska*'s home port back in the States, as Uncle Jake called our native country which we had left behind us, perhaps forever, knelt down and hugged me, and with her thin shapely fingers played a little tune on my spine, put her cheek against my cheek and made her wordless sounds of approval, adoration.

"You smell like mayonnaise," she said and laughed, the breath of her speech warming my smooth cheek. "Midnight snack? Uncle Jake's been spoiling you again?"

I nodded, I kissed her, she drew away, she looked at me with her most engaging expression: chin slightly raised, eyes serene and quick, a personal yet far-away look as if in the distance she saw some vista no one else could see, a crescent of promise which she might happily pursue and possibly attain, alone.

Quickly I dressed, watched by the two of them who were already dressed (by now Uncle Jake had donned his fedora), my haste suddenly and oddly prompted not only by the adventure that was now at hand, but by the faint sensation that I might be left behind, though even then I knew full well that I was the myth of our trio, the myth of their lives, the embodiment of the myth of the only child, and a girl as well.

"On deck everyone!" said Uncle Jake, and Sissy gave us each our coats, we quitted the cabin, gongs were sounding fore and aft. Jim, the steward, had removed our heap of luggage from the narrow corridor to the deck where the passengers' gangway was already in place for lowering.

In single file, with Uncle Jake in the lead, briskly we climbed to the upper deck where we could best watch our arrival, best see the first signs of this new place to which Uncle Jake had brought us. Standing together at the rail, holding each other's hands, bodies touching, for some odd reason we three were alone to survey the panorama spread before us, to look upon the green world slowly approaching. No other passengers, no members of the crew, only ourselves to stand together in that clear light, and to smell the air that was fresh at last, and to look to our fullest satisfaction out toward the landfall that would soon be ours. Uncle Jake squeezed my hand, and I knew that he was squeezing Sissy's; the sun came down, the deck was dry, a steady gentle wind was in our faces.

"In a moment," said Uncle Jake, and for the first time his voice was sober, more sober than I'd ever heard it, "in a moment we'll see Juneau—dead ahead."

New Directions Paperbooks—A Partial Listing